SRA Corrective Reading

Decoding A Word-Attack Basics

Siegfried Engelmann
Linda Carnine
Gary Johnson

McGraw Hill SRA

Columbus, OH

SRAonline.com

McGraw Hill SRA

Copyright © 2008 by SRA/McGraw-Hill.

All rights reserved. No part of this publication may be reproduced or distributed in any form or by any means, or stored in a database or retrieval system, without the prior written consent of The McGraw-Hill Companies, Inc., including, but not limited to, network storage or transmission, or broadcast for distance learning.

Printed in the United States of America.

Send all inquiries to this address:
SRA/McGraw-Hill
4400 Easton Commons
Columbus, OH 43219

ISBN: 978-0-07-611205-0
MHID: 0-07-611205-5

6 7 8 9 RMN 13 12 11 10

The McGraw-Hill Companies

Contents

	Page
Objectives: Lessons 31–35	1
■ Lesson 31	2
■ Lesson 32	10
■ Lesson 33	17
■ Lesson 34	23
■ Lesson 35	29
Mastery Test 8	36
Objectives: Lessons 36–40	37
■ Lesson 36	38
■ Lesson 37	45
■ Lesson 38	51
■ Lesson 39	57
■ Lesson 40	63
Mastery Test 9	69
Objectives: Lessons 41–45	70
■ Lesson 41	71
■ Lesson 42	77
■ Lesson 43	83
■ Lesson 44	89
■ Lesson 45	95
Mastery Test 10	101
Objectives: Lessons 46–50	102
■ Lesson 46	103
■ Lesson 47	109
■ Lesson 48	115
■ Lesson 49	121
■ Lesson 50	127
Mastery Test 11	132

	Page
Objectives: Lessons 51–55	133
■ Lesson 51	134
■ Lesson 52	140
■ Lesson 53	147
■ Lesson 54	154
■ Lesson 55	161
Mastery Test 12	167
Objectives: Lessons 56–60	168
■ Lesson 56	169
■ Lesson 57	176
■ Lesson 58	183
■ Lesson 59	189
■ Lesson 60	195
Mastery Test 13	201
Objectives: Lessons 61–65	202
■ Lesson 61	203
■ Lesson 62	208
■ Lesson 63	214
■ Lesson 64	220
■ Lesson 65	226
Mastery Test 14	231
End-of-Program	
Mastery Test 15	232

Lesson Objectives	LESSON 31 Exercise	LESSON 32 Exercise	LESSON 33 Exercise	LESSON 34 Exercise	LESSON 35 Exercise
Word Attack					
Phonemic Awareness					
Sound/Word Pronunciation	1–3	1–4	1–3	1–3	1–4
Identify Sounds in Words	2, 3	1, 3, 4	2, 3	2, 3	2, 4
Decoding and Word Analysis					
Letter Sounds: *w, wh, ĕ, ē, i, th, t, h, o, a*	1				
Letter Sounds: *w, wh, ĕ, ē, a, o, n, ck, i*		2			
Letter Sounds: *l, e, ē, k, wh, w, a, h, i, th, n*			1		
Letter Sounds: *ō, o, ē, e, l, c, r, a, i, sh, th, s, wh*				1	
Letter Sounds: *e, ē, ō, ŏ, r, l, d, n, h, w, ing, a, i, g*					1
Vowel Sound Discrimination: *ē, ĕ,*	2	4			
Vowel Sound Discrimination: *ō, ŏ,*		3	3	2	2
Sound Combination: *ol*					3
Word Recognition	4	5	4	4	3, 5
Assessment					
Ongoing: Individual Tests	1	2	1	1	1
Formal: Mastery Test					MT 8
Group Reading					
Decoding and Word Analysis					
Read Decodable Text	11	11	10	10	11
Comprehension					
Make Predictions					11
Access Prior Knowledge					11
Draw Inferences		11	10	10	
Note Details	11	11	10	10	11
Assessment					
Ongoing: Comprehension Check	11	11	10	10	
Ongoing: Decoding Accuracy	11	11	10	10	
Workbook Exercises					
Decoding and Word Analysis					
Word Recognition	8	8	7	7	8
Sentence Reading	9	9	8	8	9
Sound Combinations	8	8	7	7	8
Spelling: Sound/Letter Relationships	6, 7, 10, 12	6, 10, 12	5, 9, 11	5, 9, 11	6, 10, 12
Spelling: CVC, CCVC		7	6	6	7
Spelling: CVC, CCVC, CVCC	5				
Visual Discrimination	12, 13	12, 13	11, 12	11, 12	12, 13
Assessment					
Ongoing: Individual Tests	9, 10	9	8	8	9
Ongoing: Teacher-Monitored Accuracy	15	15	14	14	15
Ongoing: Workcheck	14	14	13	13	14

Lesson 31

WORD-ATTACK SKILLS

EXERCISE 1
SOUND INTRODUCTION

1. (Point to **w**:) This letter makes the sound **www**. What sound? (Touch.) *www*. Yes, **www**.
2. (Point to **wh**:) These letters also make the sound **www**. What sound? (Touch.) *www*. Yes, **www**.
3. (Point to **e**:) One sound you learned for this letter is the letter name. Everybody, what's that sound? (Touch.) *ēēē*. Yes, *ēēē*.
* What's the other sound? (Touch.) *ĕĕĕ*. Yes, *ĕĕĕ*.
4. Say each sound when I touch it.
5. (Point to **i**:) What sound? (Touch.) *ĭĭĭ*. Yes, *ĭĭĭ*.
6. (Repeat step 5 for **th, wh, t, h, ŏ, ă, w.**)

w wh
e i th
wh t h
o a w

Individual test
(Call on two or three students. Touch under each sound. Each student says all the sounds, including two sounds for **e**.)

EXERCISE 2

e

VOWEL VARIATIONS

1. (Point to **e**:) One sound you learned for this letter is the letter name. Everybody, what's that sound? (Touch.) *ēēē*.
2. What's the other sound? (Touch.) *ĕĕĕ*.
3. (Point to **e**:) In some words this letter makes the sound *ēēē*. In other words it makes the sound *ĕĕĕ*.
4. (Point to the underlined part of **mend**. Pause.) What sound in this word? (Touch.) *ĕĕĕ*.
* (Touch the ball of the arrow for **mend**. Pause.) What word? (Slash right:) *Mend*.
5. (Repeat step 4 for **then, seems, sent.**)
6. (Repeat the list until the students can correctly identify all the words in order.)

m<u>e</u>nd

th<u>e</u>n

s<u>ee</u>ms

s<u>e</u>nt

Lesson 31

7. (Point to the underlined part of **teen.** Pause.) What sound in this word? (Touch.) *ēēē.*
- (Touch the ball of the arrow for **teen.** Pause.) What word? (Slash right:) *Teen.*
8. (Repeat step 7 for **them, dent, met, meet.**)
9. (Repeat the list until the students can correctly identify all the words in order.)

t<u>ee</u>n

th<u>e</u>m

d<u>e</u>nt

m<u>e</u>t

m<u>ee</u>t

EXERCISE 3
PRONUNCIATIONS

Task A Not, net, knit

1. Listen: **not, net, knit.** Say those words. (Signal.) *Not, net, knit.* (Repeat until firm.)
2. One of those words has the middle sound **ŏŏŏ.** I'll say the words again: **not, net, knit.**
3. Which word has the middle sound **ŏŏŏ?** (Signal.) *Not.* Yes, **not.**
- Which word has the middle sound **ĕĕĕ?** (Signal.) *Net.* Yes, **net.**
- Which word has the middle sound **ĭĭĭ?** (Signal.) *Knit.* Yes, **knit.**
4. Listen: **nŏŏŏt.** What's the middle sound in the word **not?** (Signal.) *ŏŏŏ.* Yes, **ŏŏŏ.**
- Listen: **nĕĕĕt.** What's the middle sound in the word **net?** (Signal.) *ĕĕĕ.* Yes, **ĕĕĕ.**
- Listen: **knĭĭĭt.** What's the middle sound in the word **knit?** (Signal.) *ĭĭĭ.* Yes, **ĭĭĭ.**
5. (Repeat step 4 until firm.) Good job.

Task B Sand, send

1. Listen: **sand** (pause) **send.** Say those words. (Signal.) *Sand, send.* (Repeat until firm.)
2. One of those words has the middle sound **ĕĕĕ.** I'll say the words again: **sand** (pause) **send.**
3. Which word has the middle sound **ĕĕĕ?** (Signal.) *Send.* Yes, **send.**
- Which word has the middle sound **ăăă?** (Signal.) *Sand.* Yes, **sand.**
4. Listen: **săăănd.** What's the middle sound in the word **sand?** (Signal.) *ăăă.* Yes, **ăăă.**
- Listen: **sĕĕĕnd.** What's the middle sound in the word **send?** (Signal.) *ĕĕĕ.* Yes, **ĕĕĕ.**
5. (Repeat step 4 until firm.) Good job.

Task C Set, sit, sat

1. Listen: **set, sit, sat.** Say those words. (Signal.) *Set, sit, sat.* (Repeat until firm.)
2. One of those words has the middle sound **ăăă.** I'll say the words again: **set, sit, sat.**
3. Which word has the middle sound **ăăă?** (Signal.) *Sat.* Yes, **sat.**
- Which word has the middle sound **ĭĭĭ?** (Signal.) *Sit.* Yes, **sit.**
- Which word has the middle sound **ĕĕĕ?** (Signal.) *Set.* Yes, **set.**
4. Listen: **sĕĕĕt.** What's the middle sound in the word **set?** (Signal.) *ĕĕĕ.* Yes, **ĕĕĕ.**
- Listen: **sĭĭĭt.** What's the middle sound in the word **sit?** (Signal.) *ĭĭĭ.* Yes, **ĭĭĭ.**
- Listen: **săăăt.** What's the middle sound in the word **sat?** (Signal.) *ăăă.* Yes, **ăăă.**
5. (Repeat step 4 until firm.) Good job.

Lesson 31

EXERCISE 4
WORD READING THE FAST WAY

1. You're going to read these words the fast way.
2. (For each word: Touch the ball of the arrow. Pause.) What word? (Slash right.)
3. (Repeat each list until firm.)

sent

set

end

and

add

am

an

odd

in

on

it

if

is

his

has

hand

Lesson 31

4. (For each word: Touch the ball of the arrow. Pause.) **What word?** (Slash right.)
5. (Repeat the column until firm.)

had
rot
trot
track
socks

Lesson 31

WORKBOOK EXERCISES

Note: Pass out the Workbooks. Direct the students to open to Lesson 31.

(Award 6 points if the group worked well during the word attack. Remind the students of the points they can earn in their Workbook.)

EXERCISE 5
NEW SPELLING FROM DICTATION

1. Touch part 1 in your Workbook. ✓
- You're going to write words that I dictate.
2. First word: **cat.** What word? (Signal.) *Cat.*
- Listen again: **c . . . ăăă . . . t.** Write it in the first blank.
(Observe students and give feedback.)
3. Next word: **can.** What word? (Signal.) *Can.*
- Listen again: **c . . . ăăă . . . nnn.** Write it in the next blank.
(Observe students and give feedback.)
4. (Repeat step 3 for **cans, she, shed, he.**)

EXERCISE 6
WORD COMPLETION

1. Everybody, touch the first line in part 2 in your Workbook. ✓
2. You're going to write the word (pause) **ad** on the first line. What word? (Signal.) *Ad.* Yes, **ad.**
- Write (pause) **ad** on the first line.
(Observe students and give feedback.)
3. Now you're going to change (pause) **ad** to say (pause) **had.**
- Listen: **had.** What is the first sound in (pause) **had?** (Signal.) *h.* Yes, **h.**
- Fix it up to say **had.**
(Observe students and give feedback.)
4. Listen. You started with a word. What word? (Signal.) *Ad.*
- What word do you have now? (Signal.) *Had.* Yes, **had.**

Lesson 31   5

Lesson 31

5. Touch the second line. ✓
- You're going to write the word (pause) **id**. What word? (Signal.) *id*. Yes, **id**.
- Write (pause) **id** on the line.
  (Observe students and give feedback.)
6. Now you're going to change (pause) **id** to say (pause) **hid**.
- Listen: **hid**. What is the first sound in (pause) **hid**? (Signal.) *h*. Yes, **h**.
- Fix it up to say **hid**.
  (Observe students and give feedback.)
7. Listen. You started with a word. What word? (Signal.) *id*.
- What word do you have now? (Signal.) *Hid*. Yes, **hid**.
8. Touch the third line. ✓
- You're going to write the word (pause) **een**. What word? (Signal.) *een*. Yes, **een**.
- Write (pause) **een** on the line. Remember to write two **ē**'s.
  (Observe students and give feedback.)
9. Now you're going to change (pause) **een** to say (pause) **teen**.
- Listen: **teen**. What is the first sound in (pause) **teen**? (Signal.) *t*. Yes, **t**.
- Fix it up to say **teen**.
  (Observe students and give feedback.)
10. Listen. You started with a word. What word? (Signal.) *een*.
- What word do you have now? (Signal.) *Teen*. Yes, **teen**.

EXERCISE 7

NEW SOUND DICTATION

1. I'll say the sounds. You write the letters in part 3 in your Workbook.
2. First sound. Write a letter that says **www** in the first blank.
   (Observe students and give feedback.)
3. Next sound. Write two letters that go together and say **www**.
   (Observe students and give feedback.)

4. Next sound. (Pause.) **ththth**. What sound? (Signal.) *ththth*.
- Write it.
  (Observe students and give feedback.)
5. (Repeat step 4 for **ŏŏŏ, ēēē, g, ĭĭĭ, shshsh, ĕĕĕ, ăăă, t, h**.)
6. (Repeat sounds students had trouble with.)

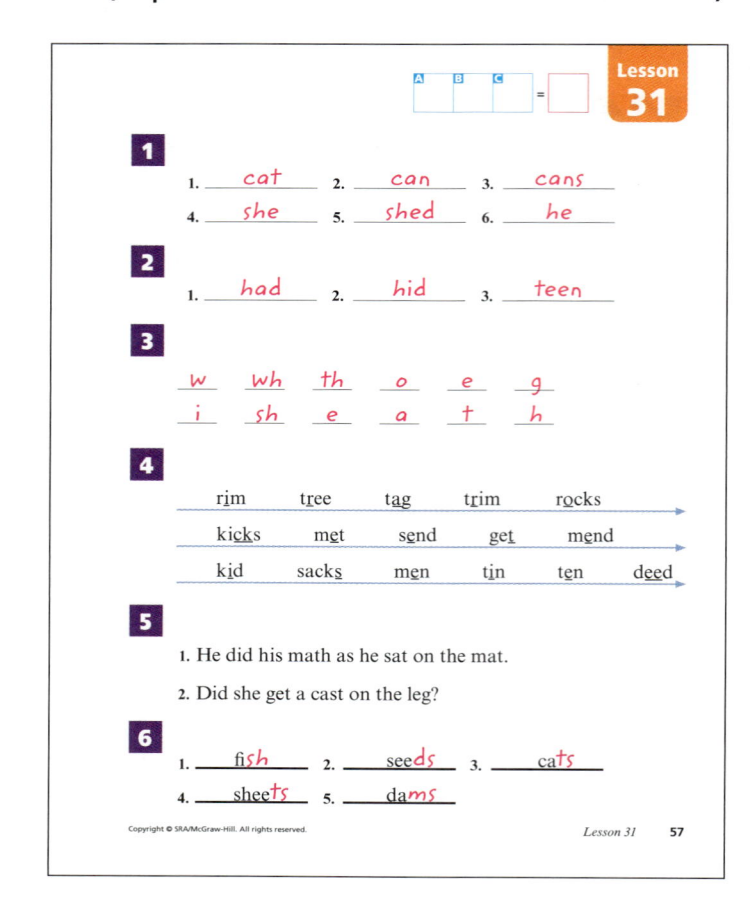

EXERCISE 8

WORD READING: Workbook

1. Touch the first word in part 4. ✓
2. Tell me the sound in the first word. (Pause.) What sound? (Signal.) *ĭĭĭ*.
- (Pause.) What word? (Signal.) *Rim*.
3. Next word. (Pause.) What sound? (Signal.) *rrr*.
- (Pause.) What word? (Signal.) *Tree*.
4. (Repeat step 3 for **tag, trim, rocks, kicks, met, send, get, mend, kids, sacks, men, tin, ten, deed**.)

Lesson 31

=== EXERCISE 9 ===
SENTENCE READING

1. Everybody, touch part 5. ✓
2. Touch under the first word in sentence 1. ✓
- What word? (Signal.) *He.*
3. Next word. ✓
- What word? (Signal.) *Did.*
4. (Repeat step 3 for **his, math, as, he, sat, on, the, mat.**)
5. (Repeat steps 2–4 until the students correctly identify all the words in the sentence in order.)
6. (Repeat steps 2–5 for sentence 2: **Did she get a cast on the leg?**)

> **Individual test**
> (Give each student a chance to read one of the sentences.)

=== EXERCISE 10 ===
WORD COMPLETION

1. Everybody, touch part 6. ✓
2. Sound out the word on the first line. Get ready. (Clap for **f, i:**) *fffĭĭĭ.*
- What word? (Signal.) *fi.* Yes, **fi.**
3. Fix it up to say (pause) **fish.** (Pause.) **Fish.** What word? (Signal.) *Fish.* Yes, **fish.**
- Fix it up.
(Observe students and give feedback.)
4. Sound out the word on the next line. Get ready. (Clap for **s, ee:**) *sssēēē.*
- What word? (Signal.) *See.* Yes, **see.**
5. Fix it up to say (pause) **seeds.** (Pause.) **Seeds.** What word? (Signal.) *Seeds.* Yes, **seeds.**
- Fix it up.
(Observe students and give feedback.)
6. Sound out the word on the third line. Get ready. (Clap for **c, a:**) *căăă.*
- What word? (Signal.) *ca.* Yes, **ca.**
7. Fix it up to say (pause) **cats.** (Pause.) **Cats.** What word? (Signal.) *Cats.* Yes, **cats.**
- Fix it up.
(Observe students and give feedback.)
8. Sound out the word on the fourth line. Get ready. (Clap for **sh, ee:**) *shshshēēē.*
- What word? (Signal.) *shee.* Yes, **shee.**
9. Fix it up to say (pause) **sheets.** (Pause.) **Sheets.** What word? (Signal.) *Sheets.* Yes, **sheets.**
- Fix it up.
(Observe students and give feedback.)
10. Sound out the word on the fifth line. Get ready. (Clap for **d, a:**) *dăăă.*
- What word? (Signal.) *da.* Yes, **da.**
11. Fix it up to say (pause) **dams.** (Pause.) **Dams.** What word? (Signal.) *Dams.* Yes, **dams.**
- Fix it up.
(Observe students and give feedback.)

> **Individual test**
> I'll call on different students to read words in part 6. First word. (Call on a student.) What word? (Call on different students to read the remaining words.)

=== EXERCISE 11 ===
STORY READING

Task A

1. Everybody, touch part 7. ✓
2. This is a story. There are problems after some of the sentences. You're going to read the sentences the fast way.
3. Touch under the first word. ✓
- What word? (Signal.) *He.*
4. Next word. ✓
- What word? (Signal.) *Did.*
5. (Repeat step 4 for **math.**)
6. (Repeat steps 3–5 until the students correctly identify all the words in the sentence.)
7. (Repeat steps 3–6 for each remaining sentence:
- **He did this.**
- **Then he did this.**
- **Can he add?**)
8. (If students miss more than four words, repeat the story reading from the beginning.)

Lesson 31

Lesson 31

Task B

1. Now I'll read the story and ask questions. Follow along.
2. **He did math. He did this.** What did he write? (Call on a student.) *One plus three equals five.*
3. Everybody, did he get the answer right? (Signal.) *No.*
- What does one plus three equal? (Signal.) *Four.*
4. **Then he did this.** What did he write? (Call on a student.) *Seven plus two equals four.*
- Everybody, is that the right answer? (Signal.) *No.*
5. Last sentence: **Can he add?** Everybody, what's the answer? (Signal.) *No.*

EXERCISE 12
MATCHING COMPLETION

1. Everybody, touch part 8. ✓
- Read the words the fast way.
2. Touch under the first word. ✓
- What word? (Signal.) *Me.*
3. Next word. ✓
- What word? (Signal.) *Met.*
4. (Repeat step 3 for **than, get, sacks.**)
5. Later, you're going to write the words in the second column.

EXERCISE 13
CIRCLE GAME

1. Everybody, touch part 9. ✓
2. What will you circle in the first two lines? (Signal.) *ck.*
3. What will you circle in the next two lines? (Signal.) *shshsh.*
4. What will you circle in the last two lines? (Signal.) *ththth.*
5. Circle the sounds and finish the rest of your Workbook lesson.

EXERCISE 14
WORKBOOK CHECK

1. (Check each student's Workbook.)
2. (Award points for Workbook performance.)
3. (Record the student's total points in Box B.)

0–2 errors	8 points
3–4 errors	4 points
5–6 errors	2 points
7 or more errors	0 points

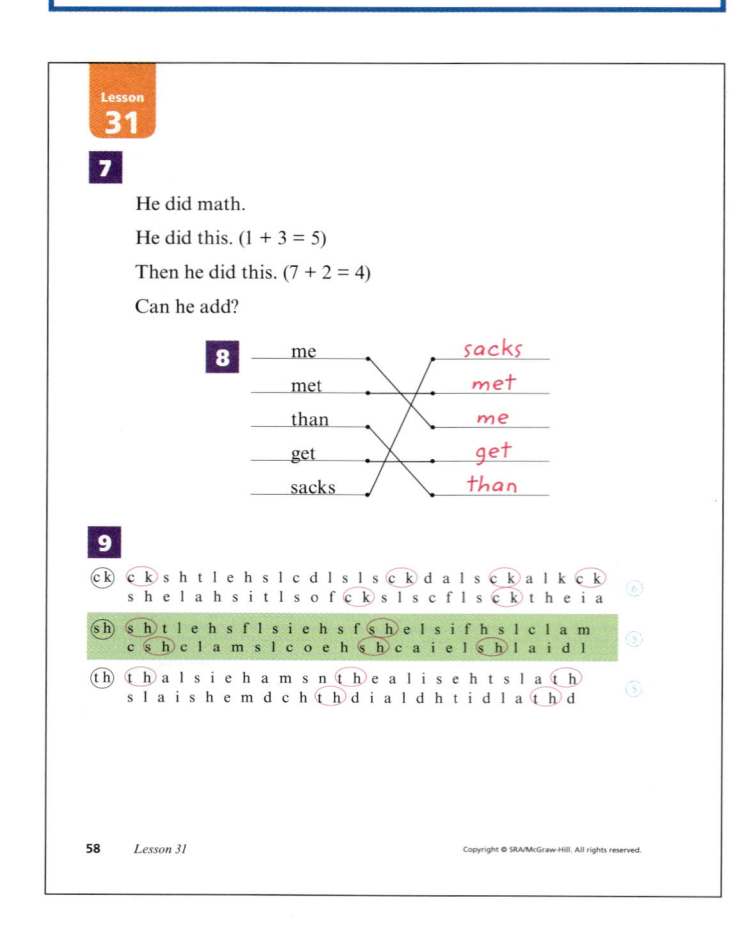

Lesson 31

7

He did math.

He did this. (1 + 3 = 5)

Then he did this. (7 + 2 = 4)

Can he add?

8

me — sacks
met — met
than — me
get — get
sacks — than

9

ck ck s h t l e h s l c d l s l s ck d a l s ck a l k ck
     s h e l a h s i t l s o f ck s l s c f l s ck t h e i a

sh sh t l e h s f l s i e h s f sh e l s i f h s l c l a m
     c sh c l a m s l c o e h sh c a i e l sh l a i d l

th th a l s i e h a m s n th e a l i s e h t s l a th
     s l a i s h e m d c h th d i a l d h t i d l a th d

Lesson 31

INDIVIDUAL READING CHECKOUTS

EXERCISE 15
STORY-READING CHECKOUT

- Study the story. If you read all the sentences with no more than 1 error, you'll earn 6 points.
- (Check the students individually.)
- (Record either 6 or 0 points in Box C.)

Lesson point total

(Tell students to write the point total in the last box at the top of the Workbook page. Maximum = 20 points.)

Point Summary Chart

(Tell students to write this point total in the box for Lesson 31 in the Point Summary Chart.)

END OF LESSON 31

Lesson 32

WORD-ATTACK SKILLS

EXERCISE 1
PRONUNCIATIONS

> **Note:** Do not write the words on the board. This is an oral exercise.

Task A

1. Say these words. Listen: **street.** Say it. (Signal.) *Street.*
2. Next word: **streets.** Say it. (Signal.) *Streets.*
3. Next word: **ringing.** Say it. (Signal.) *Ringing.*
4. (Repeat all the words until firm.)

Task B **Fill, fell, feel**

1. Listen: **fill, fell, feel.** Say those words. (Signal.) *Fill, fell, feel.* (Repeat until firm.)
2. One of those words has the middle sound ĕĕĕ. I'll say the words again: **fill, fell, feel.**
3. Which word has the middle sound ĕĕĕ? (Signal.) *Fell.* Yes, **fell.**
- Which word has the middle sound ēēē? (Signal.) *Feel.* Yes, **feel.**
- Which word has the middle sound ĭĭĭ? (Signal.) *Fill.* Yes, **fill.**

EXERCISE 2
SOUND INTRODUCTION

1. (Point to **w:**) This letter makes the sound www. What sound? (Touch.) *www.* Yes, **www.**
2. (Point to **wh:**) These letters also make the sound www. What sound? (Touch.) *www.* Yes, **www.**
3. (Point to **e:**) One sound you learned for this letter is the letter name. Everybody, what's that sound? (Touch.) *ēēē.* Yes, **ēēē.**
- What's the other sound? (Touch.) *ĕĕĕ.* Yes, **ĕĕĕ.**
4. Say each sound when I touch it.
5. (Point to **a:**) What sound? (Touch.) *ăăă.* Yes, **ăăă.**
6. (Repeat step 5 for **ŏ, n, ck, ĭ.**)

w wh e
a o
n ck i

> **Individual test**
> (Call on two or three students. Touch under each sound. Each student says all the sounds, including two sounds for **e.**)

Lesson 32

EXERCISE 3
VOWEL VARIATIONS

1. (Point to **o** in **not:**) What sound? (Touch under **o:**) ŏŏŏ.
   - (Touch the ball of the arrow. Pause.) What word? (Slash right:) *Not.*
2. (Point to **o** in **sod:**) What sound? (Touch under **o:**) ŏŏŏ.
   - (Touch the ball of the arrow. Pause.) What word? (Slash right:) *Sod.*
3. (Point to **o** in **hot:**) What sound? (Touch under **o:**) ŏŏŏ.
   - (Touch the ball of the arrow. Pause.) What word? (Slash right:) *Hot.*
4. (Point to **o** in **got:**) What sound? (Touch under **o:**) ŏŏŏ.
   - (Touch the ball of the arrow. Pause.) What word? (Slash right:) *Got.*
5. (Point to **o** in **so:**) This letter does not say ŏŏŏ in the words you're going to read now. This letter says ōōō. What sound? (Touch under **o:**) ōōō. (Repeat until firm.)
6. (Touch the ball of the arrow. Pause.) What word? (Slash right:) *So.*

> **To correct, *so*, for example:**
> a. (Say:) **so.**
> - (Point to **o:**) What sound does this letter make in this word? (Touch under **o:**) ōōō.
> b. (Touch the ball of the arrow:) Sound it out. Get ready. (Touch under **s, o:**) sssōōō. (Repeat until firm.)
> c. (Touch the ball of the arrow:) What word? (Slash right:) *So.*

7. (Point to **o** in **no:**) What sound? (Touch under **o:**) ōōō.
   - (Touch the ball of the arrow. Pause.) What word? (Slash right:) *No.*
8. (Point to **o** in **ho:**) What sound? (Touch under **o:**) ōōō.
   - (Touch the ball of the arrow. Pause.) What word? (Slash right:) *Ho.*
9. (Point to **o** in **go:**) What sound? (Touch under **o:**) ōōō.
   - (Touch the ball of the arrow. Pause.) What word? (Slash right:) *Go.*
10. (Repeat the list until the students can correctly identify all the words in order.)

not

sod

hot

got

so

no

ho

go

Lesson 32

Lesson 32

EXERCISE 4

e

VOWEL VARIATIONS

1. (Point to **e**:) One sound you learned for this letter is the letter name. Everybody, what's the sound? (Touch.) ēēē.
2. What's the other sound? (Touch.) ĕĕĕ.
3. (Point to **e**:) In some words this letter makes the sound ēēē. In other words it makes the sound ĕĕĕ.
4. (Point to the underlined part of **wet**. Pause.) What sound in this word? (Touch.) ĕĕĕ.
   - (Touch the ball of the arrow for **wet**. Pause.) What word? (Slash right:) *Wet.*
5. (Repeat step 4 for **feed, went, fed, dent, week, end, get, needs, hen**.)
6. (Repeat both lists until the students can correctly identify all the words in order.)

wet

feed

went

fed

dent

week

end

get

needs

hen

EXERCISE 5

WORD READING THE FAST WAY

1. You're going to read these words the fast way.
2. (For each word: Touch the ball of the arrow. Pause.) What word? (Slash right.)
3. (Repeat the column until firm.)

trod

how

hot

street

Lesson 32

4. (For each word: Touch the ball of the arrow. Pause.) What word? (Slash right.)
5. (Repeat each list until firm.)

odd

had

cast

his

ring

then

this

has

ringing

than

cats

fits

rags

hands

that

win

kicks

hid

Lesson 32 13

Lesson 32

WORKBOOK EXERCISES

Note: Pass out the Workbooks. Direct the students to open to Lesson 32.

(Award 6 points if the group worked well during the word attack. Remind the students of the points they can earn in their Workbook.)

EXERCISE 6
NEW SOUND DICTATION

1. I'll say the sounds. You write the letters in part 1 in your Workbook.
2. First sound. Write a letter that says **www** in the first blank.
   (Observe students and give feedback.)
3. Next sound. Write two letters that go together and say **www**.
   (Observe students and give feedback.)
4. Next sound. Write a letter that says **k**.
   (Observe students and give feedback.)
5. Next sound. Write another letter that says **k**.
   (Observe students and give feedback.)
6. Next sound. Write two letters that go together and say **k**.
   (Observe students and give feedback.)
7. Next sound. (Pause.) **g**. What sound? (Signal.) g.
- Write it.
   (Observe students and give feedback).
8. (Repeat step 7 for **ĭĭĭ, ĕĕĕ, nnn, thththe, ēēē, h**.)
9. (Repeat sounds students had trouble with.)

EXERCISE 7
SPELLING FROM DICTATION

1. Touch part 2. ✓
- You're going to write words that I dictate.

2. First word: **shed**. What word? (Signal.) *Shed*.
- Listen again: **shshsh ... ĕĕĕ ... d**. Write it in the first blank.
   (Observe students and give feedback.)
3. Next word: **red**. What word? (Signal.) *Red*.
- Listen again: **rrr ... ĕĕĕ ... d**. Write it in the next blank.
   (Observe students and give feedback.)
4. (Repeat step 3 for **dad, did, hid, had**.)

EXERCISE 8
WORD READING: Workbook

1. Touch the first word in part 3. ✓
2. Tell me the underlined sound in the first word. (Pause.) What sound? (Signal.) ăăă.
- (Pause.) What word? (Signal.) *Dad*.
3. Next word. (Pause.) What sound? (Signal.) ĭĭĭ.
- (Pause.) What word? (Signal.) *Did*.
4. (Repeat step 3 for **we, men, mend, seen, sent, with, met, meet, socks, when, send, rack**.)

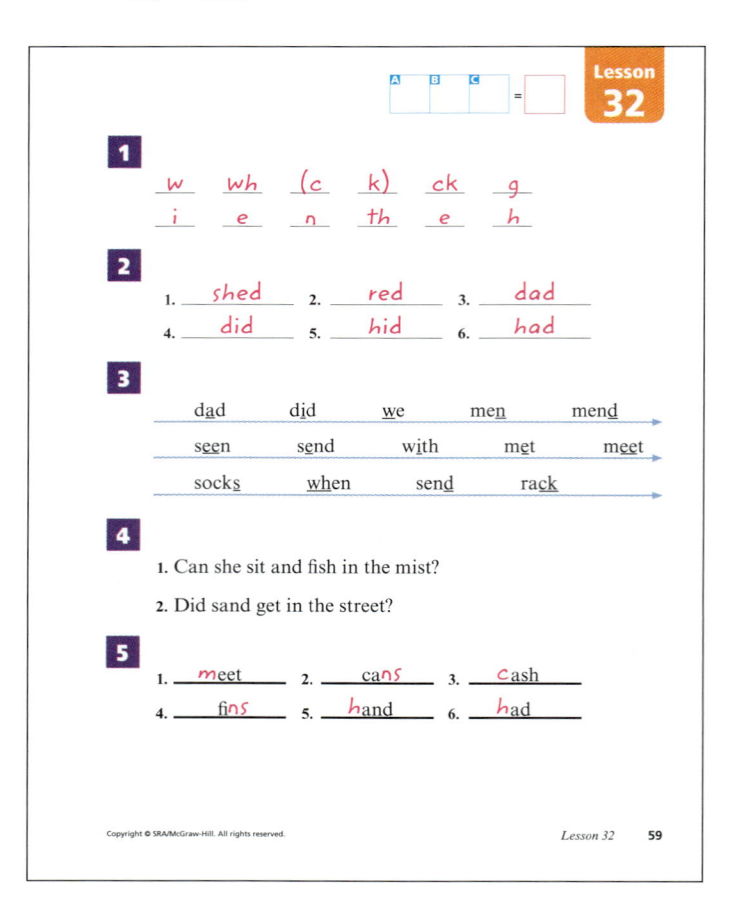

14   Lesson 32

Lesson 32

EXERCISE 9
SENTENCE READING

1. Everybody, touch part 4. ✓
2. Touch under the first word in sentence 1. ✓
- What word? (Signal.) *Can.*
3. Next word. ✓
- What word? (Signal.) *She.*
4. (Repeat step 3 for **sit, and, fish, in, the, mist.**)
5. (Repeat steps 2–4 until the students can correctly identify all the words in the sentence in order.)
6. (Repeat steps 2–5 for sentence 2: **Did sand get in the street?**)

> **Individual test**
> (Give each student a chance to read one of the sentences.)

EXERCISE 10
NEW WORD COMPLETION

1. Touch the first word in part 5. ✓
- What word? (Signal.) *eet.* Yes, **eet.**
- Fix it up to say (pause) **meet.** What word? (Signal.) *Meet.*
- Fix it up.
  (Observe students and give feedback.)
2. Touch the next word. ✓
- What word? (Signal.) *ca.* Yes, **ca.**
- Fix it up to say (pause) **cans.** What word? (Signal.) *Cans.*
- Fix it up.
  (Observe students and give feedback.)
3. Touch the next word. ✓
- What word? (Signal.) *Ash.* Yes, **ash.**
- Fix it up to say (pause) **cash.** What word? (Signal.) *Cash.*
- Fix it up.
  (Observe students and give feedback.)
4. Touch the next word. ✓
- What word? (Signal.) *fi.* Yes, **fi.**
- Fix it up to say (pause) **fins.** What word? (Signal.) *Fins.*
- Fix it up.
  (Observe students and give feedback.)
5. Touch the next word. ✓
- What word? (Signal.) *And.* Yes, **and.**
- Fix it up to say (pause) **hand.** What word? (Signal.) *Hand.*
- Fix it up.
  (Observe students and give feedback.)
6. Touch the next word. ✓
- What word? (Signal.) *Ad.* Yes, **ad.**
- Fix it up to say (pause) **had.** What word? (Signal.) *Had.*
- Fix it up.
  (Observe students and give feedback.)

EXERCISE 11
NEW STORY READING

Task A

1. Everybody, touch part 6. ✓
- You're going to read the sentences the fast way.
2. Touch under the first word. ✓
- What word? (Signal.) *She.*
3. Next word. ✓
- What word? (Signal.) *Can.*
4. (Repeat step 3 for **mend.**)
5. (Repeat steps 2–4 for each remaining sentence:
- **Can she mend a sheet?**
- **Can she mend a sock?**
- **She can not mend this.**)
6. (If the students miss more than four words, repeat the story reading from the beginning.)

Task B

1. Now I'll read the story and ask questions. Follow along.
2. **She can mend.** How would she mend something? (Call on a student.) (Idea: *By sewing it.*)
3. **Can she mend a sheet?** Everybody, what's the answer? (Signal.) *Yes.*
   Yes, if she can mend well, she can mend a sheet.
4. **Can she mend a sock?** Everybody, what's the answer? (Signal.) *Yes.*
5. **She can not mend this.** Everybody, what is that thing in the picture? (Signal.) *A rock.*
- Why can't she mend the rock? (Call on a student.) (Idea: *Because a rock is too hard.*)

Lesson 32   15

Lesson 32

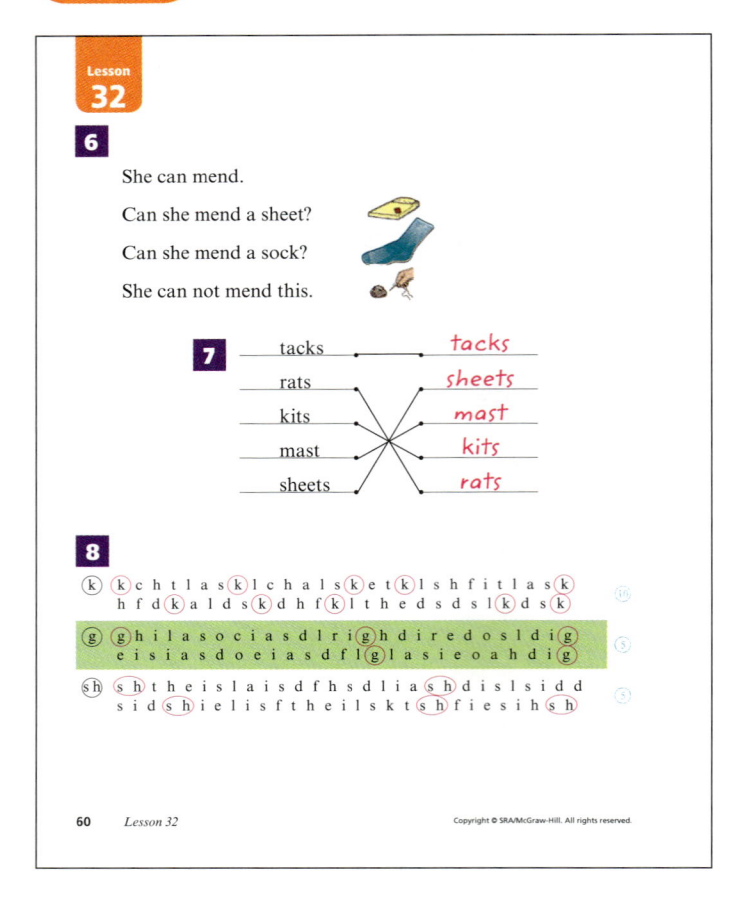

6

She can mend.
Can she mend a sheet?
Can she mend a sock?
She can not mend this.

7

tacks — tacks
rats — sheets
kits — mast
mast — kits
sheets — rats

8

k k c h t l a s k l c h a l s k e t k l s h f i t l a s k
   h f d k a l d s k d h f k l t h e d s d s l k d s k

g g h i l a s o c i a s d l r i g h d i r e d o s l d i g
   e i s i a s d o e i a s d f l g l a s i e o a h d i g

sh s h t h e i s l a i s d f h s d l i a s h d i s l s i d d
   s i d s h i e l i s f t h e i l s k t s h f i e s i h s h

EXERCISE 12
MATCHING COMPLETION

1. Everybody, touch part 7. ✓
• Read the words the fast way.
2. Touch under the first word. ✓
• What word? (Signal.) *Tacks.*
3. Next word. ✓
• What word? (Signal.) *Rats.*
4. (Repeat step 3 for **kits, mast, sheets.**)
5. Later, you're going to write the words in the second column.

EXERCISE 13
CIRCLE GAME

1. Everybody, touch part 8. ✓
2. What will you circle in the first two lines? (Signal.) *k.*
3. What will you circle in the next two lines? (Signal.) *g.*
4. What will you circle in the last two lines? (Signal.) *sh.*
5. Circle the sounds and finish the rest of your Workbook lesson.

EXERCISE 14
WORKBOOK CHECK

1. (Check each student's Workbook.)
2. (Award points for Workbook performance.)
3. (Record the student's total points in Box B.)

0–2 errors	8 points
3–4 errors	4 points
5–6 errors	2 points
7 or more errors	0 points

INDIVIDUAL READING CHECKOUTS

EXERCISE 15
STORY-READING CHECKOUT

• Study the story. If you read all the sentences with no more than 1 error, you'll earn 6 points.
• (Check the students individually.)
• (Record either 6 or 0 points in Box C.)

Lesson point total

(Tell students to write the point total in the last box at the top of the Workbook page. Maximum = 20 points.)

Point Summary Chart

(Tell students to write this point total in the box for Lesson 32 in the Point Summary Chart.)

END OF LESSON 32

WORD-ATTACK SKILLS

EXERCISE 1
SOUND IDENTIFICATION

1. (Point to **l:**) This letter makes the sound **lll**. What sound? (Touch.) *lll*. Yes, **lll**.
2. (Point to **e:**) One sound you learned for this letter is the letter name. Everybody, what's the sound? (Touch.) *ēēē*. Yes, **ēēē**.
- What's the other sound? (Touch.) *ĕĕĕ*. Yes, **ĕĕĕ**.
3. Say each sound when I touch it.
4. (Point to **k:**) What sound? (Touch.) *k*. Yes, **k**.
5. (Repeat step 4 for **wh, w, ă, h, ĭ, th, n, l.**)

l e k
wh w
a h i
th n l

Individual test
(Call on two or three students. Touch under each sound. Each student says all the sounds, including two sounds for **e.**)

EXERCISE 2
PRONUNCIATIONS

Note: Do not write the words on the board. This is an oral exercise.

Task A

1. Say these words. Listen: **trim.** Say it. (Signal.) *Trim.*
2. Next word: **treat.** Say it. (Signal.) *Treat.*
3. (Repeat step 2 for **street, singing.**)
4. (Repeat all the words until firm.)

Task B Slid, sled

1. Listen: **slid.** Say it. (Signal.) *Slid.*
- Listen: **sled.** Say it. (Signal.) *Sled.*
2. One of those words has the middle sound **ĕĕĕ**. I'll say both words again: **slid** (pause) **sled.**
3. Which word has the middle sound **ĕĕĕ**? (Signal.) *Sled.* Yes, **sled.**
- Which word has the middle sound **ĭĭĭ**? (Signal.) *Slid.* Yes, **slid.**

Task C Chip, chop

1. Listen: **chip.** Say it. (Signal.) *Chip.*
- Listen: **chop.** Say it. (Signal.) *Chop.*
2. One of those words has the middle sound **ĭĭĭ**. I'll say both words again: **chip** (pause) **chop.**
3. Which word has the middle sound **ĭĭĭ**? (Signal.) *Chip.* Yes, **chip.**
- Which word has the middle sound **ŏŏŏ**? (Signal.) *Chop.* Yes, **chop.**

Lesson 33

EXERCISE 3
VOWEL VARIATIONS

1. (Point to **o** in **sod:**) What sound? (Touch under **o:**) ŏŏŏ.
   - (Touch the ball of the arrow. Pause.) What word? (Slash right:) *Sod.*
2. (Point to **o** in **hot:**) What sound? (Touch under **o:**) ŏŏŏ.
   - (Touch the ball of the arrow. Pause.) What word? (Slash right:) *Hot.*
3. (Point to **o** in **nod:**) What sound? (Touch under **o:**) ŏŏŏ.
   - (Touch the ball of the arrow. Pause.) What word? (Slash right:) *Nod.*
4. (Point to **o** in **got:**) What sound? (Touch under **o:**) ŏŏŏ.
   - (Touch the ball of the arrow. Pause.) What word? (Slash right:) *Got.*
5. (Point to **o** in **got:**) What sound does this letter make in all the words you just read? (Touch under **o:**) ŏŏŏ.
6. (Point to **o** in **so:**) This letter does not say **ŏŏŏ** in the words you're going to read now. This letter says **ōōō**. What sound? (Touch under **o:**) ōōō. (Repeat until firm.)
7. (Touch the ball of the arrow. Pause.) What word? (Slash right:) *So.*

> **To correct, *so*, for example:**
> a. (Say:) **so.**
> - (Point to **o:**) What sound does this letter make in this word? (Touch under **o:**) ōōō.
> b. (Touch the ball of the arrow:) Sound it out. Get ready. (Touch under **s, o:**) *sssōōō.* (Repeat until firm.)
> c. (Touch the ball of the arrow:) What word? (Slash right:) *So.*

8. (Point to **o** in **ho:**) What sound? (Touch under **o:**) ōōō.
   - (Touch the ball of the arrow. Pause.) What word? (Slash right:) *Ho.*
9. (Point to **o** in **no:**) What sound? (Touch under **o:**) ōōō.
   - (Touch the ball of the arrow. Pause.) What word? (Slash right:) *No.*
10. (Point to **o** in **go:**) What sound? (Touch under **o:**) ōōō.
    - (Touch the ball of the arrow. Pause.) What word? (Slash right:) *Go.*
11. (Repeat the list until the students can correctly identify all the words in order.)

sod

hot

nod

got

so

ho

no

go

Lesson 33

EXERCISE 4
WORD READING THE FAST WAY

1. You're going to read these words the fast way.
2. (For each word: Touch the ball of the arrow. Pause.) What word? (Slash right.)
3. (Repeat each list until firm.)

tree

street

trot

cans

hams

fins

cats

cast

mast

sing

singing

ringing

dinging

has

had

hand

when

dent

wheel

Lesson 33

WORKBOOK EXERCISES

Note: Pass out the Workbooks. Direct the students to open to Lesson 33.

(Award 6 points if the group worked well during the word attack. Remind the students of the points they can earn in their Workbook.)

EXERCISE 5
SOUND DICTATION

1. I'll say the sounds. You write the letters in part 1 in your Workbook.
2. First sound. Write a letter that says **www** in the first blank.
   (Observe students and give feedback.)
3. Next sound. Write two letters that go together and say **www.**
   (Observe students and give feedback.)
4. Next sound. (Pause.) **ththth.** What sound? *ththth.*
   - Write it.
   (Observe students and give feedback.)
5. Next sound. (Pause.) **ĕĕĕ.** What sound? (Signal.) *ĕĕĕ.*
   - Write it.
   (Observe students and give feedback.)
6. (Repeat step 5 for **ĭĭĭ, sss, shshsh, ēēē, h, ĕĕĕ, ăăă, ŏŏŏ.**)
7. (Repeat sounds students had trouble with.)

EXERCISE 6
SPELLING FROM DICTATION

1. Touch part 2. ✓
   - You're going to write words that I dictate.
2. First word: **then.** Not **than.** What word? (Signal.) *Then.*
   - Listen again: **ththth . . . ĕĕĕ . . . nnn.** Write it in the first blank.
   (Observe students and give feedback.)
3. Next word: **that.** What word? (Signal.) *That.*
   - Listen again: **ththth . . . ăăă . . . t.** Write it in the next blank.
   (Observe students and give feedback.)
4. (Repeat step 3 for **did, had, red, dad.**)

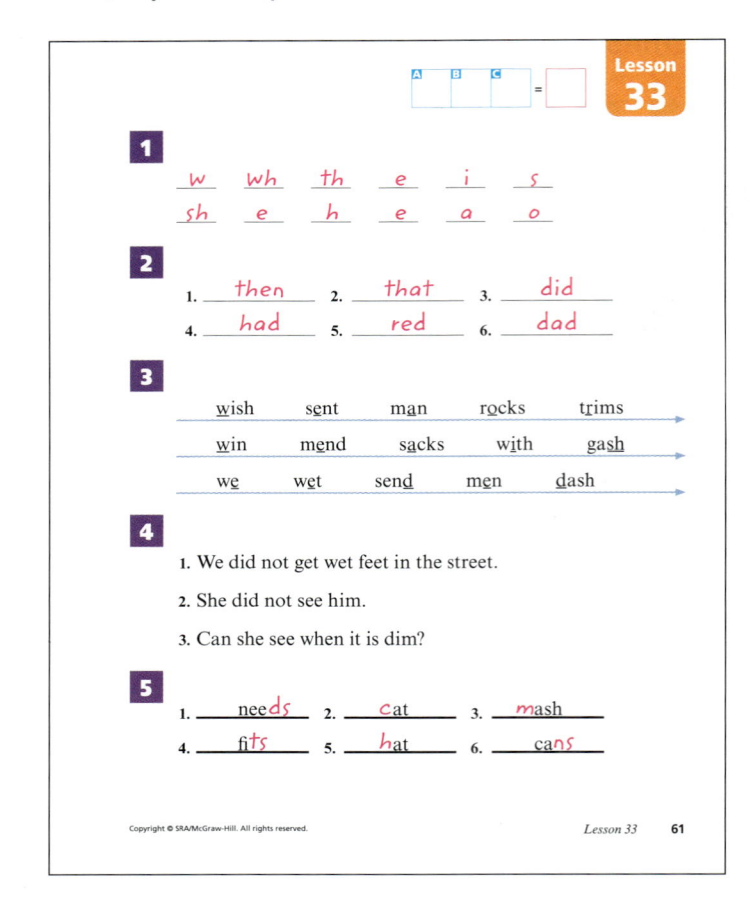

EXERCISE 7
WORD READING: Workbook

1. Touch the first word in part 3. ✓
2. Look at the underlined sound in the first word. (Pause.) What sound? (Signal.) *www.*
   - (Pause.) What word? (Signal.) *Wish.*
3. Next word. (Pause.) What sound? (Signal.) *ĕĕĕ.*
   - (Pause.) What word? (Signal.) *Sent.*
4. (Repeat step 3 for **man, rocks, trims, win, mend, sacks, with, gash, we, wet, send, men, dash.**)

Lesson 33

EXERCISE 8
SENTENCE READING

1. Everybody, touch part 4.
2. Touch under the first word in sentence 1. ✓
- What word? (Signal.) *We.*
3. Next word. ✓
- What word? (Signal.) *Did.*
4. (Repeat step 3 for **not, get, wet, feet, in, the, street.**)
5. (Repeat steps 2–4 until the students correctly identify all the words in the sentence in order.)
6. (Repeat steps 2–5 for each remaining sentence:
- **2. She did not see him.**
- **3. Can she see when it is dim?**)

> **Individual test**
> (Give each student a chance to read one of the sentences.)

EXERCISE 9
WORD COMPLETION

1. Touch the first word in part 5. ✓
- What word? (Signal.) *nee.* Yes, **nee.**
- Fix it up to say (pause) **needs.** What word? (Signal.) *Needs.*
- Fix it up.
(Observe students and give feedback.)
2. Touch the next word. ✓
- What word? (Signal.) *At.* Yes, **at.**
- Fix it up to say (pause) **cat.** What word? (Signal.) *Cat.*
- Fix it up.
(Observe students and give feedback.)
3. Touch the next word. ✓
- What word? (Signal.) *Ash.* Yes, **ash.**
- Fix it up to say (pause) **mash.** What word? (Signal.) *Mash.*
- Fix it up.
(Observe students and give feedback.)
4. Touch the next word. ✓
- What word? (Signal.) *fi.* Yes, **fi.**
- Fix it up to say (pause) **fits.** What word? (Signal.) *Fits.*
- Fix it up.
(Observe students and give feedback.)
5. Touch the next word. ✓
- What word? (Signal.) *At.* Yes, **at.**
- Fix it up to say (pause) **hat.** What word? (Signal.) *Hat.*
- Fix it up.
(Observe students and give feedback.)
6. Touch the next word. ✓
- What word? (Signal.) *ca.* Yes, **ca.**
- Fix it up to say (pause) **cans.** What word? (Signal.) *Cans.*
- Fix it up.
(Observe students and give feedback.)

EXERCISE 10
STORY READING

Task A

1. Everybody, touch part 6. ✓
- You're going to read sentences the fast way.
2. Touch under the first word. ✓
- What word? (Signal.) *A.*
3. Next word. ✓
- What word? (Signal.) *Cat.*
4. (Repeat step 3 for **had, wet, feet.**)
5. (Repeat steps 2–4 until the students correctly identify all the words in the sentence.)
6. (Repeat steps 2–5 for each remaining sentence:
- **Then the cat went in wet sand.**
- **That cat went on a street.**
- **The street has wet sand on it.**)
7. (If students miss more than four words, repeat the story reading from the beginning.)

Task B

1. Now I'll read the story and ask questions. Follow along.
2. **A cat had wet feet. Then the cat went in wet sand.** If the cat had wet feet, what would happen to the sand? (Call on a student.) (Idea: *The sand would stick to the cat's feet.*)
3. **The cat went on a street. The street has wet sand on it.** What are those funny marks in the picture? (Call on a student.) *Footprints.*

Lesson 33   21

Lesson 33

4. If you touched one of those footprints, what would it feel like? (Call on a student.) (Idea: *Wet and sandy.*)

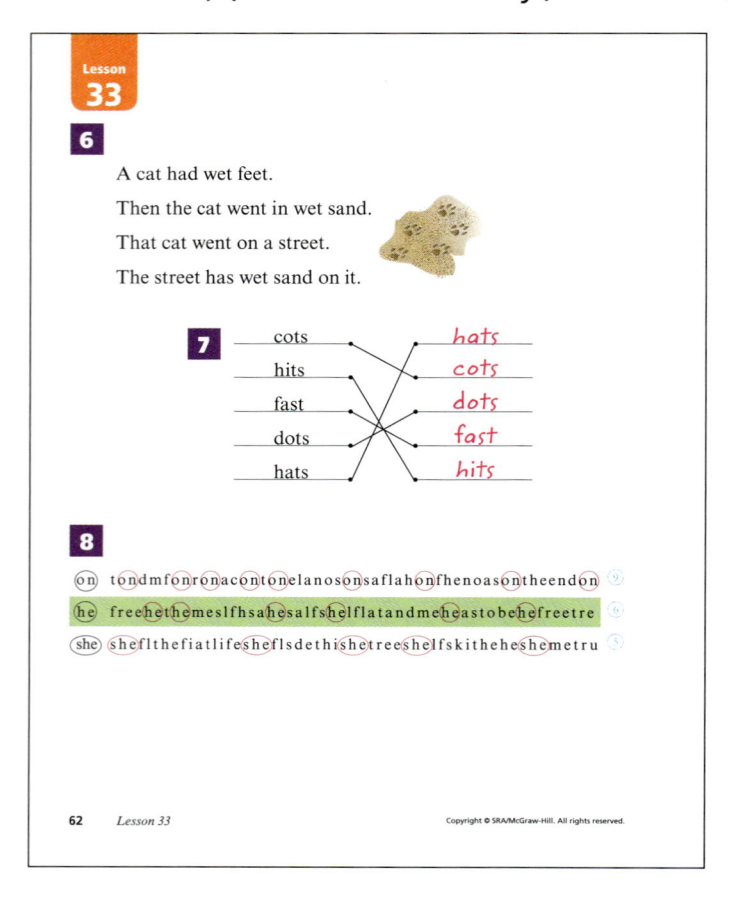

Lesson 33

6

A cat had wet feet.
Then the cat went in wet sand.
That cat went on a street.
The street has wet sand on it.

7
cots — hats
hits — cots
fast — dots
dots — fast
hats — hits

8
on tondmfonronacontonelanosonsaflahonfhenoasontheendon 9
he freehethemeslfhsahesalfshelflatandmeheastobehefreetre 6
she sheflthefiatlifesheflsdethishetreeshelfskitheheshemetru 5

62 Lesson 33

EXERCISE 11
MATCHING COMPLETION

1. Everybody, touch part 7. Read the words the fast way.
2. Touch under the first word. ✓
- What word? (Signal.) *Cots.*
3. Next word. ✓
- What word? (Signal.) *Hits.*
4. (Repeat step 3 for **fast, dots, hats.**)
5. Later, you're going to write the words in the second column.

EXERCISE 12
NEW CIRCLE GAME

1. Everybody, touch part 8.
- The circled word at the beginning of the line tells you what word to circle.
- The number at the end of the line tells how many there are.

2. What word will you circle in the first line? (Signal.) *On.*
- How many are there? (Signal.) *9.*
3. What word will you circle in the second line? (Signal.) *He.*
- How many are there? (Signal.) *6.*
4. What word will you circle in the third line? (Signal.) *She.*
- How many are there? (Signal.) *5.*
5. Circle the words and finish the rest of your Workbook lesson.

EXERCISE 13
WORKBOOK CHECK

1. (Check each student's Workbook.)
2. (Award points for Workbook performance.)
3. (Record the student's total points in Box B.)

0–2 errors	8 points
3–4 errors	4 points
5–6 errors	2 points
7 or more errors	0 points

INDIVIDUAL READING CHECKOUTS

EXERCISE 14
STORY-READING CHECKOUT

- Study the story. If you read all the sentences with no more than 1 error, you'll earn 6 points.
- (Check the students individually.)
- (Record either 6 or 0 points in Box C.)

Lesson point total

(Tell students to write the point total in the last box at the top of the Workbook page. Maximum = 20 points.)

Point Summary Chart

(Tell students to write this point total in the box for Lesson 33 in the Point Summary Chart.)

END OF LESSON 33

Lesson 34

WORD-ATTACK SKILLS

EXERCISE 1
SOUND IDENTIFICATION

Task A

1. Remember, the letter name is the name you say when you say the alphabet. I'll say the sounds. You tell me if each sound is a letter name.
2. Listen: ēēē. Is that a letter name? (Signal.) *Yes.* Right.
3. (Repeat step 2 for ĕĕĕ, ăăă, ōōō, ĭĭĭ, ŏŏŏ.)
4. (Repeat steps 2 and 3 until firm.)

Task B

1. (Point to **o**:) One sound you learned for this letter is the letter name. Everybody, what's that sound? (Touch.) *ōōō.* Yes, ōōō.
   - What's the other sound? (Touch.) *ŏŏŏ.* Yes, ŏŏŏ.
2. (Point to **e**:) One sound you learned for this letter is the letter name. Everybody, what's that sound? (Touch.) *ēēē.* Yes, ēēē.
   - What's the other sound? (Touch.) *ĕĕĕ.* Yes, ĕĕĕ.
3. (Point to **l**:) This letter makes the sound *lll.* What sound? (Touch.) *lll.* Yes, lll.
4. Say each sound when I touch it.
5. (Point to **c**:) What sound? (Touch.) *k.* Yes, k.
6. (Repeat step 5 for **r, ă, ĭ, sh, th, s, wh.**)

Individual test
(Call on two or three students. Touch under each sound. Each student says all the sounds, including two sounds for **e** and two sounds for **o**.)

EXERCISE 2

o⟶

VOWEL VARIATIONS

1. (Point to **o**:) One sound you learned for this letter is the letter name. Everybody, what's the sound? (Touch.) *ōōō.*
2. What's the other sound? (Touch.) *ŏŏŏ.*
3. (Point to **o**:) In some words this letter makes the sound ōōō. In other words it makes the sound ŏŏŏ.

o e l

c r a

i sh th

s wh

Lesson 34   23

Lesson 34

4. (Point to the underlined part of **nod**. Pause.) What sound in this word? (Touch.) ŏŏŏ.
- (Touch the ball of the arrow for **nod**. Pause.) What word? (Slash right:) *Nod.*
5. (Repeat step 4 for **s**o, **g**o**t**, **n**o, **c**o**d**, **g**o, **o**dd.)
6. (Repeat the list until the students can correctly identify all the words in order.)

n**o**d

s**o**

g**o**t

n**o**

c**o**d

g**o**

odd

EXERCISE 3
PRONUNCIATIONS

> **Note:** Do not write the words on the board. This is an oral exercise.

Task A
1. Say these words. Listen: **street.** Say it. (Signal.) *Street.*
2. Next word: **class.** Say it. (Signal.) *Class.*
3. (Repeat step 2 for **trip, ringing.**)
4. (Repeat all the words until firm.)

Task B Chip, chap
1. Listen: **chip.** Say it. (Signal.) *Chip.*
- Listen: **chap.** Say it. (Signal.) *Chap.*
2. One of those words has the middle sound ăăă. I'll say the words again: **chip** (Pause) **chap.**
3. Which word has the middle sound ăăă? (Signal.) *Chap.* Yes, **chap.**
- Which word has the middle sound ĭĭĭ? (Signal.) *Chip.* Yes, **chip.**

Task C Slip, slap
1. Listen: **slip.** Say it. (Signal.) *Slip.*
- Listen: **slap.** Say it. (Signal.) *Slap.*
2. One of those words has the middle sound ĭĭĭ. I'll say the words again: **slip** (pause) **slap.**
3. Which word has the middle sound ĭĭĭ? (Signal.) *Slip.* Yes, **slip.**
- Which word has the middle sound ăăă? (Signal.) *Slap.* Yes, **slap.**

EXERCISE 4
WORD READING THE FAST WAY

1. You're going to read these words the fast way.
2. (For each word: Touch the ball of the arrow. Pause.) What word? (Slash right.)
3. (Repeat each list until firm.)

figs

fins

fast

fist

fits

needs

we

wet

with

seed

tree

street

mend

rocks

win

hen

not

Lesson 34

Lesson 34

WORKBOOK EXERCISES

Note: Pass out the Workbooks. Direct the students to open to Lesson 34.

(Award 6 points if the group worked well during the word attack. Remind the students of the points they can earn in their Workbook.)

EXERCISE 5
SOUND DICTATION

1. I'll say the sounds. You write the letters in part 1 in your Workbook.
2. First sound. Write a letter that says **k** in the first blank.
   (Observe students and give feedback.)
3. Next sound. Write another letter that says **k**.
   (Observe students and give feedback.)
4. Next sound. Write two letters that go together and say **k**.
   (Observe students and give feedback.)
5. Next sound. (Pause.) **lll**. What sound? (Signal.) *lll*.
- Write it.
   (Observe students and give feedback).
6. (Repeat step 5 for **ĭĭĭ, ŏŏŏ, ōōō, thththth, ēēē, d, lll, ĕĕĕ**.)
7. (Repeat sounds students had trouble with.)

EXERCISE 6
SPELLING FROM DICTATION

1. Touch part 2. ✓
- You're going to write words that I dictate.
2. First word: **mad**. What word? (Signal.) *Mad*.
- Listen again: **mmm . . . ăăă . . . d**. Write it in the first blank.
   (Observe students and give feedback.)
3. Next word: **cat**. What word? (Signal.) *Cat*.
- Listen again: **c . . . ăăă . . . t**. Write it in the next blank.
   (Observe students and give feedback.)
4. (Repeat step 3 for **cans, she, shed, that**.)

EXERCISE 7
WORD READING: Workbook

1. Touch the first word in part 3. ✓
2. Tell me the underlined sound in the first word. (Pause.) What sound? (Signal.) *ĭĭĭ*
- (Pause.) What word? (Signal.) *His.*
3. Next word. (Pause.) What sound? (Signal.) *ăăă*.
- (Pause.) What word? (Signal.) *Has.*
4. (Repeat step 3 for **hams, dash, dish, mash, math, kicks, sacks, did, when, with, rods, trot, socks**.)

EXERCISE 8
SENTENCE READING

1. Everybody, touch part 4. ✓
2. Touch under the first word in sentence 1. ✓
- What word? (Signal.) *She.*
3. Next word. ✓
- What word? (Signal.) *Is.*

Lesson 34

4. (Repeat step 3 for **sad, and, sick.**)
5. (Repeat steps 2–4 until the students can correctly identify all the words in the sentence in order.)
6. (Repeat steps 2–5 for each remaining sentence:
   - **2. His fat fish is not fast.**
   - **3. She met me at the dam.**)

> **Individual test**
> (Give each student a chance to read one of the sentences.)

EXERCISE 9
NEW WORD COMPLETION

1. Touch the first word in part 5. ✓
   - What word? (Signal.) *And.* Yes, **and.**
   - Fix it up to say (pause) **land.** What word? (Signal.) *Land.*
   - Fix it up.
     (Observe students and give feedback.)
2. Touch the next word. ✓
   - What word? (Signal.) *An.* Yes, **an.**
   - Fix it up to say (pause) **than.** What word? (Signal.) *Than.*
   - Fix it up.
     (Observe students and give feedback.)
3. (Repeat step 2 for **wi [with], fi [fins], ma [math], eeds [needs].**)

EXERCISE 10
STORY READING

Task A

1. Everybody, touch part 6. ✓
   - You're going to read the sentences the fast way.
2. Touch under first word. ✓
   - What word? (Signal.) *The.*
3. Next word. ✓
   - What word? (Signal.) *Rams.*
4. (Repeat step 3 for **had, a, meet.**)
5. (Repeat steps 2–4 until the students correctly identify all the words in the sentence.)
6. (Repeat steps 2–5 for each remaining sentence:
   - **This ram can win when the rams trot.**
   - **This ram can win when the rams sing.**
   - **When can this ram win?**)
7. (If the students miss more than four words, repeat the story reading from the beginning.)

Task B

1. Now I'll read the story and ask questions. Follow along.
2. **This ram had a meet. This ram can win when the rams trot.** Why do you think that ram can win? (Call on a student.) (Idea: *The ram looks fast.*)
3. **This ram can win when the rams sing.** Everybody, what is the ram in the picture doing? (Signal.) *Singing.*
4. Last sentence. **When can this ram win?** What's the answer? (Call on a student.) (Idea: *When the rams sleep.*)
5. Yes, the ram looks like it's good at sleeping.

EXERCISE 11
MATCHING COMPLETION

1. Everybody, touch part 7. ✓
   - Read the words the fast way.
2. Touch under the first word. ✓
   - What word? (Signal.) *Mend.*
3. Next word. ✓
   - What word? (Signal.) *Them.*
4. (Repeat step 3 for **send, sick, then.**)
5. Later, you're going to write the words in the second column.

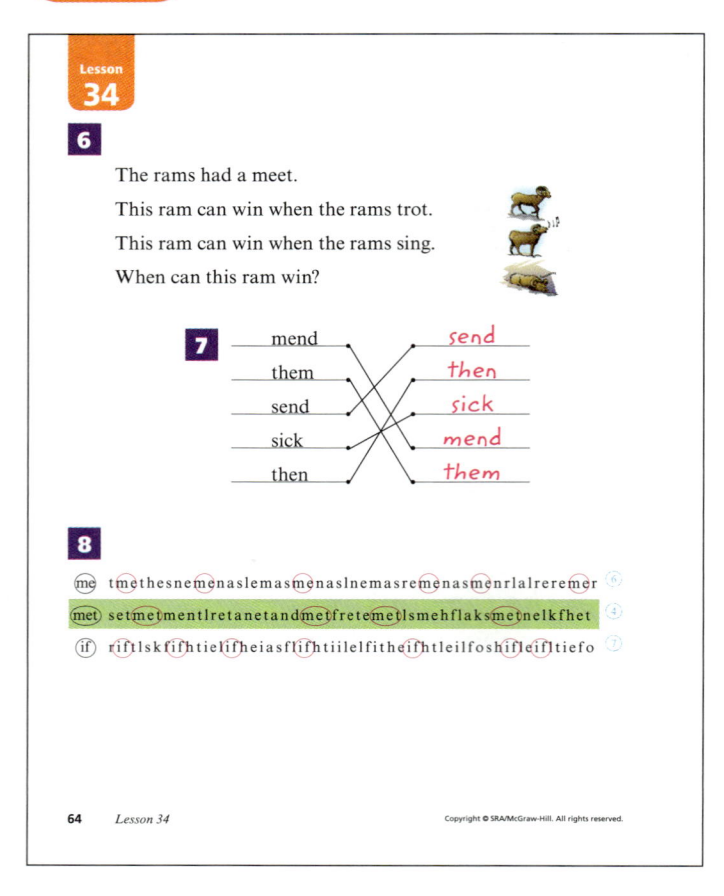

Lesson 34

Lesson 34

6

The rams had a meet.
This ram can win when the rams trot.
This ram can win when the rams sing.
When can this ram win?

7

mend — send
them — then
send — sick
sick — mend
then — them

8

(me) tmethesnemenaslemasmenaslnemasremenasmenrlalreremer 6
(met) setmetmentlretanetandmetfretemetlsmehflaksmetnelkfhet 4
(if) riftlskfifhtielifheiasflifhtiilelfitheifhtleilfoshifleifltiefo 7

EXERCISE 12
CIRCLE GAME

1. Everybody, touch part 8. The circled word at the beginning of the line tells you what word to circle. ✓
   - The number at the end of the line tells how many there are.
2. What word will you circle in the first line? (Signal.) *Me.*
3. What word will you circle in the second line? (Signal.) *Met.*
4. What word will you circle in the third line? (Signal.) *If.*
5. Circle the words and finish the rest of your Workbook lesson.

EXERCISE 13
WORKBOOK CHECK

1. (Check each student's Workbook.)
2. (Award points for Workbook performance.)
3. (Record the student's total points in Box B.)

0–2 errors	8 points
3–4 errors	4 points
5–6 errors	2 points
7 or more errors	0 points

INDIVIDUAL READING CHECKOUTS

EXERCISE 14
STORY-READING CHECKOUT

- Study the story. If you read all the sentences with no more than 1 error, you'll earn 6 points.
- (Check the students individually.)
- (Record either 6 or 0 points in Box C.)

Lesson point total

(Tell students to write the point total in the last box at the top of the Workbook page. Maximum = 20 points.)

Point Summary Chart

(Tell students to write this point total in the box for Lesson 34 in the Point Summary Chart.)

END OF LESSON 34

Lesson 35

WORD-ATTACK SKILLS

EXERCISE 1
SOUND IDENTIFICATION

1. (Point to **e**:) One sound you learned for this letter is the letter name. Everybody, what's that sound? (Touch.) *ēēē*. Yes, *ēēē*.
   - What's the other sound? (Touch.) *ěěě*. Yes, *ěěě*.
2. (Point to **o**:) One sound you learned for this letter is the letter name. Everybody, what's that sound? (Touch.) *ōōō*. Yes, *ōōō*.
   - What's the other sound? (Touch.) *ŏŏŏ*. Yes, *ŏŏŏ*.
3. Say each sound when I touch it.
4. (Point to **r**:) What sound? (Touch.) *rrr*. Yes, **rrr**.
5. (Repeat step 4 for **l, d, n, h, w, ing, ă, ĭ, g**.)

e o r
l d n h
w ing
a i g

Individual test
(Call on two or three students. Touch under each sound. Each student says all the sounds, including two sounds for **e** and two sounds for **o**.)

EXERCISE 2

o

VOWEL VARIATIONS

1. (Point to **o**:) One sound you learned for this letter is the letter name. Everybody, what's the sound? (Touch.) *ōōō*.
2. What's the other sound? (Touch.) *ŏŏŏ*.
3. (Point to **o**:) In some words this letter makes the sound *ōōō*. In other words it makes the sound *ŏŏŏ*.
4. (Point to the underlined part of **got**. Pause.) What sound in this word? (Touch.) *ŏŏŏ*.
   - (Touch the ball of the arrow for **got**. Pause.) What word? (Slash right:) *Got*.
5. (Repeat step 4 for **not, no, go**.)
6. (Repeat the list until the students can correctly identify all the words in order.)

g<u>o</u>t

n<u>o</u>t

n<u>o</u>

g<u>o</u>

Lesson 35

EXERCISE 3

ol

NEW **SOUND COMBINATION: ol**

1. (Point to **ol:**) These letters go together and say **ol**. What sound? (Signal.) *ol*.
2. You're going to read words that have the sound **ol**.
3. (Point to the underlined part of **old:**) What sound? (Touch.) *ol*.
   - What word? (Signal.) *Old*.
4. (Repeat step 3 for **gold, sold**.)

<u>ol</u>d

g<u>ol</u>d

s<u>ol</u>d

EXERCISE 4

PRONUNCIATIONS

> **Note:** Do not write the words on the board. This is an oral exercise.

Task A

1. Say these words. Listen: **clop.** Say it. (Signal.) *Clop*.
2. Next word: **sleek.** Say it. (Signal.) *Sleek*.
3. (Repeat step 2 for **sling, sleep, street**.)
4. (Repeat all the words until firm.)

Task B Slim, slam

1. Listen: **slim.** Say it. (Signal.) *Slim*.
   - Listen: **slam.** Say it. (Signal.) *Slam*.
2. One of those words has the middle sound ĭĭĭ. I'll say the words again: **slim** (pause) **slam**.
3. Which word has the middle sound ĭĭĭ? (Signal.) *Slim*. Yes, **slim**.
   - Which word has the middle sound ăăă? (Signal.) *Slam*. Yes, **slam**.

Task C Dent, dint

1. Listen: **dent.** Say it. (Signal.) *Dent*.
   - Listen: **dint.** Say it. (Signal.) *Dint*.
2. One of those words has the middle sound ĭĭĭ. I'll say the words again: **dent** (pause) **dint**.
3. Which word has the middle sound ĭĭĭ? (Signal.) *Dint*. Yes, **dint**.
   - Which word has the middle sound ĕĕĕ? (Signal.) *Dent*. Yes, **dent**.

Task D Cheek, check

1. Listen: **cheek.** Say it. (Signal.) *Cheek*.
   - Listen: **check.** Say it. (Signal.) *Check*.
2. One of those words has the middle sound ēēē. I'll say the words again: **cheek** (pause) **check**.
3. Which word has the middle sound ēēē? (Signal.) *Cheek*. Yes, **cheek**.
   - Which word has the middle sound ĕĕĕ? (Signal.) *Check*. Yes, **check**.

EXERCISE 5
WORD READING THE FAST WAY

1. You're going to read these words the fast way.
2. (For each word: Touch the ball of the arrow. Pause.) What word? (Slash right.)
3. (Repeat each word list until firm.)

lit

let

lot

lack

lock

lick

sick

will

well

fill

fell

track

trick

trot

Lesson 35 31

Lesson 35

4. (For each word: Touch the ball of the arrow. Pause.) What word? (Slash right.)
5. (Repeat the column until firm.)

when

wheel

then

get

sent

am

WORKBOOK EXERCISES

Note: Pass out the Workbooks. Direct the students to open to Lesson 35.

(Award 6 points if the group worked well during the word attack. Remind the students of the points they can earn in their Workbook.)

EXERCISE 6
SOUND DICTATION

1. I'll say the sounds. You write the letters in part 1 in your Workbook.
2. First sound. Write a letter that says **www** in the first blank.
   (Observe students and give feedback.)
3. Next sound. Write two letters that go together and say **www.**
   (Observe students and give feedback.)
4. Next sound. (Pause.) **ĕĕĕ.** What sound? (Signal.) ĕĕĕ.
   • Write it.
   (Observe students and give feedback).
5. (Repeat step 4 for **lll, ōōō, thththth, ŏŏŏ, ăăă, ĭĭĭ, lll, g, d.**)
6. (Repeat sounds students had trouble with.)

EXERCISE 7
SPELLING FROM DICTATION

1. Touch part 2. ✓
   • You're going to write words that I dictate.
2. First word: **that.** What word? (Signal.) *That.*
   • Listen again: **thththth . . . ăăă . . . t.** Write it in the first blank.
   (Observe students and give feedback.)
3. Next word: **this.** What word? (Signal.) *This.*
   • Listen again: **thththth . . . ĭĭĭ . . . sss.** Write it in the next blank.
   (Observe students and give feedback.)

Lesson 35

4. Next word: **then.** Not **than. Then.** What word? (Signal.) *Then.*
- Listen again: **ththth . . . ĕĕĕ . . . nnn.** Write it in the next blank.
(Observe students and give feedback.)
5. (Repeat step 3 for **hit** [not **hid**], **hid, sat** [not **sad**].)

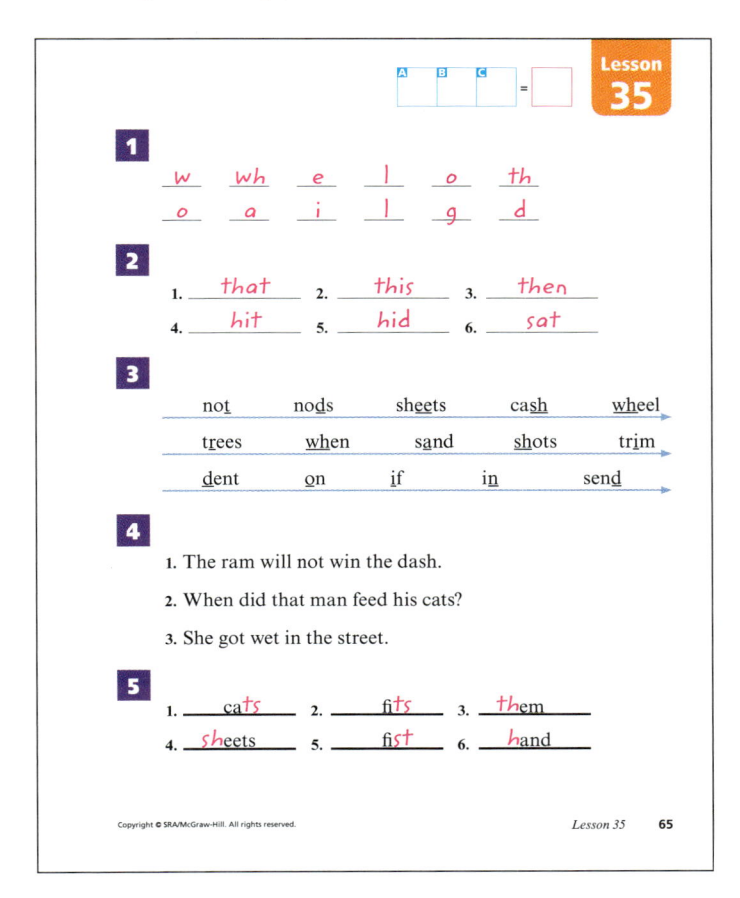

Workbook page (Lesson 35, p. 65)

Part 1:
w wh e l o th
o a i l g d

Part 2:
1. that   2. this   3. then
4. hit   5. hid   6. sat

Part 3:
not   nods   sheets   cash   wheel
trees when   sand   shots   trim
dent   on   if   in   send

Part 4:
1. The ram will not win the dash.
2. When did that man feed his cats?
3. She got wet in the street.

Part 5:
1. cats   2. fits   3. them
4. sheets 5. fist   6. hand

EXERCISE 8
WORD READING: Workbook

1. Touch the first word in part 3. ✓
2. Tell me the underlined sound in the first word. (Pause.) What sound? (Signal.) *t.*
- (Pause.) What word? (Signal.) *Not.*
3. Next word. (Pause.) What sound? (Signal.) *d.*
- (Pause.) What word? (Signal.) *Nods.*
4. (Repeat step 3 for **sheets, cash, wheel, trees, when, sand, shots, trim, dent, on, if, in, send.**)

EXERCISE 9
SENTENCE READING

1. Everybody, touch part 4. ✓
2. Touch under the first word in sentence 1. ✓
- What word? (Signal.) *The.*
3. Next word. ✓
- What word? (Signal.) *Ram.*
4. (Repeat step 3 for **will, not, win, the, dash.**)
5. (Repeat steps 2–4 until the students can correctly identify all the words in the sentence in order.)
6. (Repeat steps 2–5 for each remaining sentence:
- **2. When did that man feed his cats?**
- **3. She got wet in the street.**)

> **Individual test**
> (Give each student a chance to read one of the sentences.)

EXERCISE 10
WORD COMPLETION

1. Touch the first word in part 5. ✓
- What word? (Signal.) *ca.* Yes, **ca.**
- Fix it up to say (pause) **cats.** What word? (Signal.) *Cats.*
- Fix it up.
(Observe students and give feedback.)
2. Touch the next word. ✓
- What word? (Signal.) *fi.* Yes, **fi.**
- Fix it up to say (pause) **fits.** What word? (Signal.) *Fits.*
- Fix it up.
(Observe students and give feedback.)
3. (Repeat step 2 for **em [them], eets [sheets], fi [fist], and [hand].**)

Lesson 35

EXERCISE 11
STORY READING

Task A

1. Everybody, touch part 6. ✓
- You're going to read the sentences the fast way.
2. Touch under the first word. ✓
- What word? (Signal.) *He.*
3. Next word. ✓
- What word? (Signal.) *Has.*
4. (Repeat step 3 for **an, ant.**)
5. (Repeat steps 2–4 until the students correctly identify all the words in the sentence.)
6. (Repeat steps 2–5 for each remaining sentence:
- **That ant is trim and fast.**
- **It is as fast as a cat.**
- **And it can fit in a hand.**)
7. (If the students miss more than four words, repeat the story reading from the beginning.)

Task B

1. Now I'll read the story and ask questions. Follow along.
2. **He has an ant.** Everybody, what does he have? (Signal.) *An ant.*
3. **That ant is trim and fast.** If an ant is trim, how does it look? (Call on a student.) (Idea: *Thin, healthy.*)
4. **It is as fast as a cat.** Which is faster, the cat or the ant? (Call on a student.) (Ideas: *Neither; the ant is as fast as a cat.*)
5. **And it can fit in a hand.** I don't see the ant. Where is it? (Call on a student.) *In the hand.* Yes, in the hand.
- I wonder what that ant would do if it wanted to get out of the hand. What do you think the ant would do? (Call on a student.) (Ideas: *Squeeze out of the fist; run fast when the hand opens.*)

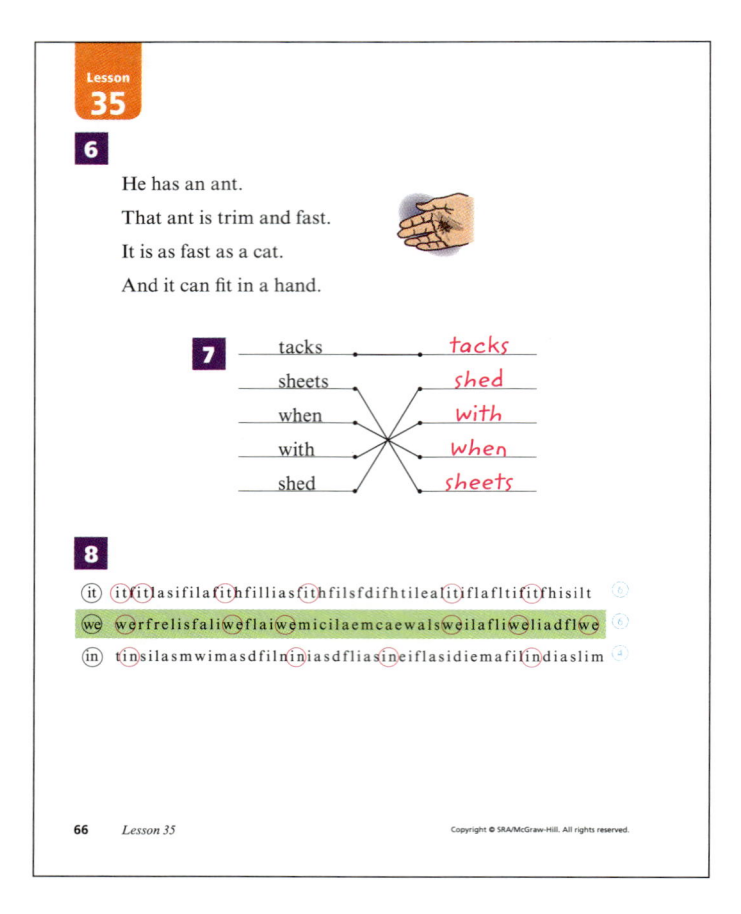

Lesson 35

6

He has an ant.
That ant is trim and fast.
It is as fast as a cat.
And it can fit in a hand.

7
tacks — tacks
sheets — shed
when — with
with — when
shed — sheets

8

(it) it it asifila ith fillias ith filsfdifhtilea it iflafltifit hisilt
(we) werfrelisfali we flai we micilaemcaewals we ilafli we liadfl we
(in) tin silasmwimasdfil n in iasdflias in eiflasidiemafil in diaslim

66 Lesson 35

34 Lesson 35

Lesson 35

EXERCISE 12
MATCHING COMPLETION

1. Everybody, touch part 7. ✓
- Read the words the fast way.
2. Touch under the first word. ✓
- What word? (Signal.) *Tacks.*
3. Next word. ✓
- What word? (Signal.) *Sheets.*
4. (Repeat step 3 for **when, with, shed.**)
5. Later, you're going to write the words in the second column.

EXERCISE 13
CIRCLE GAME

1. Everybody, touch part 8. ✓
2. What word will you circle in the first line? (Signal.) *It.*
3. What word will you circle in the second line? (Signal.) *We.*
4. What word will you circle in the third line? (Signal.) *In.*
5. Circle the words and finish the rest of your Workbook lesson.

EXERCISE 14
WORKBOOK CHECK

1. (Check each student's Workbook.)
2. (Award points for Workbook performance.)
3. (Record the student's total points in Box B.)

0–2 errors	8 points
3–4 errors	4 points
5–6 errors	2 points
7 or more errors	0 points

INDIVIDUAL READING CHECKOUTS

EXERCISE 15
STORY-READING CHECKOUT

- Study the story. If you read all the sentences with no more than one error, you'll earn 6 points.
- (Check the students individually.)
- (Record either 6 or 0 points in Box C.)

Lesson point total

(Tell students to write the point total in the last box at the top of the Workbook page. Maximum = 20 points.)

Point Summary Chart

(Tell students to write this point total in the box for Lesson 35 in the Point Summary Chart.)

Five-lesson point summary

(Tell students to add the point totals for Lessons 31 through 35 in the Point Summary Chart and to write the total for Block 7. Maximum for Block 7 = 100 points.)

END OF LESSON 35

MASTERY TEST 8

AFTER LESSON 35, BEFORE LESSON 36

> **Note:** Use students' performance on the Lesson 35 Story reading checkout for Mastery Test 8.

Scoring the test

1. (Count each student's errors on the Story reading checkout. Write these numbers in the Test 8 boxes on the *Decoding A* Mastery Test Student Profile form. Circle **P** or **F**.)
2. (When all students have been tested, circle **P** or **F** for each student on the *Decoding A* Mastery Test Group Summary form. Determine if more than 25 percent of the students failed the Story reading checkout by dividing the number of students who failed by the total number of students in the group.)

Remedies

(If more than 25 percent of the students made 2 or more errors on the Story reading checkout, [1] repeat the Story reading checkouts for Lessons 31 through 34, and [2] repeat all of Lesson 35. Permission is granted to reproduce the Workbook pages for Lesson 35 for classroom use.)

Lesson Objectives	LESSON 36 Exercise	LESSON 37 Exercise	LESSON 38 Exercise	LESSON 39 Exercise	LESSON 40 Exercise
Word Attack					
Phonemic Awareness					
Sound/Word Pronunciation	1, 4, 5	1, 2, 4	1, 2	1, 2	1, 2
Identify Sounds in Words	4, 5	2	2	2	2
Decoding and Word Analysis					
Letter Sounds: *er, ō, ŏ, ē, ĕ, w, t, l, r, a, g, i, sh, th*	1				
Letter Sounds: *l*	2				
Letter Sounds: *er, ō, ŏ, ē, ĕ, wh, r, n, l, h, a, d, w, ol*		1			
Letter Sounds: *p, ē, ĕ, ō, ŏ, c, k, i, er, th, a, d, ck*			1		
Letter Sounds: *u, ē, ĕ, ō, ŏ, p, i, d, g, wh, th, a, l, k*				1	
Letter Sounds: *u, ē, ĕ, ō, ŏ, n, a, ol, r, i, sh, wh, p, th, er*					1
Vowel Sound Discrimination: *ō, ŏ*	4				
Sound Combination: *ol*	3				
Word Recognition	3–6	3	3	3	3
Assessment					
Ongoing: Individual Tests	1	1	1	1	1
Group Reading					
Decoding and Word Analysis					
Read Decodable Text	12	9	9	9	9
Comprehension					
Make Predictions					
Access Prior Knowledge			9	9	9
Draw Inferences	12	9	9	9	
Note Details	12	9	9	9	9
Assessment					
Ongoing: Comprehension Check	12	9	9	9	9
Ongoing: Decoding Accuracy	12	9	9	9	9
Formal: Mastery Test					MT 9
Workbook Exercises					
Decoding and Word Analysis					
Word Recognition	9	6	6	6	6
Sentence Reading	10	7	7	7	7
Sound Combinations	9	6	6	6	6
Spelling: Sound/Letter Relationships	7, 11, 13	4, 8, 10	4, 8, 10	4, 8, 10	4, 8, 10
Spelling: CVC, CCVC					5
Spelling: CVC, CCVC, CVVC			5		
Spelling: CVC, CVVC, VC				5	
Spelling: CVC, CCVC, CVCC	8				
Spelling: CVV, CVCC, CCVC		5			
Visual Discrimination	13, 14	10, 11	10, 11	10, 11	10, 11
Assessment					
Ongoing: Individual Tests	10	7	7	7	7
Ongoing: Teacher-Monitored Accuracy	16	13	13	13	13
Ongoing: Workcheck	15	12	12	12	12

Objectives   *Lessons 36–40*   **37**

Lesson 36

WORD-ATTACK SKILLS

EXERCISE 1
SOUND INTRODUCTION

1. (Point to **er**:) These letters usually make the sound **er**. What sound? (Touch.) *er*.
2. (Point to **o**:) One sound you learned for this letter is the letter name. Everybody, what's that sound? (Touch.) *ōōō*. Yes, **ōōō**.
- What's the other sound? (Touch.) *ŏŏŏ*. Yes, **ŏŏŏ**.
3. (Point to **e**:) One sound you learned for this letter is the letter name. Everybody, what's that sound? (Touch.) *ēēē*. Yes, **ēēē**.
- What's the other sound? (Touch.) *ĕĕĕ*. Yes, **ĕĕĕ**.
4. Say each sound when I touch it.
5. (Point to **w**:) What sound? (Touch.) *www*. Yes, **www**.
6. (Repeat step 5 for **t, l, r, ă, g, ĭ, sh, th**.)

er   o   e
w   t   l
r   a   g
i   sh   th

Individual test
(Call on two or three students. Touch under each sound. Each student says all the sounds, including two sounds for **e** and two sounds for **o**.)

EXERCISE 2

I

NEW CAPITAL I

1. (Point to **I**.)
2. This is capital **I**. It's a word when it's in a sentence. **I**. (Pause.) It means **me**.

EXERCISE 3

ol

SOUND COMBINATION: ol

1. (Point to **ol**:) These letters go together and say **ol**. What sound? (Signal.) *ol*.
2. You're going to read words that have the sound **ol**.
3. (Point to the underlined part of **mold**:) What sound? (Touch.) *ol*.
- What word? (Signal.) *Mold*.
4. (Repeat step 3 for **told, cold**.)

m<u>o</u>ld

t<u>ol</u>d

c<u>ol</u>d

38   Lesson 36

EXERCISE 4

o

VOWEL VARIATIONS

1. (Point to **o:**) One sound you learned for this letter is the letter name. Everybody, what's the sound? (Touch.) ōōō.
2. What's the other sound? (Touch.) ŏŏŏ.
3. (Point to **o:**) In some words this letter makes the sound ōōō. In other words it makes the sound ŏŏŏ.
4. (Point to the underlined part of **got.** Pause.) What sound in this word? (Touch.) ŏŏŏ.
- (Touch the ball of the arrow for **got.** Pause.) What word? (Slash right:) *Got.*
5. (Repeat step 4 for **s**o**cks, s**o**, g**o**, n**o**d, n**o**t, n**o**.)
6. (Repeat the list until the students can correctly identify all the words in order.)

g**o**t

s**o**cks

s**o**

g**o**

n**o**d

n**o**t

n**o**

EXERCISE 5
PRONUNCIATIONS

Note: Do not write the words on the board. This is an oral exercise.

Task A

1. Say these words. Listen: **flag.** Say it. (Signal.) *Flag.*
2. Next word: **crack.** Say it. (Signal.) *Crack.*
3. (Repeat step 2 for **trot, sling, creek, stops, slip.**)
4. (Repeat all the words until firm.)

Task B Clack, click

1. Listen: **clack.** Say it. (Signal.) *Clack.*
- Listen: **click.** Say it. (Signal.) *Click.*
2. One of those words has the middle sound ăăă. I'll say both words again: **clack** (pause) **click.**
3. Which word has the middle sound ăăă? (Signal.) *Clack.* Yes, **clack.**
- Which word has the middle sound ĭĭĭ? (Signal.) *Click.* Yes, **click.**

Task C Trick, track

1. Listen: **trick.** Say it. (Signal.) *Trick.*
- Listen: **track.** Say it. (Signal.) *Track.*
2. One of those words has the middle sound ăăă. I'll say both words again: **trick** (pause) **track.**
3. Which word has the middle sound ăăă? (Signal.) *Track.* Yes, **track.**
- Which word has the middle sound ĭĭĭ? (Signal.) *Trick.* Yes, **trick.**

Lesson 36

Lesson 36

Task D Chomp, champ

1. Listen: **chomp.** Say it. (Signal.) *Chomp.*
- Listen: **champ.** Say it. (Signal.) *Champ.*
2. One of those words has the middle sound **ŏŏŏ.** I'll say both words again: **chomp** (pause) **champ.**
3. Which word has the middle sound **ŏŏŏ?** (Signal.) *Chomp.* Yes, **chomp.**
- Which word has the middle sound **ăăă?** (Signal.) *Champ.* Yes, **champ.**

EXERCISE 6
WORD READING THE FAST WAY

1. You're going to read these words the fast way.
2. (For each word: Touch the ball of the arrow. Pause.) What word? (Slash right.)
3. (Repeat each word list until firm.)

rack

track

lack

tack

lick

click

how

kits

kills

mills

add

and

we

with

slid

40 *Lesson 36*

Lesson 36

4. (For each word: Touch the ball of the arrow. Pause.) **What word?** (Slash right.)
5. (Repeat the column until firm.)

sled

wheel

wet

went

hands

lands

sacks

WORKBOOK EXERCISES

Note: Pass out the Workbooks. Direct the students to open to Lesson 36.

(Award 6 points if the group worked well during the word attack. Remind the students of the points they can earn in their Workbook.)

EXERCISE 7
SOUND DICTATION

1. I'll say the sounds. You write the letters in part 1 in your Workbook.
2. First sound. Write a letter that says **k** in the first blank.
   (Observe students and give feedback.)
3. Next sound. Write another letter that says **k**.
   (Observe students and give feedback.)
4. Next sound. Write two letters that go together and say **k**.
   (Observe students and give feedback.)
5. Next sound. (Pause.) **shshsh.** What sound? (Signal.) *shshsh.*
   • Write it.
   (Observe students and give feedback).
6. Next sound. (Pause.) **ăăă.** What sound? (Signal.) *ăăă.*
   • Write it.
   (Observe students and give feedback).
7. (Repeat step 6 for **ŏŏŏ, ĭĭĭ, ōōō, ĕĕĕ, d, ēēē, lll.**)
8. (Repeat sounds students had trouble with.)

EXERCISE 8
SPELLING FROM DICTATION

1. Touch part 2. ✓
   • You're going to write words that I dictate.
2. First word: **dad.** What word? (Signal.) *Dad.*
   • Listen again: **d . . . ăăă . . . d.** Write it in the first blank. (Observe students and give feedback.)

Lesson 36   41

Lesson 36

3. Next word: **she.** What word? (Signal.) *She.*
- Listen again: **shshsh . . . ēēē.** Write it in the next blank.
(Observe students and give feedback.)
4. (Repeat step 3 for **that, did, fans, cats.**)

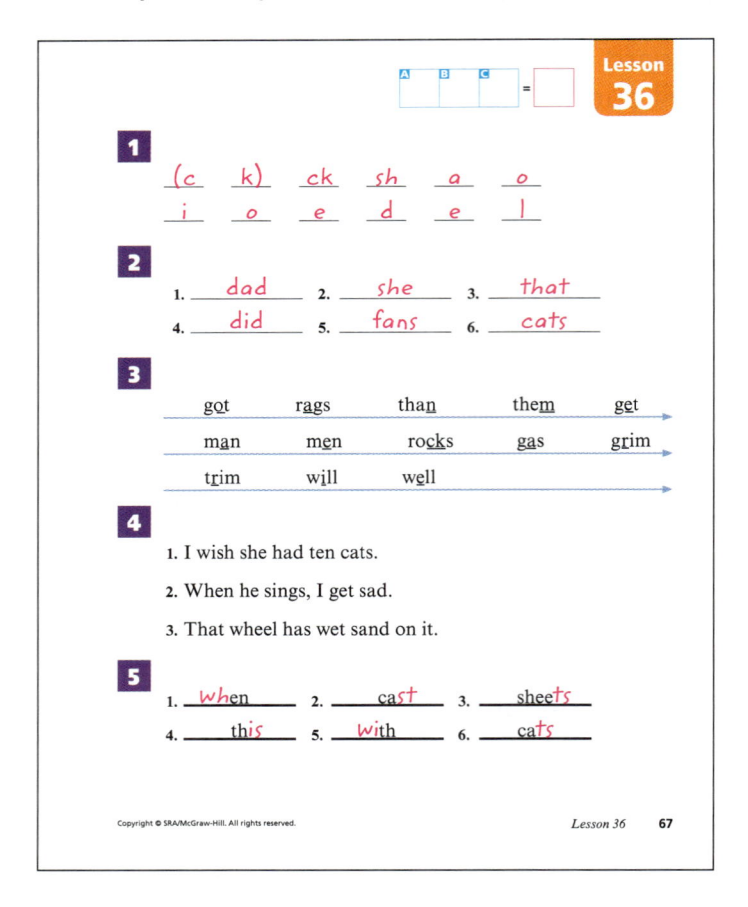

Lesson 36 Workbook

1
(c k) ck sh a o
i o e d e l

2
1. dad 2. she 3. that
4. did 5. fans 6. cats

3
got rags than them get
man men rocks gas grim
trim will well

4
1. I wish she had ten cats.
2. When he sings, I get sad.
3. That wheel has wet sand on it.

5
1. when 2. cast 3. sheets
4. this 5. with 6. cats

Lesson 36 67

EXERCISE 9
WORD READING: Workbook

1. Touch the first word in part 3. ✓
2. Tell me the underlined sound in the first word. (Pause.) What sound? (Signal.) ŏŏŏ.
- (Pause.) What word? (Signal.) *Got.*
3. Next word. (Pause.) What sound? (Signal.) ăăă.
- (Pause.) What word? (Signal.) *Rags.*
4. (Repeat step 3 for **than, them, get, man, men, rocks, gas, grim, trim, will, well.**)

EXERCISE 10
SENTENCE READING

1. Everybody, touch part 4. ✓
2. Touch under the first word in sentence 1. ✓
- What word? (Signal.) *I.*
3. Next word. ✓
- What word? (Signal.) *Wish.*
4. (Repeat step 3 for **she, had, ten, cats.**)
5. (Repeat steps 2–4 until the students can correctly identify all the words in the sentence in order.)
6. (Repeat steps 2–5 for each remaining sentence:
- **2. When he sings, I get sad.**
- **3. That wheel has wet sand on it.**)

Individual test
(Give each student a chance to read one of the sentences.)

EXERCISE 11
WORD COMPLETION

1. Touch the first word in part 5. ✓
- What word? (Signal.) *en.* Yes, **en.**
- Fix it up to say (pause) **when.** What word? (Signal.) *When.*
- Fix it up.
(Observe students and give feedback.)
2. Touch the next word. ✓
- What word? (Signal.) *ca.* Yes, **ca.**
- Fix it up to say (pause) **cast.** What word? (Signal.) *Cast.*
- Fix it up.
(Observe students and give feedback.)
3. (Repeat step 2 for **shee [sheets], th [this], th [with], ca [cats].**)

42 *Lesson 36*

EXERCISE 12
STORY READING

Task A

1. **Everybody, touch part 6.** ✓
- **You're going to read the sentences the fast way.**
2. **Touch under the first word.** ✓
- **What word?** (Signal.) *A.*
3. **Next word.** ✓
- **What word?** (Signal.) *Tack.*
4. (Repeat step 3 for **sat, on, the, track.**)
5. (Repeat steps 2–4 until the students correctly identify all the words in the sentence.)
6. (Repeat steps 2–5 for each remaining sentence:)
- **This wheel went on the track.**
- **The tack got in the wheel.**
- **And that wheel did this.**
7. (If the students miss more than four words, repeat the story reading from the beginning.)

Task B

1. **Now I'll read the story and ask questions. Follow along.**
2. **A tack sat on the track.** The track is like a racetrack.
3. **This wheel went on the track.** That wheel is part of something. What's that? (Call on a student.) (Ideas: *Car; truck.*)
4. **The tack got in the wheel.** How did that happen? (Call on a student.) (Idea: *The car drove over the tack, and the tack stuck in the wheel.*)
5. **And that wheel did this.** Why did that happen? (Call on a student.) (Idea: *The air leaked out the hole that the tack made.*)
- **Everybody, touch the flat tire in the picture.** ✓

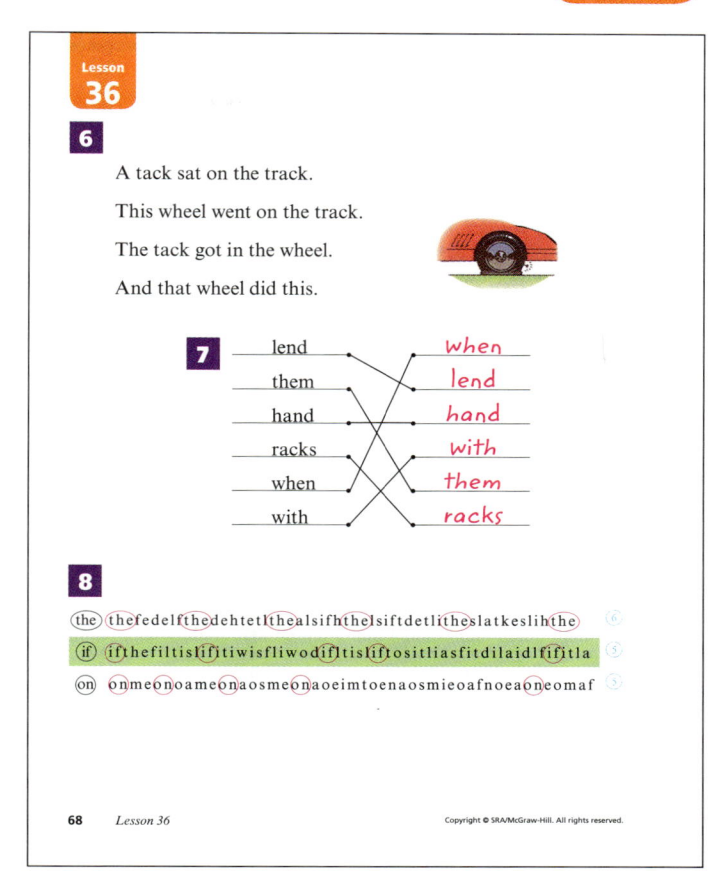

EXERCISE 13
MATCHING COMPLETION

1. **Everybody, touch part 7.** ✓
- **Read the words the fast way.**
2. **Touch under the first word.** ✓
- **What word?** (Signal.) *Lend.*
3. **Next word.** ✓
- **What word?** (Signal.) *Them.*
4. (Repeat step 3 for **hand, racks, when, with.**)
5. **Later, you're going to write the words in the second column.**

Lesson 36   43

Lesson 36

EXERCISE 14
CIRCLE GAME

1. Everybody, touch part 8. ✓
2. What word will you circle in the first line? (Signal.) *The.*
3. What word will you circle in the second line? (Signal.) *If.*
4. What word will you circle in the third line? (Signal.) *On.*
5. Circle the words and finish the rest of your Workbook lesson.

EXERCISE 15
WORKBOOK CHECK

1. (Check each student's Workbook.)
2. (Award points for Workbook performance.)
3. (Record the student's total points in Box B.)

0–2 errors	8 points
3–4 errors	4 points
5–6 errors	2 points
7 or more errors	0 points

INDIVIDUAL READING CHECKOUTS

EXERCISE 16
STORY-READING CHECKOUT

- Study the story. If you read all the sentences with no more than 1 error, you'll earn 6 points.
- (Check the students individually.)
- (Record either 6 or 0 points in Box C.)

Lesson point total
(Tell students to write the point total in the last box at the top of the Workbook page. Maximum = 20 points.)

Point Summary Chart
(Tell students to write this point total in the box for Lesson 36 in the Point Summary Chart.)

END OF LESSON 36

Lesson 37

WORD-ATTACK SKILLS

EXERCISE 1
SOUND INTRODUCTION

1. (Point to **er:**) These letters usually make the sound **er.** What sound? (Touch.) *er.*
2. (Point to **o:**) One sound you learned for this letter is the letter name. Everybody, what's that sound? (Touch.) *ōōō.* Yes, **ōōō.**
- What's the other sound? (Touch.) *ŏŏŏ.* Yes, **ŏŏŏ.**
3. (Point to **e:**) One sound you learned for this letter is the letter name. Everybody, what's that sound? (Touch.) *ēēē.* Yes, **ēēē.**
- What's the other sound? (Touch.) *ĕĕĕ.* Yes, **ĕĕĕ.**
4. Say each sound when I touch it.
5. (Point to **wh:**) What sound? (Touch.) *www.* Yes, **www.**
6. (Repeat step 5 for **r, n, l, h, ă, d, w, er, ĭ, ol.**)

er o e
wh r n
l h a d
w er i
ol

Individual test
(Call on two or three students. Touch under each sound. Each student says all the sounds, including two sounds for **o** and two sounds for **e.**)

EXERCISE 2
PRONUNCIATIONS

Note: Do not write the words on the board. This is an oral exercise.

Task A

1. Say these words. Listen: **crack.** Say it. (Signal.) *Crack.*
2. Next word: **clack.** Say it. (Signal.) *Clack.*
3. (Repeat step 2 for **track, sleek, pots, slick.**)
4. (Repeat all the words until firm.)

Task B Slip, sleep

1. Listen: **slip.** Say it. (Signal.) *Slip.*
- Listen: **sleep.** Say it. (Signal.) *Sleep.*
2. One of those words has the middle sound **ēēē.** I'll say the words again: **slip** (pause) **sleep.**
3. Which word has the middle sound **ēēē**? (Signal.) *Sleep.* Yes, **sleep.**
- Which word has the middle sound **ĭĭĭ**? (Signal.) *Slip.* Yes, **slip.**

Task C Chomp, champ

1. Listen: **chomp.** Say it. (Signal.) *Chomp.*
- Listen: **champ.** Say it. (Signal.) *Champ.*
2. One of those words has the middle sound **ăăă.** I'll say the words again: **chomp** (pause) **champ.**
3. Which word has the middle sound **ăăă**? (Signal.) *Champ.* Yes, **champ.**
- Which word has the middle sound **ŏŏŏ**? (Signal.) *Chomp.* Yes, **chomp.**

Task D List, last

1. Listen: **list.** Say it. (Signal.) *List.*
- Listen: **last.** Say it. (Signal.) *Last.*
2. One of those words has the middle sound **ĭĭĭ.** I'll say both words again: **list** (pause) **last.**
3. Which word has the middle sound **ĭĭĭ**? (Signal.) *List.* Yes, **list.**
- Which word has the middle sound **ăăă**? (Signal.) *Last.* Yes, **last.**

Lesson 37

Lesson 37

EXERCISE 3
WORD READING THE FAST WAY

1. You're going to read these words the fast way.
2. (For each word: Touch the ball of the arrow. Pause.) What word? (Slash right.)
3. (Repeat each word list until firm.)

sack

rack

crack

kits

list

go

got

sad

seed

ten

teen

so

clam

no

went

when

4. (For each word: Touch the ball of the arrow. Pause.) What word? (Slash right.)
5. (Repeat the column until firm.)

well

with

wish

will

sleek

Lesson 37

WORKBOOK EXERCISES

Note: Pass out the Workbooks. Direct the students to open to Lesson 37.

(Award 6 points if the group worked well during the word attack. Remind the students of the points they can earn in their Workbook.)

EXERCISE 4
SOUND DICTATION

1. I'll say the sounds. You write the letters in part 1 in your Workbook.
2. First sound. (Pause.) **ēēē.** What sound? (Signal.) *ēēē.*
- Write it.
   (Observe students and give feedback.)
3. Next sound. (Pause.) **rrr.** What sound? (Signal.) *rrr.*
- Write it.
   (Observe students and give feedback.)
4. Next sound. Write a letter that says **www.**
   (Observe students and give feedback.)
5. Next sound. Write two letters that go together and say **www.**
   (Observe students and give feedback.)
6. Next sound. (Pause.) **thththth.** What sound? (Signal.) *thththth.*
- Write it.
   (Observe students and give feedback).
7. Next sound. (Pause.) **fff.** What sound? (Signal.) *fff.*
- Write it.
   (Observe students and give feedback).
8. (Repeat step 7 for **ĕĕĕ, ĭĭĭ, ŏŏŏ, ăăă, g, d.**)
9. (Repeat sounds students had trouble with.)

Lesson 37

Lesson 37

EXERCISE 5
SPELLING FROM DICTATION

1. Touch part 2. ✓
- You're going to write words that I dictate.
2. First word: **see**. What word? (Signal.) *See.*
- Listen again: **sss . . . ēēē**. Write it in the first blank. Remember to write two **ē**'s. (Observe students and give feedback.)
3. Next word: **seem**. What word? (Signal.) *Seem.*
- Listen again: **sss . . . ēēē . . . mmm**. Write it in the next blank. Remember to write two **ē**'s. (Observe students and give feedback.)
4. (Repeat step 3 for **than** [not **then**], **this, cats**.)

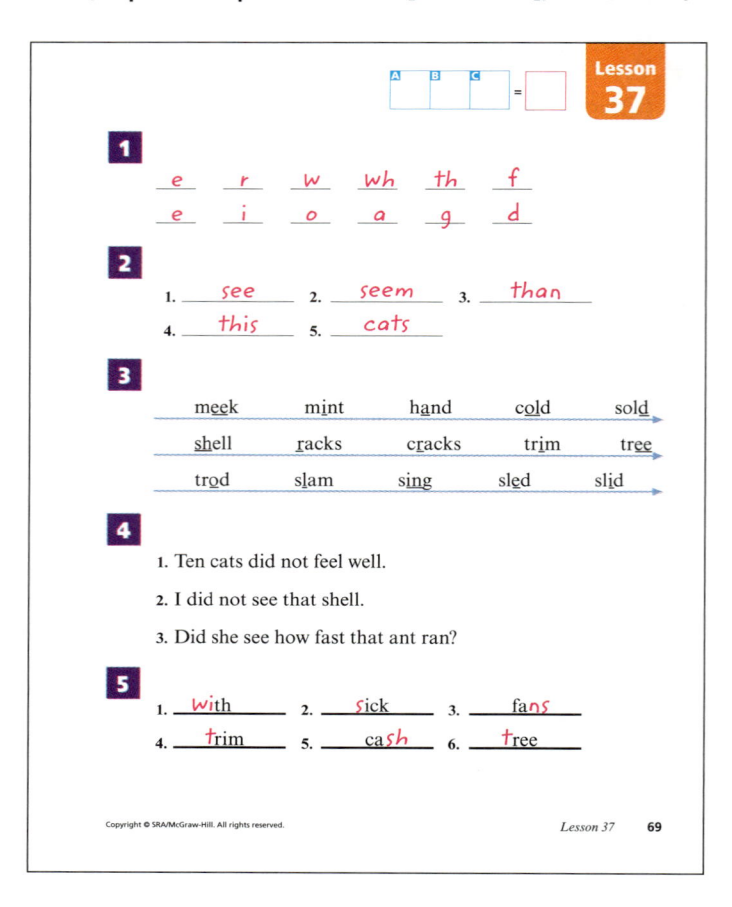

EXERCISE 6
WORD READING: Workbook

1. Touch the first word in part 3. ✓
2. Tell me the underlined sound in the first word. (Pause.) What sound? (Signal.) *ēēē.*
- (Pause.) What word? (Signal.) *Meek.*
3. Next word. (Pause.) What sound? (Signal.) *ĭĭĭ.*
- (Pause.) What word? (Signal.) *Mint.*

4. (Repeat step 3 for **hand, cold, sold, shell, racks, cracks, trim, tree, trod, slam, sing, sled, slid**.)

EXERCISE 7
SENTENCE READING

1. Everybody, touch part 4. ✓
2. Touch under the first word in sentence 1. ✓
- What word? (Signal.) *Ten.*
3. Next word. ✓
- What word? (Signal.) *Cats.*
4. (Repeat step 3 for **did, not, feel, well**.)
5. (Repeat steps 2–4 until the students can correctly identify all the words in the sentence in order.)
6. (Repeat steps 2–5 for each remaining sentence:
- 2. **I did not see that shell.**
- 3. **Did she see how fast that ant ran?**)

> **Individual test**
> (Give each student a chance to read one of the sentences.)

EXERCISE 8
WORD COMPLETION

1. Touch the first sound in part 5. ✓
- What sound? (Signal.) *thththth.* Yes, **thththth**.
- Fix it up to say (pause) **with**. What word? (Signal.) *With.*
- Fix it up. (Observe students and give feedback.)
2. Touch the next word. ✓
- What word? (Signal.) *ick.* Yes, **ick**.
- Fix it up to say (pause) **sick**. What word? (Signal.) *Sick.*
- Fix it up. (Observe students and give feedback.)
3. (Repeat step 2 for **fa [fans], rim [trim], ca [cash], ree [tree]**.)

48 Lesson 37

Lesson 37

EXERCISE 9
STORY READING

Task A

1. Everybody, touch part 6. ✓
   - You're going to read the sentences the fast way.
2. Touch under the first word. ✓
   - What word? (Signal.) *A.*
3. Next word. ✓
   - What word? (Signal.) *Crack.*
4. (Repeat step 3 for **is, in, the, street.**)
5. (Repeat steps 2–4 until the students correctly identify all the words in the sentence.)
6. (Repeat steps 2–5 for each remaining sentence:
   - **A ram is in the crack.**
   - **A rat is on the ram.**
   - **This is on the rat.**)
7. (If students miss more than four words, repeat the story reading from the beginning.)

Task B

1. Now I'll read the story and ask questions. Follow along.
2. **A crack is in the street. A ram is in the crack.** Everybody, is that a big crack or a little crack? (Signal.) *A big crack.*
3. **A rat is on the ram.** Everybody, what's on the ram? (Signal.) *A rat.*
   - Where is the ram? (Call on a student.) (Ideas: *In the crack; in the street.*)
4. **This is on the rat.** What is in the picture? (Call on a student.) (Idea: *A bug.*)
   - Everybody, where is that bug? (Signal.) *On the rat.*
5. Where is the rat? (Signal.) *On the ram.*
   - Where is the ram? (Call on a student.) (Ideas: *In the crack; in the street.*)

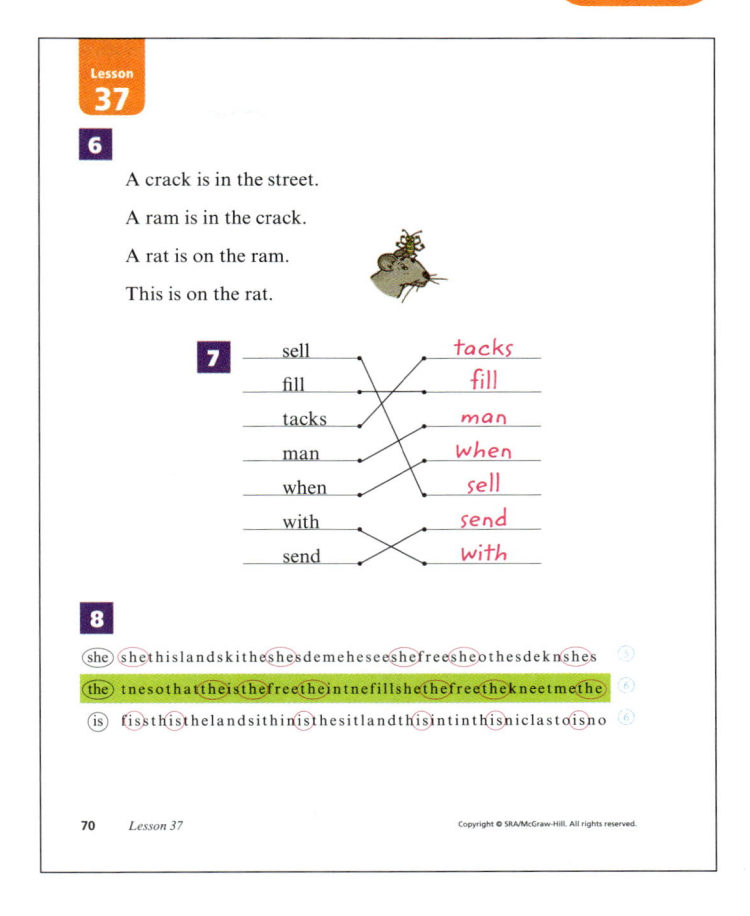

EXERCISE 10
MATCHING COMPLETION

1. Everybody, touch part 7. ✓
   - Read the words the fast way.
2. Touch under the first word. ✓
   - What word? (Signal.) *Sell.*
3. Next word. ✓
   - What word? (Signal.) *Fill.*
4. (Repeat step 3 for **tacks, man, when, with, send.**)
5. Later, you're going to write the words in the second column.

Lesson 37

EXERCISE 11
CIRCLE GAME

1. Everybody, touch part 8. ✓
2. What word will you circle in the first line? (Signal.) *She.*
3. What word will you circle in the second line? (Signal.) *The.*
4. What word will you circle in the third line? (Signal.) *Is.*
5. Circle the words and finish the rest of your Workbook lesson.

EXERCISE 12
WORKBOOK CHECK

1. (Check each student's Workbook.)
2. (Award points for Workbook performance.)
3. (Record the student's total points in Box B.)

0–2 errors	8 points
3–4 errors	4 points
5–6 errors	2 points
7 or more errors	0 points

INDIVIDUAL READING CHECKOUTS

EXERCISE 13
STORY-READING CHECKOUT

- Study the story. If you read all the sentences with no more than 1 error, you'll earn 6 points.
- (Check the students individually.)
- (Record either 6 or 0 points in Box C.)

Lesson point total
(Tell students to write the point total in the last box at the top of the Workbook page. Maximum = 20 points.)

Point Summary Chart
(Tell students to write this point total in the box for Lesson 37 in the Point Summary Chart.)

END OF LESSON 37

Lesson 38

WORD-ATTACK SKILLS

EXERCISE 1
SOUND INTRODUCTION

1. (Point to **p**:) This letter usually makes the sound **p**. What sound? (Touch.) *p.*
2. (Point to **e**:) One sound you learned for this letter is the letter name. Everybody, what's that sound? (Touch.) *ēēē. Yes, ēēē.*
 - What's the other sound? (Touch.) *ĕĕĕ. Yes, ĕĕĕ.*
3. (Point to **o**:) One sound you learned for this letter is the letter name. Everybody, what's that sound? (Touch.) *ōōō. Yes, ōōō.*
 - What's the other sound? (Touch.) *ŏŏŏ. Yes, ŏŏŏ.*
4. Say each sound when I touch it.
5. (Point to **c**:) What sound? (Touch.) *k. Yes,* **k.**
6. (Repeat step 5 for **k, ĭ, er, th, ă, d, ck, p.**)

p e o

c k i

er th a

d ck p

Individual test
(Call on two or three students. Touch under each sound. Each student says all the sounds, including two sounds for **e** and two sounds for **o.**)

EXERCISE 2
PRONUNCIATIONS

Note: Do not write the words on the board. This is an oral exercise.

Task A

1. Say these words. Listen: **clocks.** Say it. (Signal.) *Clocks.*
2. Next word: **crocks.** Say it. (Signal.) *Crocks.*
3. (Repeat step 2 for **clams, claps, slips, trips, sadder.**)
4. (Repeat all the words until firm.)

Task B Flip, flop

1. Listen: **flip.** Say it. (Signal.) *Flip.*
 - Listen: **flop.** Say it. (Signal.) *Flop.*
2. One of those words has the middle sound *ŏŏŏ.* I'll say both words again: **flip** (pause) **flop.**
3. Which word has the middle sound *ŏŏŏ?* (Signal.) *Flop. Yes,* **flop.**
 - Which word has the middle sound *ĭĭĭ?* (Signal.) *Flip. Yes,* **flip.**

Task C Trim, tram

1. Listen: **trim** (pause) **tram.** Say it. (Signal.) *Trim, tram.* (Repeat until firm.)
2. One of those words has the middle sound *ĭĭĭ.* I'll say both words again: **trim** (pause) **tram.**
3. Which word has the middle sound *ĭĭĭ?* (Signal.) *Trim. Yes,* **trim.**
 - Which word has the middle sound *ăăă?* (Signal.) *Tram. Yes,* **tram.**
4. Listen: **trĭĭĭm.** What's the middle sound in the word **trim?** (Signal.) *ĭĭĭ. Yes, ĭĭĭ.*
 - Listen: **trăăăm.** What's the middle sound in the word **tram?** (Signal.) *ăăă. Yes, ăăă.*
5. (Repeat step 4 until firm.) Good job.

Lesson 38

Lesson 38

EXERCISE 3
WORD READING THE FAST WAY

1. You're going to read these words the fast way.
2. (For each word: Touch the ball of the arrow. Pause.) What word? (Slash right.)
3. (Repeat each word list until firm.)

hot

no

mast

mist

cold

now

last

list

class

clock

lock

lick

click

rack

track

crack

lags

4. (For each word: Touch the ball of the arrow. Pause.) What word? (Slash right.)
5. (Repeat each word list until firm.)

- street
- shell
- tells
- will
- wish
- when
- went
- her
- sad
- sadder

WORKBOOK EXERCISES

Note: Pass out the Workbooks. Direct the students to open to Lesson 38.

(Award 6 points if the group worked well during the word attack. Remind the students of the points they can earn in their Workbook.)

EXERCISE 4
SOUND DICTATION

1. I'll say the sounds. You write the letters in part 1 in your Workbook.
2. First sound. (Pause.) **p.** What sound? (Signal.) *p.*
- Write it in the first blank.
 (Observe students and give feedback.)
3. Next sound. (Pause.) **mmm.** What sound? (Signal.) *mmm.*
- Write it.
 (Observe students and give feedback.)
4. Next sound. Write a letter that says **k.**
 (Observe students and give feedback.)
5. Next sound. Write another letter that says **k.**
 (Observe students and give feedback.)
6. Next sound. Write two letters that go together and say **k.**
 (Observe students and give feedback.)
7. Next sound. (Pause.) **shshsh.** What sound? (Signal.) *shshsh.*
- Write it.
 (Observe students and give feedback).
8. (Repeat step 7 for **ēēē, ōōō, ĕĕĕ, ŏŏŏ, rrr, g.**)
9. (Repeat sounds students had trouble with.)

Lesson 38   53

Lesson 38

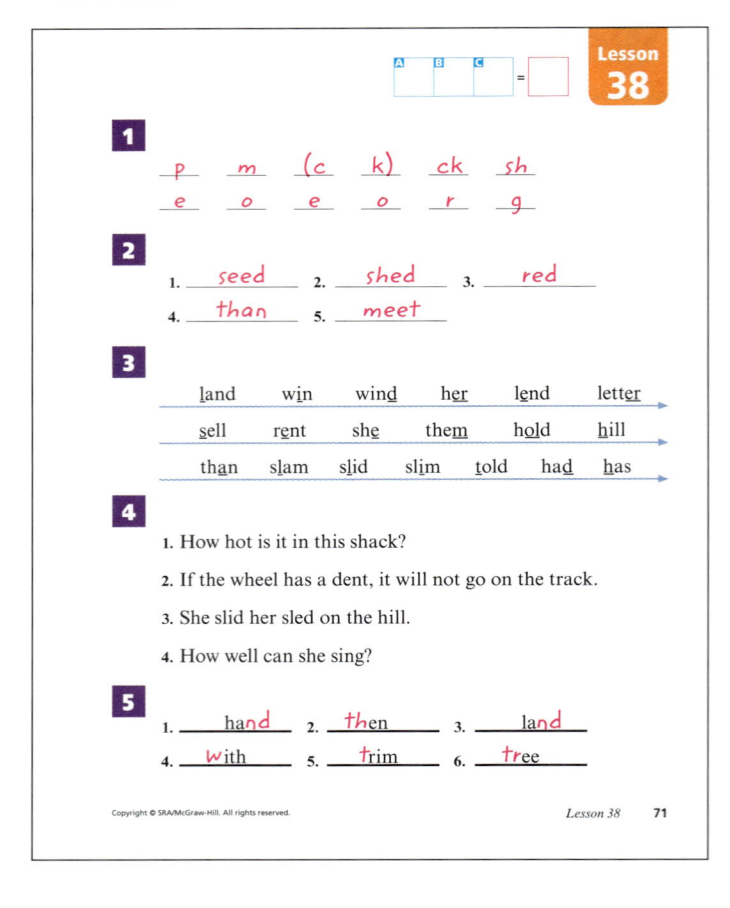

Worksheet (Lesson 38)

1
p_ m_ (c_ k_) ck_ sh_
_e _o _e _o _r _g

2
1. seed 2. shed 3. red
4. than 5. meet

3
land win wind her lend letter
sell rent she them hold hill
than slam slid slim told had has

4
1. How hot is it in this shack?
2. If the wheel has a dent, it will not go on the track.
3. She slid her sled on the hill.
4. How well can she sing?

5
1. hand 2. then 3. land
4. with 5. trim 6. tree

EXERCISE 5
SPELLING FROM DICTATION

1. Touch part 2. ✓
- You're going to write words that I dictate.
2. First word: **seed.** What word? (Signal.) *Seed.*
- Listen again: **sss . . . ēēē . . . d.** Write it in the first blank. Remember to write two **ē**'s.
(Observe students and give feedback.)
3. Next word: **shed.** What word? (Signal.) *Shed.*
- Listen again: **shshsh . . . ĕĕĕ . . . d.** Write it in the next blank.
(Observe students and give feedback.)
4. (Repeat step 3 for **red, than** [not **then**], **meet.**)

EXERCISE 6
WORD READING: Workbook

1. Touch the first word in part 3. ✓
2. Tell me the underlined sound in the first word. (Pause.) What sound? (Signal.) *lll.*
- (Pause.) What word? (Signal.) *Land.*
3. Next word. (Pause.) What sound? (Signal.) *ĭĭĭ.*
- (Pause.) What word? (Signal.) *Win.*
4. (Repeat step 3 for **wind, her, lend, letter, sell, rent, she, them, hold, hill, than, slam, slid slim, told, had, has.**)

EXERCISE 7
SENTENCE READING

1. Everybody, touch part 4. ✓
2. Touch under the first word in sentence 1. ✓
- What word? (Signal.) *How.*
3. Next word. ✓
- What word? (Signal.) *Hot.*
4. (Repeat step 3 for **is, it, in, this, shack.**)
5. (Repeat steps 2–4 until the students can correctly identify all the words in the sentence in order.)
6. (Repeat steps 2–5 for each remaining sentence:
- **2. If the wheel has a dent, it will not go on the track.**
- **3. She slid her sled on the hill.**
- **4. How well can she sing?**)

> **Individual test**
> (Give each student a chance to read one of the sentences.)

EXERCISE 8
WORD COMPLETION

1. Touch the first word in part 5. ✓
- What word? (Signal.) *ha.* Yes, **hă.**
- Fix it up to say (pause) **hand.** What word? (Signal.) *Hand.*
- Fix it up.
(Observe students and give feedback.)
2. Touch the next word. ✓
- What word? (Signal.) *en.* Yes, **en.**
- Fix it up to say (pause) **then.** What word? (Signal.) *Then.*
- Fix it up.
(Observe students and give feedback.)
3. (Repeat step 2 for **la [land], ith [with], rim [trim], ee [tree].**)

Lesson 38

EXERCISE 9
STORY READING

Task A

1. Everybody, touch part 6. ✓
   - You're going to read the sentences the fast way.
2. Touch under the first word. ✓
   - What word? (Signal.) *A.*
3. Next word. ✓
   - What word? (Signal.) *Seed.*
4. (Repeat step 3 for **sat, on, a rock.**)
5. (Repeat steps 2–4 until the students correctly identify all the words in the sentence.)
6. (Repeat steps 2–5 for each remaining sentence:
   - **The seed fell in the sand.**
   - **The sand got wet.**
   - **A tree is in the sand.**)
7. (If students miss more than four words, repeat the story reading from the beginning.)

Task B

1. Now I'll read the story and ask questions. Follow along.
   - **A seed sat on a rock.** Everybody, where is the seed? (Signal.) *On a rock.*
2. **The seed fell in the sand. The sand got wet.** The seed also got wet. What do you think happened to make the seed wet? (Call on a student.) (Idea: *It rained.*)
   - What happens to seeds when they are in wet sand? (Call on a student.) (Idea: *Seeds grow.*)
3. **A tree is in the sand.** Where did that tree come from? (Call on a student.) (Idea: *It grew from the seed.*)
   - Everybody, is the tree in the picture a big tree or a little tree? (Signal.) *A little tree.*

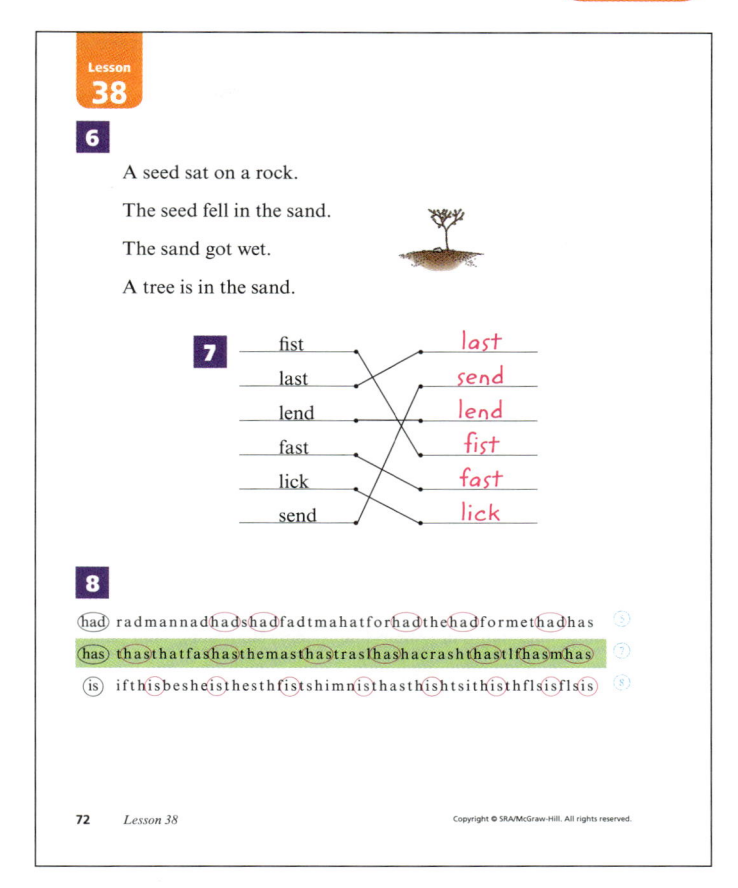

EXERCISE 10
MATCHING COMPLETION

1. Everybody, touch part 7. ✓
   - Read the words the fast way.
2. Touch under the first word. ✓
   - What word? (Signal.) *Fist.*
3. Next word. ✓
   - What word? (Signal.) *Last.*
4. (Repeat step 3 for **lend, fast, lick, send.**)
5. Later, you're going to write the words in the second column.

Lesson 38

EXERCISE 11
CIRCLE GAME

1. Everybody, touch part 8. ✓
2. What word will you circle in the first line? (Signal.) *Had.*
3. What word will you circle in the second line? (Signal.) *Has.*
4. What word will you circle in the third line? (Signal.) *Is.*
5. Circle the words and finish the rest of your Workbook lesson.

EXERCISE 12
WORKBOOK CHECK

1. (Check each student's Workbook.)
2. (Award points for Workbook performance.)
3. (Record the student's total points in Box B.)

0–2 errors	8 points
3–4 errors	4 points
5–6 errors	2 points
7 or more errors	0 points

INDIVIDUAL READING CHECKOUTS

EXERCISE 13
STORY-READING CHECKOUT

- Study the story. If you read all the sentences with no more than 1 error, you'll earn 6 points.
- (Check the students individually.)
- (Record either 6 or 0 points in Box C.)

Lesson point total

(Tell students to write the point total in the last box at the top of the Workbook page. Maximum = 20 points.)

Point Summary Chart

(Tell students to write this point total in the box for Lesson 38 in the Point Summary Chart.)

END OF LESSON 38

WORD-ATTACK SKILLS

EXERCISE 1
SOUND INTRODUCTION

1. (Point to **u**:) One sound this letter makes is **ŭŭŭ**. What sound? (Touch.) *ŭŭŭ.*
2. (Point to **e**:) One sound you learned for this letter is the letter name. Everybody, what's that sound? (Touch.) *ēēē.* Yes, **ēēē**.
- What's the other sound? (Touch.) *ĕĕĕ.* Yes, **ĕĕĕ**.
3. (Point to **o**:) One sound you learned for this letter is the letter name. Everybody, what's that sound? (Touch.) *ōōō.* Yes, **ōōō**.
- What's the other sound? (Touch.) *ŏŏŏ.* Yes, **ŏŏŏ**.
4. Say each sound when I touch it.
5. (Point to **u**:) What sound? (Touch.) *ŭŭŭ.* Yes, **uuu**.
6. (Repeat step 5 for **p, ĭ, d, g, wh, th, ă, l, k**.)

u e o u
p i d g
wh th a
l k

Individual test
(Call on two or three students. Touch under each sound. Each student says all the sounds, including two sounds for **e** and two sounds for **o**.)

EXERCISE 2
PRONUNCIATIONS

Note: Do not write the words on the board. This is an oral exercise.

Task A

1. Say these words. Listen: **caster.** Say it. (Signal.) *Caster.*
2. Next word: **peeks.** Say it. (Signal.) *Peeks.*
3. (Repeat step 2 for **singer, flags, dents, slips, streets, clod, cold.**)
4. (Repeat all the words until firm.)

Task B Pit, pat, pot

1. Listen: **pit, pat, pot.** Say those words. (Signal.) *Pit, pat, pot.* (Repeat until firm.)
2. One of those words has the middle sound **ăăă**. I'll say the words again: **pit, pat, pot.**
3. Which word has the middle sound **ăăă**? (Signal.) *Pat.* Yes, **pat**.
- Which word has the middle sound **ĭĭĭ**? (Signal.) *Pit.* Yes, **pit**.
- Which word has the middle sound **ŏŏŏ**? (Signal.) *Pot.* Yes, **pot**.

Task C Sill, sell

1. Listen: **sill** (pause) **sell.** Say those words. (Signal.) *Sill, sell.* (Repeat until firm.)
2. One of those words has the middle sound **ĕĕĕ**. I'll say the words again: **sill** (pause) **sell.**
3. Which word has the middle sound **ĕĕĕ**? (Signal.) *Sell.* Yes, **sell**.
- Which word has the middle sound **ĭĭĭ**? (Signal.) *Sill.* Yes, **sill**.
4. Listen: **sĭĭĭll.** What's the middle sound in the word **sill**? (Signal.) *ĭĭĭ.* Yes, **ĭĭĭ**.
- Listen: **sĕĕĕll.** What's the middle sound in the word **sell**? (Signal.) *ĕĕĕ.* Yes, **ĕĕĕ**.
5. (Repeat step 4 until firm.) Good job.

Lesson 39

EXERCISE 3
WORD READING THE FAST WAY

1. You're going to read these words the fast way.
2. (For each word: Touch the ball of the arrow. Pause.) What word? (Slash right.)
3. (Repeat each word list until firm.)

sell

well

shop

odd

cod

men

will

rent

sod

how

tracks

then

than

this

last

so

list

58   Lesson 39

4. (For each word: Touch the ball of the arrow. Pause.) **What word?** (Slash right.)
5. (Repeat the column until firm.)

mist
lip
slip
peek
pit
pet

Lesson 39

WORKBOOK EXERCISES

Note: Pass out the Workbooks. Direct the students to open to Lesson 39.

(Award 6 points if the group worked well during the word attack. Remind the students of the points they can earn in their Workbook.)

EXERCISE 4
SOUND DICTATION

1. **I'll say the sounds. You write the letters in part 1 in your Workbook.**
2. **First sound. (Pause.) ŭŭŭ. What sound?** (Signal.) *ŭŭŭ.*
- **Write it in the first blank.**
   (Observe students and give feedback.)
3. **Next sound. (Pause.) p. What sound?** (Signal.) *p.*
- **Write it.**
   (Observe students and give feedback.)
4. (Repeat step 3 for **d, ĭĭĭ, ŏŏŏ, thththth, ĕĕĕ, ōōō, ĭĭĭ, ēēē, d, g**.)
5. (Repeat sounds students had trouble with.)

EXERCISE 5
SPELLING FROM DICTATION

1. **Touch part 2.** ✓
- **You're going to write words that I dictate.**
2. **First word: on. What word?** (Signal.) *On.*
- **Listen again: ŏŏŏ . . . nnn. Write it in the first blank.**
   (Observe students and give feedback.)
3. **Next word: had. What word?** (Signal.) *Had.*
- **Listen again: h . . . ăăă . . . d. Write it in the next blank.**
   (Observe students and give feedback.)
4. (Repeat step 3 for **meet, rod, hid, met**.)

Lesson 39 59

Lesson 39

Workbook Page

1
u	p	d	i	o	th
e	o	i	e	d	g

2
1. on 2. had 3. meet
4. rod 5. hid 6. met

3

her	dig	digger	win	winner	with
how	cast	caster	fold	dinner	has
tree	slam	pack	hold	thing	

4
1. If it is not hot, we will sleep.
2. How did he get so slim?
3. She has a ring on her hand.
4. That cat is slim and sleek.

5
1. ca**st** 2. **s**end 3. **tr**im
4. ha**nd** 5. ca**ts** 6. **t**ree

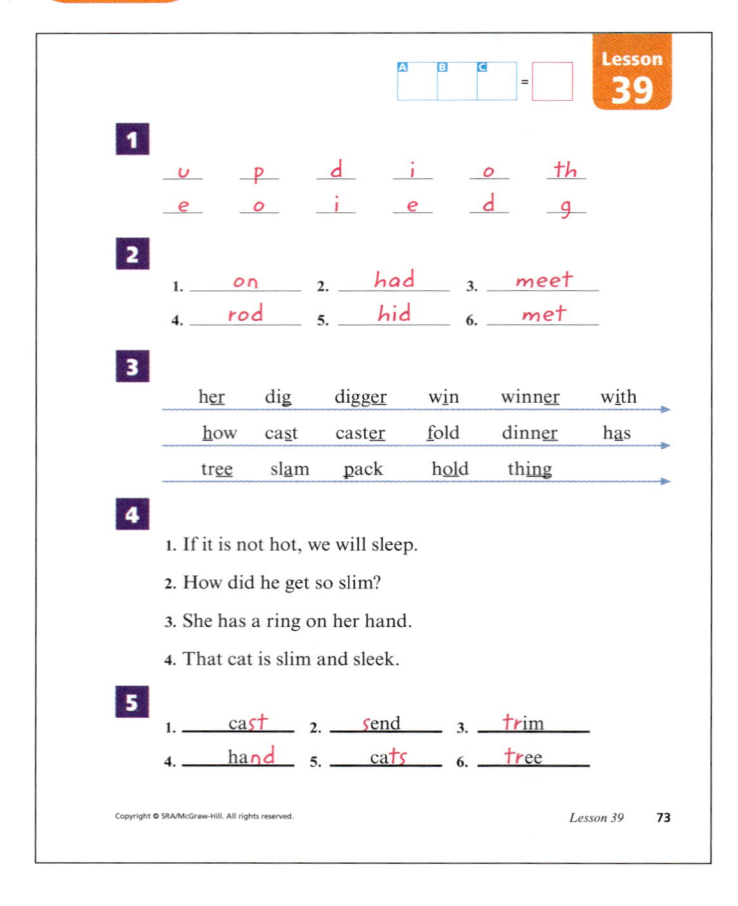

EXERCISE 6
WORD READING: Workbook

1. Touch the first word in part 3. ✓
2. Tell me the underlined sound in the first word. (Pause.) What sound? (Signal.) *er.*
   - (Pause.) What word? (Signal.) *Her.*
3. Next word. (Pause.) What sound? (Signal.) *g.*
   - (Pause.) What word? (Signal.) *Dig.*
4. (Repeat step 3 for **digger, win, winner, with, how, cast, caster, fold, dinner, has, tree, slam, pack, hold, thing.**)

EXERCISE 7
SENTENCE READING

1. Everybody, touch part 4. ✓
2. Touch under the first word in sentence 1. ✓
   - What word? (Signal.) *If.*
3. Next word. ✓
   - What word? (Signal.) *It.*
4. (Repeat step 3 for **is, not, hot, we, will, sleep.**)
5. (Repeat steps 2–4 until the students can correctly identify all the words in the sentence in order.)
6. (Repeat steps 2–5 for each remaining sentence:
   - 2. **How did he get so slim?**
   - 3. **She has a ring on her hand.**
   - 4. **That cat is slim and sleek.**)

Individual test
(Give each student a chance to read one of the sentences.)

EXERCISE 8
WORD COMPLETION

1. Touch the first word in part 5. ✓
   - What word? (Signal.) *ca.* Yes, **ca.**
   - Fix it up to say (pause) **cast.** What word? (Signal.) *Cast.*
   - Fix it up.
     (Observe students and give feedback.)
2. Touch the next word. ✓
   - What word? (Signal.) *End.* Yes, **end.**
   - Fix it up to say (pause) **send.** What word? (Signal.) *Send.*
   - Fix it up. (Observe students and give feedback.)
3. (Repeat step 2 for **im [trim], ha [hand], ca [ats], ee [tree].**)

Lesson 39

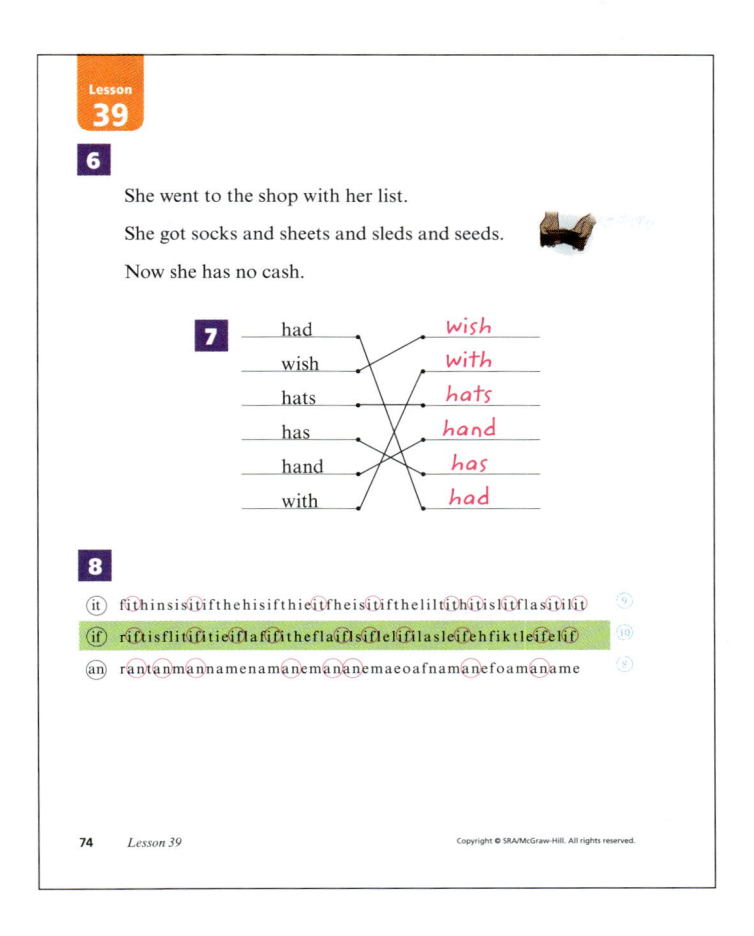

[Worksheet page 74, Lesson 39:

6
She went to the shop with her list.
She got socks and sheets and sleds and seeds.
Now she has no cash.

7 Matching:
had — wish
wish — with
hats — hats
has — hand
hand — has
with — had

8
- it) fithinsisitifthehisifthieitfheisitifthelilitithitislitflasitilit
- if) riftisflitifitieiflafifitheflaiflsiflelifilasleifehfiktleifelif
- an) rantanmannamenamanemananemaeoafnamanefoamaname
]

EXERCISE 9
STORY READING

Task A

1. Everybody, touch part 6. ✓
- You're going to read the sentences the fast way.
2. Touch under the first word. ✓
- What word? (Signal.) *She.*
3. Next word. ✓
- What word? (Signal.) *Went.*
4. (Repeat step 3 for **to, the, shop, with, her, list.**)
5. (Repeat steps 2–4 until the students correctly identify all the words in the sentence.)
6. (Repeat steps 2–5 for each remaining sentence:
- **She got socks and sheets and sleds and seeds.**
- **Now she has no cash.**)
7. (If students miss more than four words, repeat the story reading from the beginning.)

Task B

1. Now I'll read the story and ask questions. Follow along.
2. **She went to the shop with her list.** Everybody, where did she go? (Signal.) *To the shop.*
3. What did she take with her? (Signal.) *Her list.*
- What is a list? (Call on a student.) (Accept reasonable responses.)
4. **She got socks and sheets and sleds and seeds.** Name all the things she got. (Call on a student.) *Socks, sheets, sleds, and seeds.*
5. **Now she has no cash.** Why doesn't she have any cash? (Call on a student.) (Idea: *She spent her cash at the shop.*)
6. What's in the picture? (Call on a student.) *A wallet.*
- What's inside the wallet? (Call on a student.) (Idea: *Nothing.*)
- Was there anything in the wallet before she went into the shop? (Call on a student.) (Idea: *Yes, cash.*)

Lesson 39   61

Lesson 39

EXERCISE 10
MATCHING COMPLETION

1. Everybody, touch part 7. ✓
 - Read the words the fast way.
2. Touch under the first word. ✓
 - What word? (Signal.) *Had.*
3. Next word. ✓
 - What word? (Signal.) *Wish.*
4. (Repeat step 3 for **hats, has, hand, with.**)
5. Later, you're going to write the words in the second column.

EXERCISE 11
CIRCLE GAME

1. Everybody, touch part 8. ✓
2. What word will you circle in the first line? (Signal.) *It.*
3. What word will you circle in the second line? (Signal.) *If.*
4. What word will you circle in the third line? (Signal.) *An.*
5. Circle the words and finish the rest of your Workbook lesson.

EXERCISE 12
WORKBOOK CHECK

1. (Check each student's Workbook.)
2. (Award points for Workbook performance.)
3. (Record the student's total points in Box B.)

0–2 errors	8 points
3–4 errors	4 points
5–6 errors	2 points
7 or more errors	0 points

INDIVIDUAL READING CHECKOUTS

EXERCISE 13
STORY-READING CHECKOUT

- Study the story. If you read all the sentences with no more than 1 error, you'll earn 6 points.
- (Check the students individually.)
- (Record either 6 or 0 points in Box C.)

Lesson point total

(Tell students to write the point total in the last box at the top of the Workbook page. Maximum = 20 points.)

Point Summary Chart

(Tell students to write this point total in the box for Lesson 39 in the Point Summary Chart.)

END OF LESSON 39

WORD-ATTACK SKILLS

EXERCISE 1
SOUND INTRODUCTION

1. (Point to **u**:) One sound this letter makes is *ŭŭŭ*. What sound? (Touch.) *ŭŭŭ*.
2. (Point to **e**:) One sound you learned for this letter is the letter name. Everybody, what's that sound? (Touch.) *ēēē*. Yes, *ēēē*.
   - What's the other sound? (Touch.) *ĕĕĕ*. Yes, *ĕĕĕ*.
3. (Point to **o**:) One sound you learned for this letter is the letter name. Everybody, what's that sound? (Touch.) *ōōō*. Yes, *ōōō*.
   - What's the other sound? (Touch.) *ŏŏŏ*. Yes, *ŏŏŏ*.
4. Say each sound when I touch it.
5. (Point to **n**:) What sound? (Touch.) *nnn*. Yes, *nnn*.
6. (Repeat step 5 for **ă, ŭ, ol, r, ĭ, sh, wh, p, th, er**.)

u e o

n a u

ol r i

sh wh

p th er

Individual test
(Call on two or three students. Touch under each sound. Each student says all the sounds, including two sounds for **e** and two sounds for **o**.)

EXERCISE 2
PRONUNCIATIONS

Note: Do not write the words on the board. This is an oral exercise.

Task A

1. Say these words. Listen: **hod.** Say it. (Signal.) *Hod.*
2. Next word: **hold.** Say it. (Signal.) *Hold.*
3. (Repeat step 2 for **cot, colt, cold, seller, lags, dents, winner, winning.**)
4. (Repeat all the words until firm.)

Task B Slip, slap, slop

1. Listen: **slip, slap, slop.** Say those words. (Signal.) *Slip, slap, slop.* (Repeat until firm.)
2. One of those words has the middle sound *ăăă*. I'll say the words again: **slip, slap, slop.**
3. Which word has the middle sound *ăăă*? (Signal.) *Slap.* Yes, **slap.**
   - Which word has the middle sound *ĭĭĭ*? (Signal.) *Slip.* Yes, **slip.**
   - Which word has the middle sound *ŏŏŏ*? (Signal.) *Slop.* Yes, **slop.**

Task C Ran, run

1. Listen: **ran.** Say it. (Signal.) *Ran.*
   - Listen: **run.** Say it. (Signal.) *Run.*
2. One of those words has the middle sound *ŭŭŭ*. I'll say the words again: **ran** (pause) **run.**
3. Which word has the middle sound *ŭŭŭ*? (Signal.) *Run.* Yes, **run.**
   - Which word has the middle sound *ăăă*? (Signal.) *Ran.* Yes, **ran.**

Lesson 40

Lesson 40

EXERCISE 3
WORD READING THE FAST WAY

1. You're going to read these words the fast way.
2. (For each word: Touch the ball of the arrow. Pause.) What word? (Slash right.)
3. (Repeat each word list until firm.)

lag

flag

clam

clap

class

clock

trap

crack

trip

when

went

no

con

mast

mats

Lesson 40

4. (For each word: Touch the ball of the arrow. Pause.) What word? (Slash right.)
5. (Repeat each word list until firm.)

pats

pills

lip

slip

dents

packs

pig

dig

rest

now

hot

how

down

Lesson 40 65

Lesson 40

WORKBOOK EXERCISES

Note: Pass out the Workbooks. Direct the students to open to Lesson 40.

(Award 6 points if the group worked well during the word attack. Remind the students of the points they can earn in their Workbook.)

EXERCISE 4
SOUND DICTATION

1. I'll say the sounds. You write the letters in part 1 in your Workbook.
2. First sound. (Pause.) **lll.** What sound? (Signal.) *lll.*
- Write it in the first blank.
  (Observe students and give feedback.)
3. Next sound. Write two letters that go together and say **www.**
  (Observe students and give feedback.)
4. Next sound. Write another letter that says **www.**
  (Observe students and give feedback.)
5. Next sound. (Pause.) **ŭŭŭ.** What sound? (Signal.) *ŭŭŭ.*
- Write it.
  (Observe students and give feedback.)
6. (Repeat step 5 for **rrr, ēēē, ŏŏŏ, ĭĭĭ, thththth, p, ĕĕĕ, ĭĭĭ.**)
7. (Repeat sounds students had trouble with.)

EXERCISE 5
SPELLING FROM DICTATION

1. Touch part 2. ✓
- You're going to write words that I dictate.
2. First word: **not.** Not **nod.** Not. What word? (Signal.) *Not.*
- Listen again: **nnn . . . ŏŏŏ . . . t.** Write it in the first blank.
  (Observe students and give feedback.)
3. Next word: **red.** What word? (Signal.) *Red.*
- Listen again: **rrr . . . ĕĕĕ . . . d.** Write it in the next blank.
  (Observe students and give feedback.)
4. (Repeat step 3 for **then** [not **than**], **nod** [not **not**], **that, shed.**)

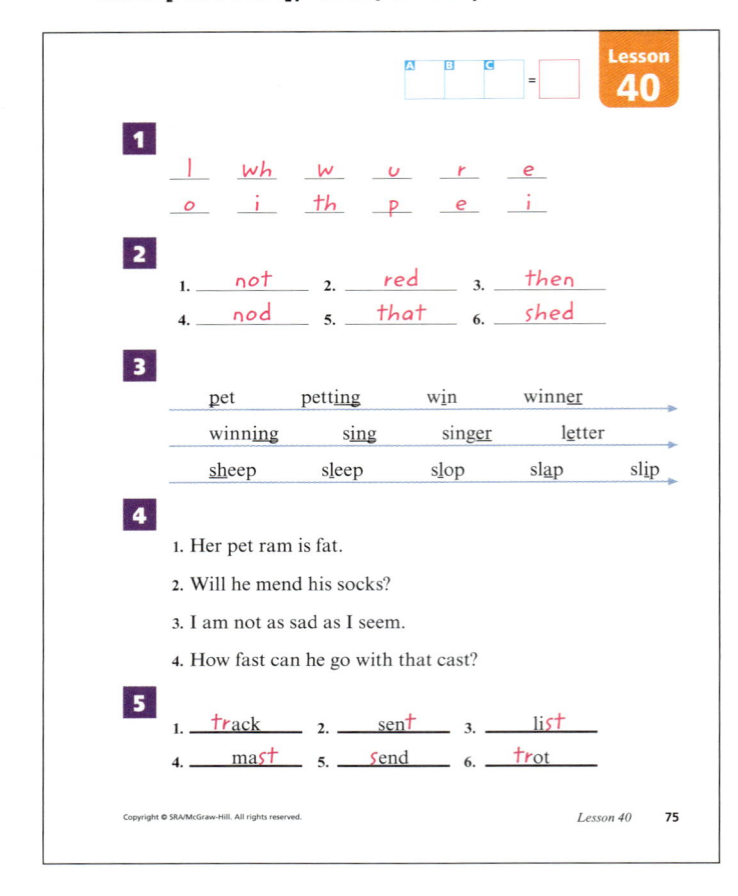

EXERCISE 6
WORD READING: Workbook

1. Touch the first word in part 3. ✓
2. Tell me the underlined sound in the first word. (Pause.) What sound? (Signal.) *p.*
- (Pause.) What word? (Signal.) *Pet.*
3. Next word. (Pause.) What sound? (Signal.) *ing.*
- (Pause.) What word? (Signal.) *Petting.*
4. (Repeat step 3 for **win, winner, winning, sing, singer, letter, sheep, sleep, slop, slap, slip.**)

EXERCISE 7
SENTENCE READING

1. Everybody, touch part 4. ✓
2. Touch under the first word in sentence 1. ✓
- What word? (Signal.) *Her.*
3. Next word. ✓
- What word? (Signal.) *Pet.*
4. (Repeat step 3 for **ram, is, fat.**)
5. (Repeat steps 2–4 until the students can correctly identify all the words in the sentence in order.)
6. (Repeat steps 2–5 for each remaining sentence:
- **2. Will he mend his socks?**
- **3. I am not as sad as I seem.**
- **4. How fast can he go with that cast?**)

Individual test
(Give each student a chance to read one of the sentences.)

EXERCISE 8
WORD COMPLETION

1. Touch the first word in part 5. ✓
- What word? (Signal.) *ack.* Yes, **ack.**
- Fix it up to say (pause) **track.** What word? (Signal.) *Track.*
- Fix it up.
  (Observe students and give feedback.)
2. Touch the next word. ✓
- What word? (Signal.) *sen.* Yes, **sen.**
- Fix it up to say (pause) **sent.** What word? (Signal.) *Sent.*
- Fix it up.
  (Observe students and give feedback.)
3. (Repeat step 2 for **li [list], ma [mast], end [send], ot [trot].**)

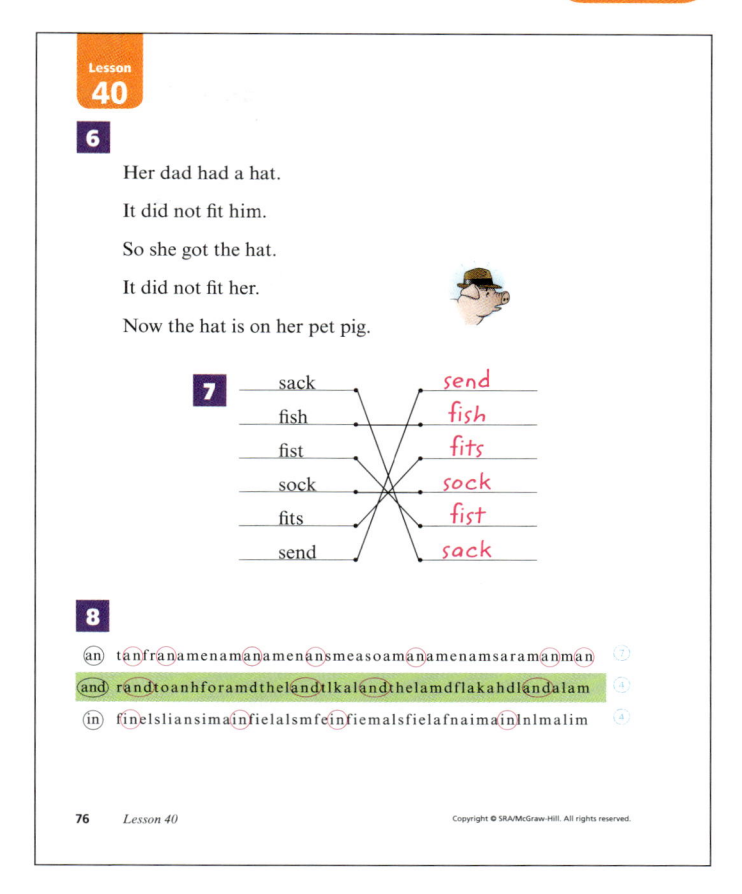

EXERCISE 9
STORY READING

Task A

1. Everybody, touch part 6. ✓
- You're going to read the sentences the fast way.
2. Touch under the first word. ✓
- What word? (Signal.) *Her.*
3. Next word. ✓
- What word? (Signal.) *Dad.*
4. (Repeat step 3 for **had, a, hat.**)
5. (Repeat steps 2–4 until the students correctly identify all the words in the sentence.)
6. (Repeat steps 2–5 for each remaining sentence:
- **It did not fit him.**
- **So she got the hat.**
- **It did not fit her.**
- **Now the hat is on her pet pig.**)
7. (If students miss more than four words, repeat the story reading from the beginning.)

Lesson 40

Task B

1. Now I'll read the story and ask questions. Follow along.
2. **Her dad had a hat. It did not fit him.** If a hat does not fit you, what does it look like on your head? (Call on a student.) (Ideas: *Too big or too small; silly.*)
3. **So she got the hat.** Why did she get the hat? (Call on a student.) (Idea: *Because it did not fit her dad.*)
4. **It did not fit her. Now the hat is on her pet pig.** Who gave the hat to her pig? (Call on a student.) (Idea: *The girl.*)
   - Why did she give the hat to her pig? (Call on a student.) (Idea: *Because it did not fit her.*)

EXERCISE 10
MATCHING COMPLETION

1. Everybody, touch part 7. ✓
   - Read the words the fast way.
2. Touch under the first word. ✓
   - What word? (Signal.) *Sack.*
3. Next word. ✓
   - What word? (Signal.) *Fish.*
4. (Repeat step 3 for **fist, sock, fits, send.**)
5. Later, you're going to write the words in the second column.

EXERCISE 11
CIRCLE GAME

1. Everybody, touch part 8. ✓
2. What word will you circle in the first line? (Signal.) *An.*
3. What word will you circle in the second line? (Signal.) *And.*
4. What word will you circle in the third line? (Signal.) *In.*
5. Circle the words and finish the rest of your Workbook lesson.

EXERCISE 12
WORKBOOK CHECK

1. (Check each student's Workbook.)
2. (Award points for Workbook performance.)
3. (Record the student's total points in Box B.)

0–2 errors	8 points
3–4 errors	4 points
5–6 errors	2 points
7 or more errors	0 points

INDIVIDUAL READING CHECKOUTS

EXERCISE 13
STORY-READING CHECKOUT

- Study the story. If you read all the sentences with no more than 1 error, you'll earn 6 points.
- (Check the students individually.)
- (Record either 6 or 0 points in Box C.)

Lesson point total

(Tell students to write the point total in the last box at the top of the Workbook page. Maximum = 20 points.)

Point Summary Chart

(Tell students to write this point total in the box for Lesson 40 in the Point Summary Chart.)

Five-lesson point summary

(Tell students to add the point totals for Lessons 36 through 40 in the Point Summary Chart and to write the total for Block 8. Maximum for Block 8 = 100 points.)

END OF LESSON 40

MASTERY TEST 9
— AFTER LESSON 40, BEFORE LESSON 41 —

> **Note:** Use students' performance on the Lesson 40 Story reading checkout for Mastery Test 9.

Scoring the test

1. (Count each student's errors on the Story reading checkout. Write these numbers in the Test 9 boxes on the *Decoding A* Mastery Test Student Profile form. Circle **P** or **F**.)
2. (When all students have been tested, circle **P** or **F** for each student on the *Decoding A* Mastery Test Group Summary form. Determine if more than 25 percent of the students failed the Story reading checkout by dividing the number of students who failed by the total number of students in the group.)

Remedies

(If more than 25 percent of the students made 2 or more errors on the Story reading checkout, [1] repeat the Story reading checkouts for Lessons 36 through 39, and [2] repeat all of Lesson 40. Permission is granted to reproduce the Workbook pages for Lesson 40 for classroom use.)

Mastery Test 9

Lesson Objectives	LESSON 41 Exercise	LESSON 42 Exercise	LESSON 43 Exercise	LESSON 44 Exercise	LESSON 45 Exercise
Word Attack					
Phonemic Awareness					
Sound/Word Pronunciation	1, 2	1, 3	1, 2	1, 2	1, 2
Identify Sounds in Words	2	2, 3	2, 3	2	2
Decoding and Word Analysis					
Letter Sounds: x, ē, ĕ, ō, ŏ, ing, h, w, d, g, u, l, p, er	1				
Letter Sounds: x, d, g, p, u, w, a, n, h, ol		1			
Letter Sounds: ŏ, ō, x, d, p, g, u, w, n, h, wh			1		
Letter Sounds: b, ō, ŏ, ē, ĕ, g, th, wh, d, c, p, x, u				1	
Letter Sounds: b, d, sh, s, er, wh, i, a, l, x					1
Sound Combination: or		2	3		
Word Recognition	3	2, 4	3, 4	3	3
Assessment					
Ongoing: Individual Tests	1	1	1	1	1
Group Reading					
Decoding and Word Analysis					
Read Decodable Text	9	10	10	9	9
Comprehension					
Make Predictions		10			
Access Prior Knowledge		10	10	9	
Draw Inferences	9	10	10	9	9
Note Details	9	10		9	9
Assessment					
Ongoing: Comprehension Check	9	10	10	9	9
Ongoing: Decoding Accuracy	9	10	10	9	9
Formal: Mastery Test					MT 10
Workbook Exercises					
Decoding and Word Analysis					
Word Recognition	6	7		6	6
Sentence Reading	7	8	9	7	7
Sound Combinations	6	7		6	6
Spelling: Sound/Letter Relationships	4, 8, 10	5, 9, 11	5, 7, 8	4, 8, 10	4, 8, 10
Spelling: CVC, CCVC				5	
Spelling: CVCC, CVVC					5
Spelling: CVC, CCVC, CVVC	5	6			
Spelling: CVC, CCVC, CVCC, CVVC			6		
Visual Discrimination	10, 11	11, 12		10, 11	10, 11
Assessment					
Ongoing: Individual Tests	6	8	9	7	7
Ongoing: Teacher-Monitored Accuracy	13	14	12	13	13
Ongoing: Workcheck	12	13	11	12	12

Lesson 41

WORD-ATTACK SKILLS

EXERCISE 1
SOUND INTRODUCTION

1. (Point to **x:**) This letter makes the sound **kss.** What sound? (Touch.) *kss.*
2. (Point to **e:**) One sound you learned for this letter is the letter name. Everybody, what's that sound? (Touch.) *ēēē.* Yes, **ēēē.**
   - What's the other sound? (Touch.) *ĕĕĕ.* Yes, **ĕĕĕ.**
3. (Point to **o:**) One sound you learned for this letter is the letter name. Everybody, what's that sound? (Touch.) *ōōō.* Yes, **ōōō.**
   - What's the other sound? (Touch.) *ŏŏŏ.* Yes, **ŏŏŏ.**
4. Say each sound when I touch it.
5. (Point to **ing:**) What sound? (Touch.) *ing.* Yes, **ing.**
6. (Repeat step 5 for **h, w, d, g, u, l, p, er, x.**)

x e o
ing h w
d g u l
p er x

Individual test
(Call on two or three students. Touch under each sound. Each student says all the sounds, including two sounds for **e** and two sounds for **o.**)

EXERCISE 2
PRONUNCIATIONS

Note: Do not write the words on the board. This is an oral exercise.

Task A

1. Listen: **wisher.** Say it. (Signal.) *Wisher.*
2. Next word: **wishing.** Say it. (Signal.) *Wishing.*
3. (Repeat step 2 for **claps, seller, filler, feeling, drops.**)
4. (Repeat all the words until firm.)

Task B Stop, step, steep

1. Listen: **stop, step, steep.** Say those words. (Signal.) *Stop, step, steep.* (Repeat until firm.)
2. One of those words has the middle sound **ĕĕĕ.** I'll say the words again: **stop, step, steep.**
3. Which word has the middle sound **ĕĕĕ**? (Signal.) *Step.* Yes, **step.**
   - Which word has the middle sound **ŏŏŏ**? (Signal.) *Stop.* Yes, **stop.**
   - Which word has the middle sound **ēēē**? (Signal.) *Steep.* Yes, **steep.**

Task C Must, mist

1. Listen: **must.** Say it. (Signal.) *Must.*
   - Listen: **mist.** Say it. (Signal.) *Mist.*
2. One of those words has the middle sound **ŭŭŭ.** I'll say both words again: **must** (pause) **mist.**
3. Which word has the middle sound **ŭŭŭ**? (Signal.) *Must.* Yes, **must.**
   - Which word has the middle sound **ĭĭĭ**? (Signal.) *Mist.* Yes, **mist.**

Task D Then, than

1. Listen: **then** (pause) **than.** Say those words. (Signal.) *Then, than.* (Repeat until firm.)
2. One of those words has the middle sound **ăăă.** I'll say the words again: **then** (pause) **than.**

Lesson 41

3. **Which word has the middle sound ăăă?** (Signal.) *Than.* Yes, **than.**
- **Which word has the middle sound ĕĕĕ?** (Signal.) *Then.* Yes, **then.**
4. **Listen: thĕĕĕn. What's the middle sound in the word then?** (Signal.) *ĕĕĕ.* Yes, **ĕĕĕ.**
- **Listen: thăăăn. What's the middle sound in the word than?** (Signal.) *ăăă.* Yes, **ăăă.**
5. (Repeat step 4 until firm.) **Good job.**

EXERCISE 3
WORD READING THE FAST WAY

1. **You're going to read these words the fast way.**
2. (For each word: Touch the ball of the arrow. Pause.) **What word?** (Slash right.)
3. (Repeat each word list until firm.)

up

us

rust

must

truck

flag

flip

slip

clap

cracks

pets

ten

tents

go

so

stop

4. (For each word: Touch the ball of the arrow. Pause.) **What word?** (Slash right.)
5. (Repeat each word list until firm.)

steep →

rest →

last →

hill →

well →

now →

how →

WORKBOOK EXERCISES

Note: Pass out the Workbooks. Direct the students to open to Lesson 41.

(Award 6 points if the group worked well during the word attack. Remind the students of the points they can earn in their Workbook.)

EXERCISE 4
SOUND DICTATION

1. I'll say the sounds. You write the letters in part 1 in your Workbook.
2. First sound. (Pause.) **kss.** What sound? (Signal.) *kss [x]*.
- Write it in the first blank.
   (Observe students and give feedback.)
3. Next sound. (Pause.) **shshsh.** What sound? (Signal.) *shshsh*.
- Write it.
   (Observe students and give feedback.)
4. (Repeat step 3 for **p, ĭĭĭ, ăăă, ēēē, ŭŭŭ, ĕĕĕ, ōōō, ing, nnn, ththth.**)
5. (Repeat sounds students had trouble with.)

EXERCISE 5
SPELLING FROM DICTATION

1. Touch part 2. ✓
- You're going to write words that I dictate.
2. First word: **hot.** What word? (Signal.) *Hot.*
- Listen again: **h . . . ŏŏŏ . . . t.** Write it in the first blank.
   (Observe students and give feedback.)
3. Next word: **she.** What word? (Signal.) *She.*
- Listen again: **shshsh . . . ēēē.** Write it in the next blank.
   (Observe students and give feedback.)
4. (Repeat step 3 for **see, not, seem, shot.**)

Lesson 41 73

Lesson 41

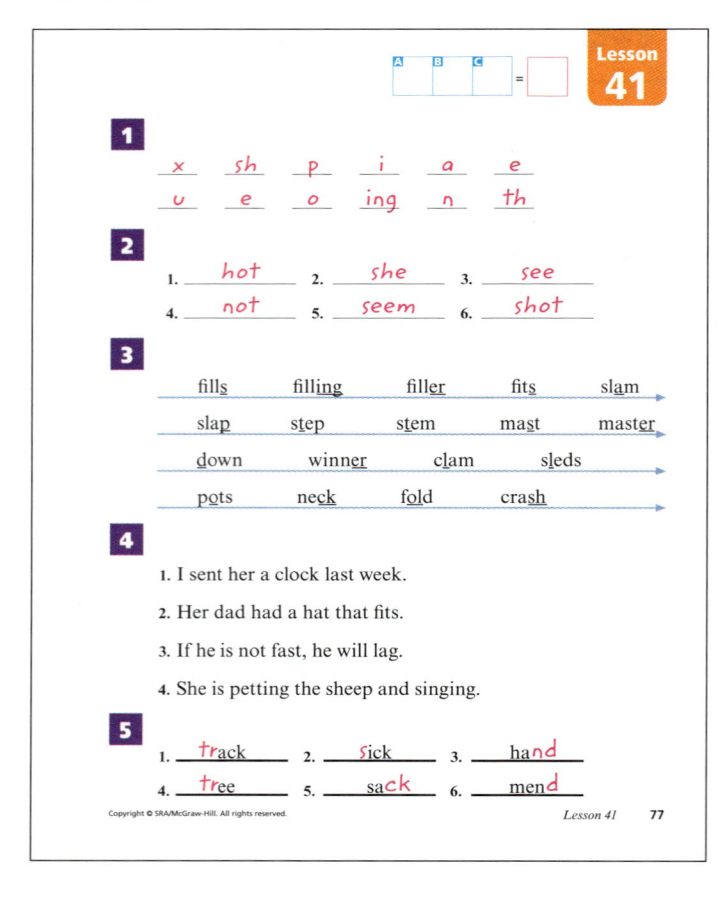

EXERCISE 6
WORD READING: Workbook

1. Touch the first word in part 3. ✓
2. Tell me the underlined sound in the first word. (Pause.) What sound? (Signal.) *sss.*
• (Pause.) What word? (Signal.) *Fills.*
3. Next word. (Pause.) What sound? (Signal.) *ing.*
• (Pause.) What word? (Signal.) *Filling.*
4. (Repeat step 3 for **filler, fits, slam, slap, step, stem, mast, master, down, winner, clam, sleds, pots, neck, fold, crash.**)

EXERCISE 7
SENTENCE READING

1. Everybody, touch part 4. ✓
2. Touch under the first word in sentence 1. ✓
• What word? (Signal.) *I.*
3. Next word. ✓
• What word? (Signal.) *Sent.*
4. (Repeat step 3 for **her, a, clock, last, week.**)
5. (Repeat steps 2–4 until the students can correctly identify all the words in the sentence in order.)
6. (Repeat steps 2–5 for each remaining sentence:
• 2. Her dad had a hat that fits.
• 3. If he is not fast, he will lag.
• 4. She is petting the sheep and singing.)

> **Individual test**
> (Give each student a chance to read one of the sentences.)

EXERCISE 8
WORD COMPLETION

1. Touch the first word in part 5. ✓
• What word? (Signal.) *ack.* Yes, **ack.**
• Fix it up to say (pause) **track.** What word? (Signal.) *Track.*
• Fix it up.
  (Observe students and give feedback.)
2. Touch the next word. ✓
• What word? (Signal.) *ick.* Yes, **ick.**
• Fix it up to say (pause) **sick.** What word? (Signal.) *Sick.*
• Fix it up.
  (Observe students and give feedback.)
3. (Repeat step 2 for **ha [hand], ee [tree], sa [sack], men [mend].**)

EXERCISE 9
STORY READING

Task A

1. Everybody, touch part 6. ✓
• You're going to read the sentences the fast way.
2. Touch under the first word. ✓
• What word? (Signal.) *His.*
3. Next word. ✓
• What word? (Signal.) *Truck.*
4. (Repeat step 3 for **has, no, gas.**)

5. (Repeat steps 2–4 for each remaining sentence:
   - **So he got a can and went for gas.**
   - **He did not get gas.**
   - **He had no cash.**
   - **So this is how he must get up the hill.**)
6. (If students miss more than four words, repeat the story reading from the beginning.)

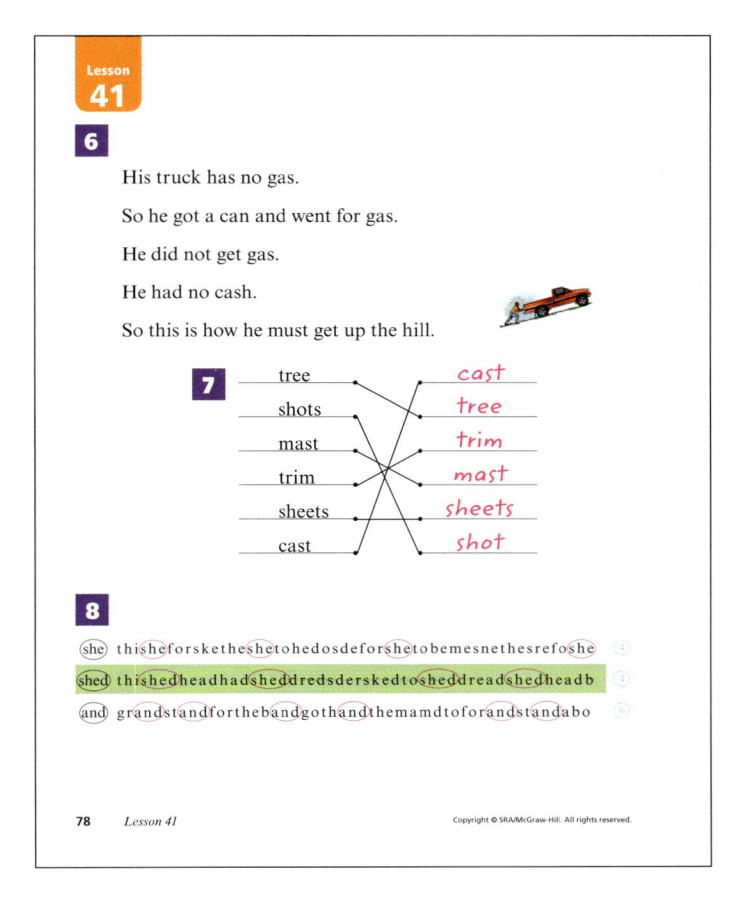

Task B

1. **Now I'll read the story and ask questions. Follow along.**
2. **His truck has no gas.** What happens to a truck when it has no gas? (Call on a student.) (Idea: *It won't run.*)
3. **So he got a can and went for gas.** What was he going to do with the can? (Call on a student.) (Idea: *Get gas.*)
4. **He did not get gas. He had no cash.** Why didn't he get gas? (Call on a student.) (Idea: *He didn't have money to pay for gas.*)
5. **So this is how he must get up the hill.** Everybody, is he driving the truck? (Signal.) *No.*
   - What is he doing? (Call on a student.) (Idea: *Pushing the truck up the hill.*)

EXERCISE 10
MATCHING COMPLETION

1. Everybody, touch part 7. ✓
   - Read the words the fast way.
2. Touch under the first word. ✓
   - What word? (Signal.) *Tree.*
3. Next word. ✓
   - What word? (Signal.) *Shots.*
4. (Repeat step 3 for **mast, trim, sheets, cast.**)
5. Later, you're going to write the words in the second column.

EXERCISE 11
CIRCLE GAME

1. Everybody, touch part 8. ✓
2. What word will you circle in the first line? (Signal.) *She.*
3. What word will you circle in the second line? (Signal.) *Shed.*
4. What word will you circle in the third line? (Signal.) *And.*
5. Circle the words and finish the rest of your Workbook lesson.

Lesson 41

EXERCISE 12
WORKBOOK CHECK

1. (Check each student's Workbook.)
2. (Award points for Workbook performance.)
3. (Record the student's total points in Box B.)

0–2 errors	8 points
3–4 errors	4 points
5–6 errors	2 points
7 or more errors	0 points

INDIVIDUAL READING CHECKOUTS

EXERCISE 13
STORY-READING CHECKOUT

- Study the story. If you read all the sentences with no more than one error, you'll earn 6 points.
- (Check the students individually.)
- (Record either 6 or 0 points in Box C.)

Lesson point total

(Tell students to write the point total in the last box at the top of the Workbook page. Maximum = 20 points.)

Point Summary Chart

(Tell students to write this point total in the box for Lesson 41 in the Point Summary Chart.)

END OF LESSON 41

Lesson 42

WORD-ATTACK SKILLS

EXERCISE 1
SOUND INTRODUCTION

1. (Point to **x**:) This letter makes the sound **kss**. What sound? (Touch.) *kss*.
2. Say each sound when I touch it.
3. (Point to **x**:) What sound? (Touch.) *kss*. Yes, **kss**.
4. (Repeat step 3 for **d, g, p, ŭ, w, ă, n, h, ol, x**.)

x d g p

u w a n

h ol x

> **Individual test**
> (Call on two or three students. Touch under each sound. Each student says all the sounds.)

EXERCISE 2

or

NEW **SOUND COMBINATION: or**

1. (Point to **or**:) These letters go together and say **or**. What sound? (Signal.) *or*.
2. You're going to read words that have the sound **or**.
3. (Point to the underlined part of **for**:) What sound? (Touch.) *or*.
   - What word? (Signal.) *For*.
4. (Repeat step 3 for **form, torn**.)

for

form

torn

EXERCISE 3
PRONUNCIATIONS

> **Note:** Do not write the words on the board. This is an oral exercise.

Task A

1. Listen: **sender**. Say it. (Signal.) *Sender*.
2. Next word: **must**. Say it. (Signal.) *Must*.
3. (Repeat step 2 for **rust, rush, truck, slim, sling, sleek, slips**.)
4. (Repeat all the words until firm.)

Lesson 42 77

Lesson 42

Task B Dell, dull

1. Listen: **dell.** Say it. (Signal.) *Dell.*
- Listen: **dull.** Say it. (Signal.) *Dull.*
2. One of those words has the middle sound **ŭŭŭ.** I'll say the words again: **dell** (pause) **dull.**
3. Which word has the middle sound **ŭŭŭ?** (Signal.) *Dull.* Yes, **dull.**
- Which word has the middle sound **ĕĕĕ?** (Signal.) *Dell.* Yes, **dell.**

Task C Than, then

1. Listen: **than** (pause) **then.** Say those words. (Signal.) *Than, then.* (Repeat until firm.)
2. One of those words has the middle sound **ăăă.** I'll say the words again: **than** (pause) **then.**
3. Which word has the middle sound **ăăă?** (Signal.) *Than.* Yes, **than.**
- Which word has the middle sound **ĕĕĕ?** (Signal.) *Then.* Yes, **then.**
4. Listen: **thăăăn.** What's the middle sound in the word **than?** (Signal.) *ăăă.* Yes, **ăăă.**
- Listen: **thĕĕĕn.** What's the middle sound in the word **then?** (Signal.) *ĕĕĕ.* Yes, **ĕĕĕ.**
5. (Repeat step 4 until firm.) Good job.

Task D Rust, rest

1. Listen: **rust.** Say it. (Signal.) *Rust.*
- Listen: **rest.** Say it. (Signal.) *Rest.*
2. One of those words has the middle sound **ŭŭŭ.** I'll say the words again: **rust** (pause) **rest.**
3. Which word has the middle sound **ŭŭŭ?** (Signal.) *Rust.* Yes, **rust.**
- Which word has the middle sound **ĕĕĕ?** (Signal.) *Rest.* Yes, **rest.**

EXERCISE 4
WORD READING THE FAST WAY

1. You're going to read these words the fast way.
2. (For each word: Touch the ball of the arrow. Pause.) What word? (Slash right.)
3. (Repeat the column until firm.)

rug

dug

stops

steps

not

selling

Lesson 42

4. (For each word: Touch the ball of the arrow. Pause.) **What word?** (Slash right.)
5. (Repeat each word list until firm.)

drop

dock

flag

well

will

streets

lags

claps

clams

did

track

trees

dad

go

wish

rest

crack

rocks

Lesson 42 79

Lesson 42

WORKBOOK EXERCISES

Note: Pass out the Workbooks. Direct the students to open to Lesson 42.

(Award 6 points if the group worked well during the word attack. Remind the students of the points they can earn in their Workbook.)

EXERCISE 5
SOUND DICTATION

1. I'll say the sounds. You write the letters in part 1 in your Workbook.
2. First sound. (Pause.) ōōō. What sound? (Signal.) ōōō.
- Write it in the first blank.
  (Observe students and give feedback.)
3. Next sound. (Pause.) ŭŭŭ. What sound? (Signal.) ŭŭŭ.
- Write it.
  (Observe students and give feedback.)
4. (Repeat step 3 for **nnn, ĭĭĭ, h, ăăă, ŏŏŏ, d, ōōō, ēēē, ĕĕĕ, kss [x]**.)
5. (Repeat sounds students had trouble with.)

EXERCISE 6
SPELLING FROM DICTATION

1. Touch part 2. ✓
- You're going to write words that I dictate.
2. First word: **seem**. What word? (Signal.) *Seem.*
- Listen again: **sss . . . ēēē . . . mmm.** Write it in the first blank.
  (Observe students and give feedback.)
3. Next word: **seed**. What word? (Signal.) *Seed.*
- Listen again: **sss . . . ēēē . . . d.** Write it in the next blank. Remember to write two ē's.
  (Observe students and give feedback.)
4. (Repeat step 3 for **then** [not **than**], **shot, meet, hot.**)

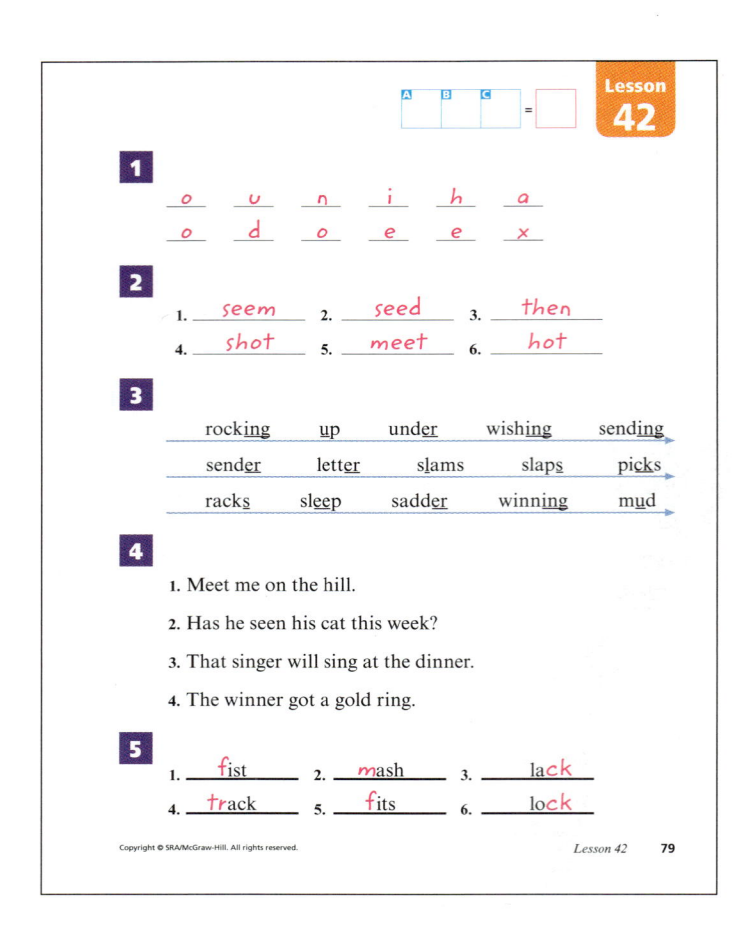

Workbook Page

1
| o | u | n | i | h | a |
| o | d | o | e | e | x |

2
1. seem 2. seed 3. then
4. shot 5. meet 6. hot

3
rock<u>ing</u>   <u>u</u>p   und<u>er</u>   wish<u>ing</u>   send<u>ing</u>
send<u>er</u>   lett<u>er</u>   s<u>l</u>ams   s<u>l</u>aps   pi<u>c</u>ks
rack<u>s</u>   s<u>l</u>eep   sadd<u>er</u>   winn<u>ing</u>   m<u>u</u>d

4
1. Meet me on the hill.
2. Has he seen his cat this week?
3. That singer will sing at the dinner.
4. The winner got a gold ring.

5
1. <u>f</u>ist 2. <u>m</u>ash 3. la<u>ck</u>
4. <u>tr</u>ack 5. <u>f</u>its 6. lo<u>ck</u>

EXERCISE 7
WORD READING: Workbook

1. Touch the first word in part 3. ✓
2. Look at the underlined sound in the first word. (Pause.) What sound? (Signal.) *ing.*
- (Pause.) What word? (Signal.) *Rocking.*
3. Next word. (Pause.) What sound? (Signal.) *ŭŭŭ.*
- (Pause.) What word? (Signal.) *Up.*
4. (Repeat step 3 for **und<u>er</u>, wish<u>ing</u>, send<u>ing</u>, send<u>er</u>, lett<u>er</u>, s<u>l</u>ams, s<u>l</u>aps, pi<u>c</u>ks, rack<u>s</u>, s<u>l</u>eep, sadd<u>er</u>, winn<u>ing</u>, m<u>u</u>d.**)

80   Lesson 42

EXERCISE 8
SENTENCE READING

1. Everybody, touch part 4. ✓
2. Touch under the first word in sentence 1. ✓
   - What word? (Signal.) *Meet.*
3. Next word. ✓
   - What word? (Signal.) *Me.*
4. (Repeat step 3 for **on, the, hill.**)
5. (Repeat steps 2–4 until the students can correctly identify all the words in the sentence in order.)
6. (Repeat steps 2–5 for each remaining sentence:
   - **2. Has he seen his cat this week?**
   - **3. That singer will sing at the dinner.**
   - **4. The winner got a gold ring.**)

> **Individual test**
> (Give each student a chance to read one of the sentences.)

EXERCISE 9
WORD COMPLETION

1. Touch the first word in part 5. ✓
   - What word? (Signal.) *ist.* Yes, **ist.**
   - Fix it up to say (pause) **fist.** What word? (Signal.) *Fist.*
   - Fix it up.
     (Observe students and give feedback.)
2. Touch the next word. ✓
   - What word? (Signal.) *Ash.* Yes, **ash.**
   - Fix it up to say (pause) **mash.** What word? (Signal.) *Mash.*
   - Fix it up.
     (Observe students and give feedback.)
3. (Repeat step 2 for **la [lack], ack [track], its [fits], lo [lock].**)

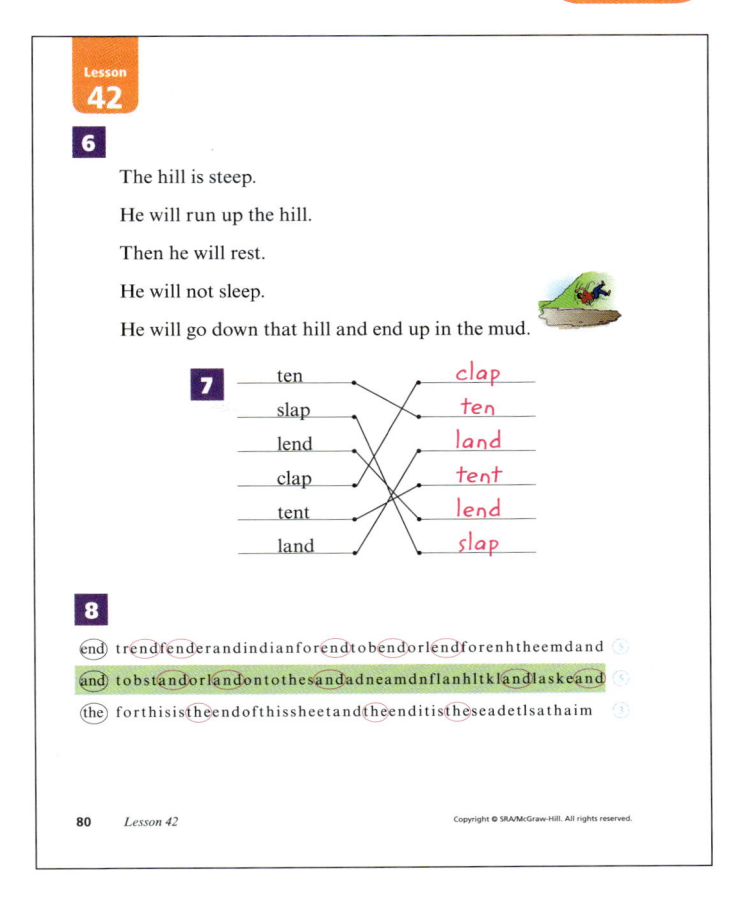

EXERCISE 10
STORY READING

Task A

1. Everybody, touch part 6. ✓
   - You're going to read the sentences the fast way.
2. Touch under the first word. ✓
   - What word? (Signal.) *The.*
3. Next word. ✓
   - What word? (Signal.) *Hill.*
4. (Repeat step 3 for **is, steep.**)
5. (Repeat steps 2–4 until the students correctly identify all the words in the sentence.)
6. (Repeat steps 2–5 for each remaining sentence.)
7. (If students miss more than four words, repeat the story reading from the beginning.)

Lesson 42

Task B

1. Now I'll read the story and ask questions. Follow along.
2. **The hill is steep.** Everybody, is it easy to climb a steep hill? (Signal.) *No.*
3. **He will run up the hill.** Do you think it would be easy to run up a hill? (Call on a student.) *No.*
4. **Then he will rest.** Why does he need to rest? (Call on a student.) (Idea: *He is tired after running uphill.*)
5. **He will not sleep.** Everybody, what won't he do? (Signal.) *Sleep.*
6. **He will go down that hill and end up in the mud.** The picture shows him going down the hill. What is he doing? (Call on a student.) (Idea: *Rolling.*)
- Where will he end up? (Call on a student.) *In the mud.*

EXERCISE 11
MATCHING COMPLETION

1. Everybody, touch part 7. ✓
- Read the words the fast way.
2. Touch under the first word. ✓
- What word? (Signal.) *Ten.*
3. Next word. ✓
- What word? (Signal.) *Slap.*
4. (Repeat step 3 for **lend, clap, tent, land.**)
5. Later, you're going to write the words in the second column.

EXERCISE 12
CIRCLE GAME

1. Everybody, touch part 8. ✓
2. What word will you circle in the first line? (Signal.) *End.*
3. What word will you circle in the second line? (Signal.) *And.*
4. What word will you circle in the third line? (Signal.) *The.*
5. Circle the words and finish the rest of your Workbook lesson.

EXERCISE 13
WORKBOOK CHECK

1. (Check each student's Workbook.)
2. (Award points for Workbook performance.)
3. (Record the student's total points in Box B.)

0–2 errors	8 points
3–4 errors	4 points
5–6 errors	2 points
7 or more errors	0 points

INDIVIDUAL READING CHECKOUTS

EXERCISE 14
STORY-READING CHECKOUT

- Study the story. If you read all the sentences with no more than 1 error, you'll earn 6 points.
- (Check the students individually.)
- (Record either 6 or 0 points in Box C.)

Lesson point total

(Tell students to write the point total in the last box at the top of the Workbook page. Maximum = 20 points.)

Point Summary Chart

(Tell students to write this point total in the box for Lesson 42 in the Point Summary Chart.)

END OF LESSON 42

Lesson 43

WORD-ATTACK SKILLS

EXERCISE 1
SOUND IDENTIFICATION

1. (Point to **o**:) One sound you learned for this letter is the letter name. Everybody, what's that sound? (Touch.) ōōō. Yes, **ōōō**.
   - What's the other sound? (Touch.) ŏŏŏ. Yes, **ŏŏŏ**.
2. Say each sound when I touch it.
3. (Point to **x**:) What sound? (Touch.) kss. Yes, **kss**.
4. (Repeat step 3 for **d, p, g, ŭ, w, n, h, wh**.)

o x
d p
g u w
n h wh

Individual test
(Call on two or three students. Touch under each sound. Each student says all the sounds, including two sounds for **o**.)

EXERCISE 2
PRONUNCIATIONS

Note: Do not write the words on the board. This is an oral exercise.

Task A Click, clock

1. Listen: **click**. Say it. (Signal.) *Click.*
   - Listen: **clock**. Say it. (Signal.) *Clock.*
2. One of those words has the middle sound ĭĭĭ. I'll say the words again: **click** (pause) **clock**.
3. Which word has the middle sound ĭĭĭ? (Signal.) *Click.* Yes, **click**.
   - Which word has the middle sound ŏŏŏ? (Signal.) *Clock.* Yes, **clock**.

Task B Crab, crib

1. Listen: **crab**. Say it. (Signal.) *Crab.*
   - Listen: **crib**. Say it. (Signal.) *Crib.*
2. One of those words has the middle sound ĭĭĭ. I'll say the words again: **crab** (pause) **crib**.
3. Which word has the middle sound ĭĭĭ? (Signal.) *Crib.* Yes, **crib**.
   - Which word has the middle sound ăăă? (Signal.) *Crab.* Yes, **crab**.

Task C Step, stop

1. Listen: **step**. Say it. (Signal.) *Step.*
   - Listen: **stop**. Say it. (Signal.) *Stop.*
2. One of those words has the middle sound ŏŏŏ. I'll say the words again: **step** (pause) **stop**.
3. Which word has the middle sound ŏŏŏ? (Signal.) *Stop.* Yes, **stop**.
   - Which word has the middle sound ĕĕĕ? (Signal.) *Step.* Yes, **step**.

Lesson 43

EXERCISE 3

or

SOUND COMBINATION: or

1. (Point to **or**:) These letters go together and say **or**. What sound? (Signal.) *or*.
2. You're going to read words that have the sound **or**.
3. (Point to the underlined part of **for**:) What sound? (Touch.) *ōr*.
   • What word? (Signal.) *For*.
4. (Repeat step 3 for **short, corn**.)

f<u>or</u>

sh<u>or</u>t

c<u>or</u>n

EXERCISE 4
WORD READING THE FAST WAY

1. You're going to read these words the fast way.
2. (For each word: Touch the ball of the arrow. Pause.) What word? (Slash right.)
3. (Repeat each word list until firm.)

run

an

ship

fold

well

picks

sleep

lids

racks

trees

Lesson 43

4. (For each word: Touch the ball of the arrow. Pause.) **What word?** (Slash right.)
5. (Repeat each word list until firm.)

slip

fast

tracks

thing

went

dinner

sadder

matter

when

will

fun

ox

fox

fix

cats

week

cast

sings

sled

sand

Lesson 43

WORKBOOK EXERCISES

Note: Pass out the Workbooks. Direct the students to open to Lesson 43.

(Award 6 points if the group worked well during the word attack. Remind the students of the points they can earn in their Workbook.)

EXERCISE 5
SOUND DICTATION

1. I'll say the sounds. You write the letters in part 1 in your Workbook.
2. First sound. (Pause.) **ăăă**. What sound? (Signal.) *ăăă*.
- Write it in the first blank.
  (Observe students and give feedback.)
3. Next sound. (Pause.) **h**. What sound? (Signal.) *h*.
- Write it.
  (Observe students and give feedback.)
4. (Repeat step 3 for **ŭŭŭ, p, ththth, ŏŏŏ, ĕĕĕ, shshsh, ĭĭĭ, ōōō, ththth, ēēē**.)
5. (Repeat sounds students had trouble with.)

EXERCISE 6
SPELLING FROM DICTATION

1. Touch part 2. ✓
- You're going to write words that I dictate.
2. First word: **red**. What word? (Signal.) *Red*.
- Listen again: **rrr . . . ĕĕĕ . . . d**. Write it in the first blank.
  (Observe students and give feedback.)
3. Next word: **not**. What word? (Signal.) *Not*.
- Listen again: **nnn . . . ŏŏŏ . . . t**. Write it in the next blank.
  (Observe students and give feedback.)
4. (Repeat step 3 for **she, then** [not **than**], **meet, cats, hid, how**.)

EXERCISE 7
WORD COMPLETION

1. Touch the first word in part 3. ✓
- What word? (Signal.) *hă*. Yes, **hă**.
- Fix it up to say (pause) **hats**. What word? (Signal.) *Hats*.
- Fix it up.
  (Observe students and give feedback.)

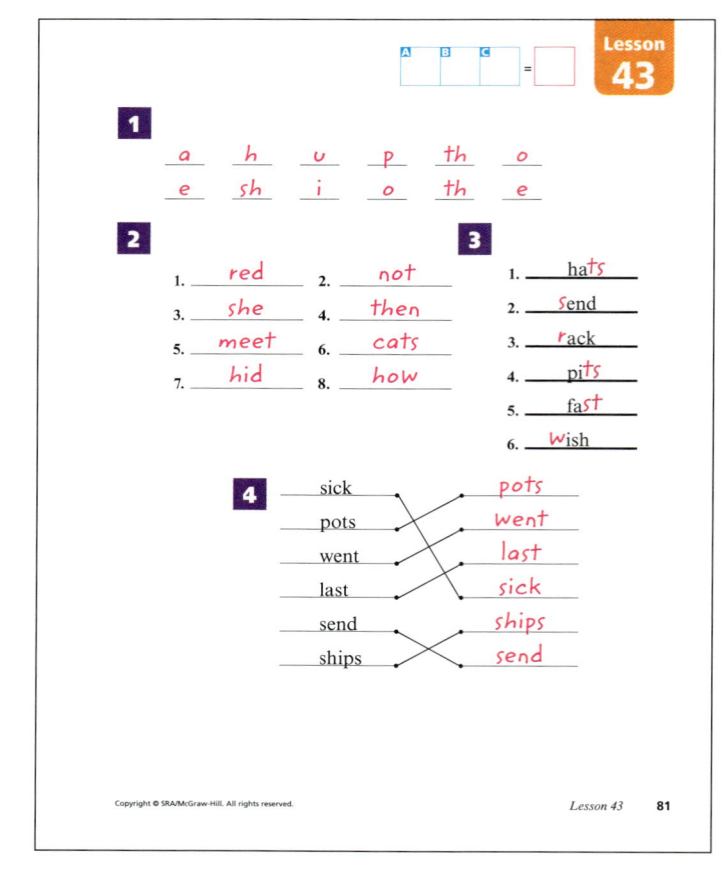

2. Touch the next word. ✓
- What word? (Signal.) *End*. Yes, **end**.
- Fix it up to say (pause) **send**. What word? (Signal.) *Send*.
- Fix it up.
  (Observe students and give feedback.)
3. (Repeat step 2 for **ack** [rack], **pi** [pits], **fa** [fast], **ish** [wish].)

Lesson 43

EXERCISE 8
MATCHING COMPLETION

1. Everybody, touch part 4. ✓
- Read the words the fast way.
2. Touch under the first word. ✓
- What word? (Signal.) *Sick.*
3. Next word. ✓
- What word? (Signal.) *Pots.*
4. (Repeat step 3 for **went, last, send, ship.**)
5. Later, you're going to write the words in the second column.

EXERCISE 9
SENTENCE READING

1. Everybody, touch part 5. ✓
2. Touch under the first word in sentence 1. ✓
- What word? (Signal.) *She.*
3. Next word. ✓
- What word? (Signal.) *Has.*
4. (Repeat step 3 for **a, cast, on, her, leg.**)
5. (Repeat steps 2–4 until the students can correctly identify all the words in the sentence in order.)
6. (Repeat steps 2–5 for each remaining sentence.)

> **Individual test**
> (Give each student a chance to read one of the sentences.)

EXERCISE 10
STORY READING

Task A

1. Everybody, touch part 6. ✓
- You're going to read the sentences the fast way.
2. Touch under the first word. ✓
- What word? (Signal.) *We.*
3. Next word. ✓
- What word? (Signal.) *Fill.*
4. (Repeat step 3 for **pots, with, clams.**)
5. (Repeat steps 2–4 until the students correctly identify all the words in the sentence.)
6. (Repeat steps 2–5 for each remaining sentence.)
7. (If students miss more than four words, repeat the story reading from the beginning.)

Task B

1. Now I'll read the story and ask questions. Follow along.
2. **We fill pots with clams.** Did you ever eat clams or clam chowder? (Call on individual students to respond.)
- They have more than one pot. So they must plan to have a lot of clam chowder.

Lesson 43

5
1. She has a cast on her leg.
2. Is his pet sheep sick?
3. How can she sleep in the sand?
4. This is a fast sled.
5. Send me the clock this week.
6. I get sadder and sadder when she sings.
7. How will we get dinner on this ship?
8. I wish I had ten cents.

6
We fill pots with clams.
We fit lids on the pots.
We can get the pots hot.
That is how we fix a clam dish.

---

3. **We fit lids on the pots.** What are lids? (Call on a student.) (Idea: *Tops for pots.*)
4. **We can get the pots hot.** How would you get pots hot? (Call on a student.) (Idea: *Put the pots on a fire or a stove.*)
5. **That is how we fix a clam dish.** Would you like to have some of that clam dish? (Call on individual students to respond.)

Lesson 43

EXERCISE 11
WORKBOOK CHECK

1. (Check each student's Workbook.)
2. (Award points for Workbook performance.)
3. (Record the student's total points in Box B.)

0–2 errors	8 points
3–4 errors	4 points
5–6 errors	2 points
7 or more errors	0 points

INDIVIDUAL READING CHECKOUTS

EXERCISE 12
STORY-READING CHECKOUT

- Study the story. If you read all the sentences with no more than 1 error, you'll earn 6 points.
- (Check the students individually.)
- (Record either 6 or 0 points in Box C.)

Lesson point total

(Tell students to write the point total in the last box at the top of the Workbook page. Maximum = 20 points.)

Point Summary Chart

(Tell students to write this point total in the box for Lesson 43 in the Point Summary Chart.)

END OF LESSON 43

Lesson 44

WORD-ATTACK SKILLS

EXERCISE 1
SOUND INTRODUCTION

1. (Point to **b**:) This letter makes the sound **b.** What sound? (Touch.) *b.*
2. (Point to **o**:) One sound you learned for this letter is the letter name. Everybody, what's that sound? (Touch.) *ōōō.* Yes, **ōōō.**
 * What's the other sound? (Touch.) *ŏŏŏ.* Yes, **ŏŏŏ.**
3. (Point to **e**:) One sound you learned for this letter is the letter name. Everybody, what's that sound? (Touch.) *ēēē.* Yes, **ēēē.**
 * What's the other sound? (Touch.) *ĕĕĕ.* Yes, **ĕĕĕ.**
4. Say each sound when I touch it.
5. (Point to **b**:) What sound? (Touch.) *b.* Yes, **b.**
6. (Repeat step 5 for **g, th, wh, d, c, p, x, ŭ.**)

b o e
b g th
wh d c
p x u

> **Individual test**
> (Call on two or three students. Touch under each sound. Each student says all the sounds, including two sounds for **o** and two sounds for **e.**)

EXERCISE 2
PRONUNCIATIONS

> **Note:** Do not write the words on the board. This is an oral exercise.

Task A

1. Listen: **crush.** Say it. (Signal.) *Crush.*
2. Next word: **rust.** Say it. (Signal.) *Rust.*
3. (Repeat step 2 for **crust, crusts, form, thorn, dorms, steep, sleeps.**)
4. (Repeat all the words until firm.)

Task B **Creek, crack**

1. Listen: **creek** (pause) **crack.** Say those words. (Signal.) *Creek, crack.* (Repeat until firm.)
2. One of those words has the middle sound **ăăă.** I'll say the words again: **creek** (pause) **crack.**
3. Which word has the middle sound **ăăă?** (Signal.) *Crack.* Yes, **crack.**
 * Which word has the middle sound **ēēē?** (Signal.) *Creek.* Yes, **creek.**
4. Listen: **crēēēk.** What's the middle sound in the word **creek?** (Signal.) *ēēē.* Yes, **ēēē.**
 * Listen: **crăăăck.** What's the middle sound in the word **crack?** (Signal.) *ăăă.* Yes, **ăăă.**
5. (Repeat step 4 until firm.) Good job.

Task C **Lag, lug**

1. Listen: **lag.** Say it. (Signal.) *Lag.*
 * Listen: **lug.** Say it. (Signal.) *Lug.*
2. One of those words has the middle sound **ŭŭŭ.** I'll say the words again: **lag** (pause) **lug.**
3. Which word has the middle sound **ŭŭŭ?** (Signal.) *Lug.* Yes, **lug.**
 * Which word has the middle sound **ăăă?** (Signal.) *Lag.* Yes, **lag.**

Task D **Step, steep**

1. Listen: **step** (pause) **steep.** Say those words. (Signal.) *Step, steep.* (Repeat until firm.)
2. One of those words has the middle sound **ĕĕĕ.** I'll say the words again: **step** (pause) **steep.**

Lesson 44 89

Lesson 44

3. Which word has the middle sound ĕĕĕ? (Signal.) *Step.* Yes, **step.**
- Which word has the middle sound ēēē? (Signal.) *Steep.* Yes, **steep.**
4. Listen: **stĕĕĕp.** What's the middle sound in the word **step?** (Signal.) *ĕĕĕ.* Yes, **ĕĕĕ.**
- Listen: **stēēēp.** What's the middle sound in the word **steep?** (Signal.) *ēēē.* Yes, **ēēē.**
5. (Repeat step 4 until firm.) Good job.

EXERCISE 3
WORD READING THE FAST WAY

1. You're going to read these words the fast way.
2. (For each word: Touch the ball of the arrow. Pause.) What word? (Slash right.)
3. (Repeat each word list until firm.)

her

up

sun

runs

cut

so

dot

go

sleep

slip

peel

pal

fix

pens

pins

picking

4. (For each word: Touch the ball of the arrow. Pause.) **What word?** (Slash right.)
5. (Repeat each word list until firm.)

or

form

claps

flags

mist

mast

must

trap

get

Lesson 44

WORKBOOK EXERCISES

Note: Pass out the Workbooks. Direct the students to open to Lesson 44.

(Award 6 points if the group worked well during the word attack. Remind the students of the points they can earn in their Workbook.)

EXERCISE 4
SOUND DICTATION

1. I'll say the sounds. You write the letters in part 1 in your Workbook.
2. First sound. (Pause.) **d.** What sound? (Signal.) *d.*
- Write it in the first blank.
  (Observe students and give feedback.)
3. Next sound. (Pause.) **ēēē.** What sound? (Signal.) *ēēē.*
- Write it.
  (Observe students and give feedback.)
4. (Repeat step 3 for **ōōō, ĕĕĕ, ĭĭĭ, ŭŭŭ, ăăă, p, lll, g, ing, nnn.**)
5. (Repeat sounds students had trouble with.)

EXERCISE 5
SPELLING FROM DICTATION

1. Touch part 2. ✓
- You're going to write words that I dictate.
2. First word: **dad.** What word? (Signal.) *Dad.*
- Listen again: **d . . . ăăă . . . d.** Write it in the first blank.
  (Observe students and give feedback.)
3. Next word: **hid.** What word? (Signal.) *Hid.*
- Listen again: **h . . . ĭĭĭ . . . d.** Write it in the next blank.
  (Observe students and give feedback.)
4. (Repeat step 3 for **this, did, not, hit.**)

Lesson 44 91

Lesson 44

Workbook (Lesson 44, p. 83)

1.
d	e	o	e	i	u
a	p	l	g	ing	n

2.
1. dad 2. hid 3. this
4. did 5. not 6. hit

3.
clam   slam   mend   street   for
handing   lending   clapping   rug   then
them   under   than   get   crash   corn

4.
1. The old man fell on the dock and got wet.
2. She will fish or sing.
3. Stop filling that gas can with sand.
4. No man will rent that shack.

5.
1. hats   2. mast   3. send
4. sheets   5. mend   6. sand

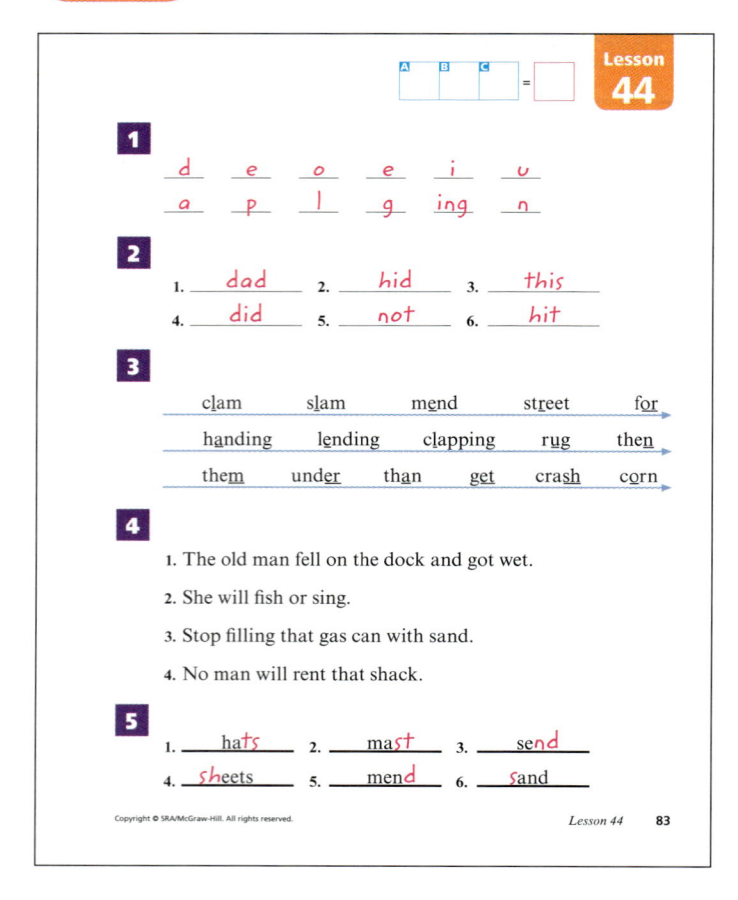

EXERCISE 6
WORD READING: Workbook

1. Touch the first word in part 3. ✓
2. Look at the underlined sound in the first word. (Pause.) What sound? (Signal.) *lll.*
- (Pause.) What word? (Signal.) *Clam.*
3. Next word. (Pause.) What sound? (Signal.) *lll.*
- (Pause.) What word? (Signal.) *Slam.*
4. (Repeat step 3 for remaining words.)

EXERCISE 7
SENTENCE READING

1. Everybody, touch part 4. ✓
2. Touch under the first word in sentence 1. ✓
- What word? (Signal.) *The.*
3. Next word. ✓
- What word? (Signal.) *Old.*
4. (Repeat step 3 for **man, fell, on, the, dock, and, got, wet.**)
5. (Repeat steps 2–4 until the students can correctly identify all the words in the sentence in order.)
6. (Repeat steps 2–5 for each remaining sentence:
- **2. She will fish or sing.**
- **3. Stop filling that gas can with sand.**
- **4. No man will rent that shack.**)

Individual test
(Give each student a chance to read one of the sentences.)

EXERCISE 8
WORD COMPLETION

1. Touch the first word in part 5. ✓
- Fix it up to say (pause) **hats.** What word? (Signal.) *Hats.*
- Fix it up.
  (Observe students and give feedback.)
2. Touch the next word. ✓
- Fix it up to say (pause) **mast.** What word? (Signal.) *Mast.*
- Fix it up.
  (Observe students and give feedback.)
3. (Repeat step 2 for **se [send], eets [sheets], men [mend], and [sand].**)

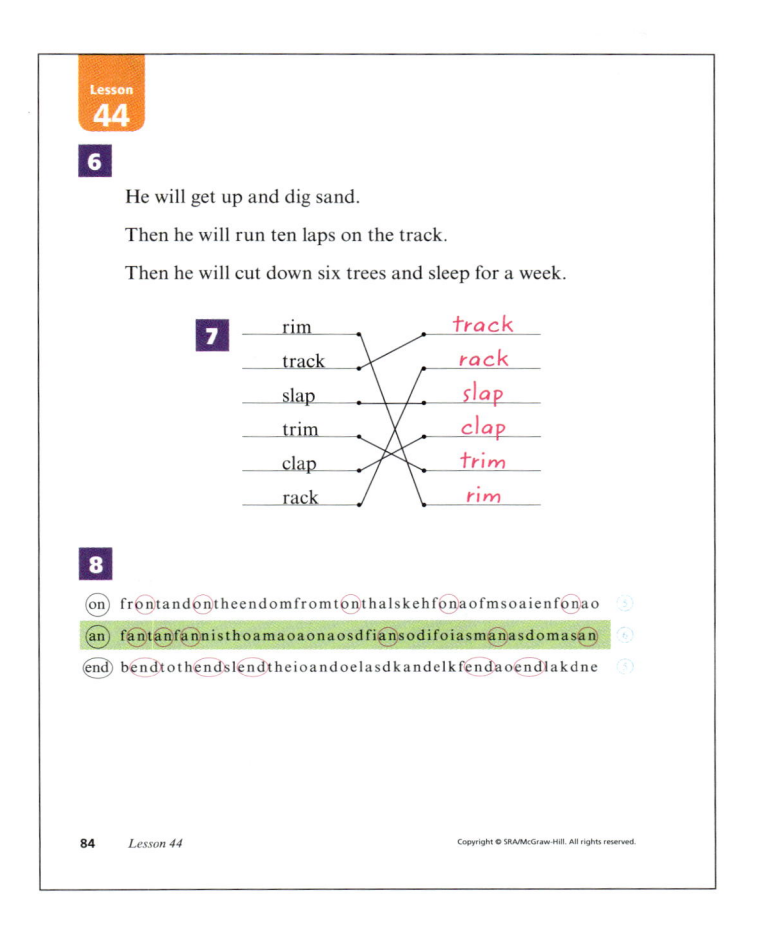

Lesson 44

Lesson 44

6

He will get up and dig sand.

Then he will run ten laps on the track.

Then he will cut down six trees and sleep for a week.

7
- rim — rim
- track — track
- slap — slap
- trim — trim
- clap — clap
- rack — rack

8
- (on) frontandontheendomfromt(on)thalskehf(on)aofmsoaienf(on)ao 3
- (an) fant(an)f(an)nisthoamaoaonaosdfi(an)sodifoiasm(an)asdomas(an) 6
- (end) b(end)toth(end)sl(end)theioandoelasdkand(end)elkf(end)aoo(end)lakdne 5

84   Lesson 44

EXERCISE 9
STORY READING

Task A

1. Everybody, touch part 6. ✓
- You're going to read the sentences the fast way.
2. Touch under the first word. ✓
- What word? (Signal.) *He.*
3. Next word. ✓
- What word? (Signal.) *Will.*
4. (Repeat step 3 for **get, up, and, dig, sand.**)
5. (Repeat steps 2–4 until the students correctly identify all the words in the sentence.)
6. (Repeat steps 2–5 for each remaining sentence:
- **Then he will run ten laps on the track.**
- **Then he will cut down six trees and sleep for a week.**)
7. (If students miss more than four words, repeat the story reading from the beginning.)

Task B

1. Now I'll read the story and ask questions. Follow along.
2. **He will get up and dig sand.** It must be morning and he's just getting up. What is he going to do after he gets up? (Call on a student.) (Idea: *Dig sand.*)
3. **Then he will run ten laps on the track.** What will he do first? (Call on a student.) *Dig sand.*
- Then what will he do? (Call on a student.) (Idea: *Run ten laps.*)
4. **Then he will cut down six trees and sleep for a week.** How do you cut down trees? (Call on a student.) (Idea: *With a saw or an ax.*)
- Is that easy work? (Call on a student.) *No.*
5. After he cuts down six trees, what will he do? (Call on a student.) *Sleep for a week.*
- Why will he sleep so much? (Call on a student.) (Idea: *He did so many hard things.*)
6. Who can name all the things he did before he went to sleep? (Call on a student.) (Idea: *He dug sand, ran ten laps, and cut down six trees.*)

Lesson 44   93

Lesson 44

EXERCISE 10
MATCHING COMPLETION

1. Everybody, touch part 7. ✓
- Read the words the fast way.
2. Touch under the first word. ✓
- What word? (Signal.) *Rim.*
3. Next word. ✓
- What word? (Signal.) *Track.*
4. (Repeat step 3 for **slap, trim, clap, rack.**)
5. Later, you're going to write the words in the second column.

EXERCISE 11
CIRCLE GAME

1. Everybody, touch part 8. ✓
2. What word will you circle in the first line? (Signal.) *On.*
3. What word will you circle in the second line? (Signal.) *An.*
4. What word will you circle in the third line? (Signal.) *End.*
5. Circle the words and finish the rest of your Workbook lesson.

EXERCISE 12
WORKBOOK CHECK

1. (Check each student's Workbook.)
2. (Award points for Workbook performance.)
3. (Record the student's total points in Box B.)

0–2 errors	8 points
3–4 errors	4 points
5–6 errors	2 points
7 or more errors	0 points

INDIVIDUAL READING CHECKOUTS

EXERCISE 13
STORY-READING CHECKOUT

- Study the story. If you read all the sentences with no more than 1 error, you'll earn 6 points.
- (Check the students individually.)
- (Record either 6 or 0 points in Box C.)

Lesson point total

(Tell students to write the point total in the last box at the top of the Workbook page. Maximum = 20 points.)

Point Summary Chart

(Tell students to write this point total in the box for Lesson 44 in the Point Summary Chart.)

END OF LESSON 44

Lesson 45

WORD-ATTACK SKILLS

EXERCISE 1
SOUND INTRODUCTION

1. (Point to **b:**) This letter makes the sound **b.** What sound? (Touch.) *b.*
2. Say each sound when I touch it.
3. (Point to **b:**) What sound? (Touch.) *b.* Yes, **b.**
4. (Repeat step 3 for **d, sh, s, er, wh, ĭ, ă, l, x.**)

b d
sh s
er wh
i a l x

> **Individual test**
> (Call on two or three students. Touch under each sound. Each student says all the sounds.)

EXERCISE 2
PRONUNCIATIONS

> **Note:** Do not write the words on the board. This is an oral exercise.

Task A

1. Listen: **crusts.** Say it. (Signal.) *Crusts.*
2. Next word: **clip.** Say it. (Signal.) *Clip.*
3. (Repeat step 2 for **drip, trip, slug, flip, flush.**)
4. (Repeat all the words until firm.)

Task B Pills, pals, peels

1. Listen: **pills, pals, peels.** Say those words. (Signal.) *Pills, pals, peels.* (Repeat until firm.)
2. One of those words has the middle sound ăăă. I'll say the words again: **pills, pals, peels.**
3. Which word has the middle sound ăăă? (Signal.) *Pals.* Yes, **pals.**
- Which word has the middle sound ēēē? (Signal.) *Peels.* Yes, **peels.**
- Which word has the middle sound ĭĭĭ? (Signal.) *Pills.* Yes, **pills.**

Task C Clock, click, clack

1. Listen: **clock, click, clack.** Say those words. (Signal.) *Clock, click, clack.* (Repeat until firm.)
2. One of those words has the middle sound ĭĭĭ. I'll say the words again: **clock, click, clack.**
3. Which word has the middle sound ĭĭĭ? (Signal.) *Click.* Yes, **click.**
- Which word has the middle sound ŏŏŏ? (Signal.) *Clock.* Yes, **clock.**
- Which word has the middle sound ăăă? (Signal.) *Clack.* Yes, **clack.**

Task D Tint, tent

1. Listen: **tint** (pause) **tent.** Say those words. (Signal.) *Tint, tent.* (Repeat until firm.)
2. One of those words has the middle sound ĕĕĕ. I'll say the words again: **tint** (pause) **tent.**
3. Which word has the middle sound ĕĕĕ? (Signal.) *Tent.* Yes, **tent.**
- Which word has the middle sound ĭĭĭ? (Signal.) *Tint.* Yes, **tint.**
4. Listen: **tĭĭĭnt.** What's the middle sound in the word **tint**? (Signal.) *ĭĭĭ.* Yes, **ĭĭĭ.**
- Listen: **tĕĕĕnt.** What's the middle sound in the word **tent**? (Signal.) *ĕĕĕ.* Yes, **ĕĕĕ.**

Lesson 45

EXERCISE 3
NEW ▸ WORD READING THE FAST WAY

Note: Starting in this lesson, the correction procedure for errors on words displayed in the Teacher Presentation Book changes from a sound-out to a whole-word procedure.

1. You're going to read these words the fast way.
2. (For each word: Touch the ball of the arrow. Pause.) What word? (Slash right.)

To correct:
  a. (Say the correct word.)
  b. What word? (Slash right.) Yes, _____. Remember that word.
  c. (Return to the first word in each list and present the words in order.)

3. (Repeat each word list until firm.)

up

but

fill

fell

class

dug

under

click

big

dig

mend

lend

crack

street

Lesson 45

4. (For each word: Touch the ball of the arrow. Pause.) **What word?** (Slash right.)
5. (Repeat each word list until firm.)

track

told

torn

more

flags

pills

men

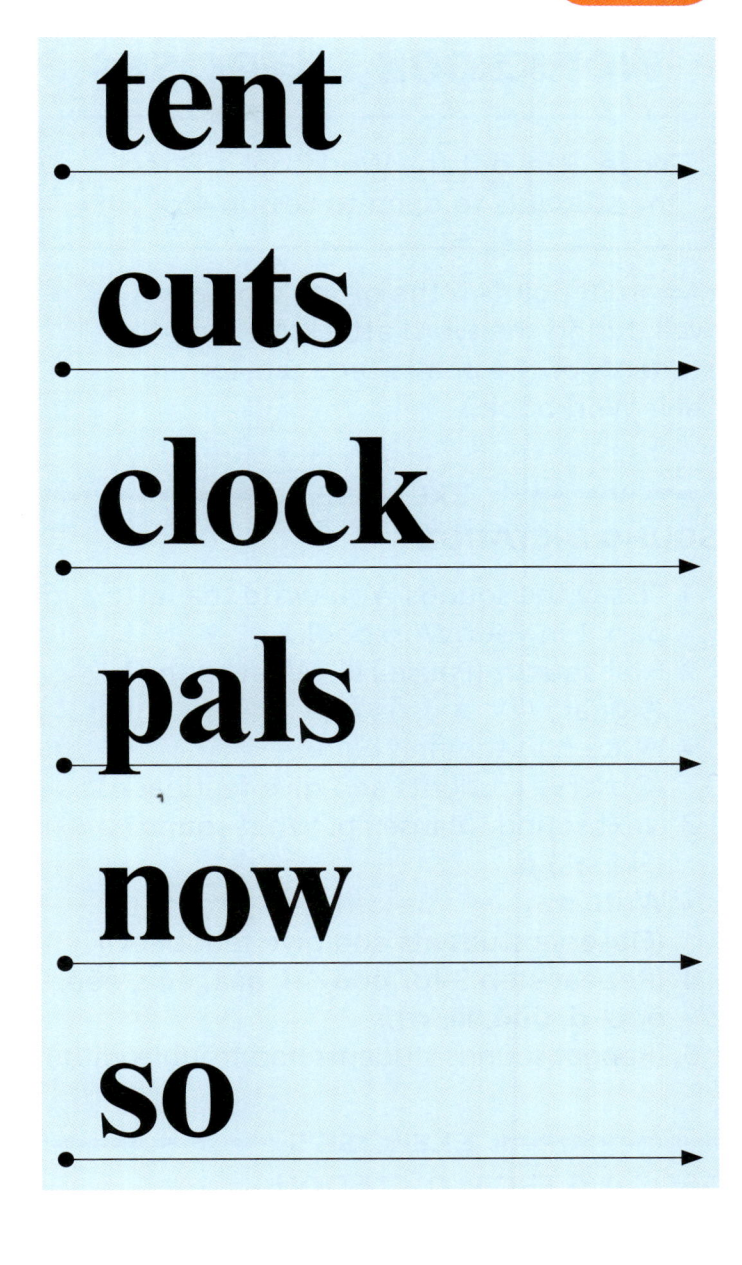

tent

cuts

clock

pals

now

so

Lesson 45

WORKBOOK EXERCISES

Note: Pass out the Workbooks. Direct the students to open to Lesson 45.

(Award 6 points if the group worked well during the word attack. Remind the students of the points they can earn in their Workbook.)

EXERCISE 4
SOUND DICTATION

1. I'll say the sounds. You write the letters in part 1 in your Workbook.
2. First sound. (Pause.) **lll.** What sound? (Signal.) *lll.*
   - Write it in the first blank.
     (Observe students and give feedback.)
3. Next sound. (Pause.) **p.** What sound? (Signal.) *p.*
   - Write it.
     (Observe students and give feedback.)
4. (Repeat step 3 for **ōōō, ĭĭĭ, ăăă, ěěě, ēēē, ŏŏŏ, d, ŭŭŭ, lll, rrr.**)
5. (Repeat sounds students had trouble with.)

EXERCISE 5
SPELLING FROM DICTATION

1. Touch part 2. ✓
   - You're going to write words that I dictate.
2. First word: **meet.** What word? (Signal.) *Meet.*
   - Listen again: **mmm . . . ēēē . . . t.** Write it in the first blank. Remember to write two **ē**'s.
     (Observe students and give feedback.)
3. Next word: **hits.** What word? (Signal.) *Hits.*
   - Listen again: **h . . . ĭĭĭ . . . t . . . sss.** Write it in the next blank.
     (Observe students and give feedback.)
4. (Repeat step 3 for **cans, seen, cats, seed.**)

EXERCISE 6
WORD READING: Workbook

1. Touch the first word in part 3. ✓
2. Look at the underlined sound in the first word. (Pause.) What sound? (Signal.) *ēēē.*
   - (Pause.) What word? (Signal.) *Sleep.*

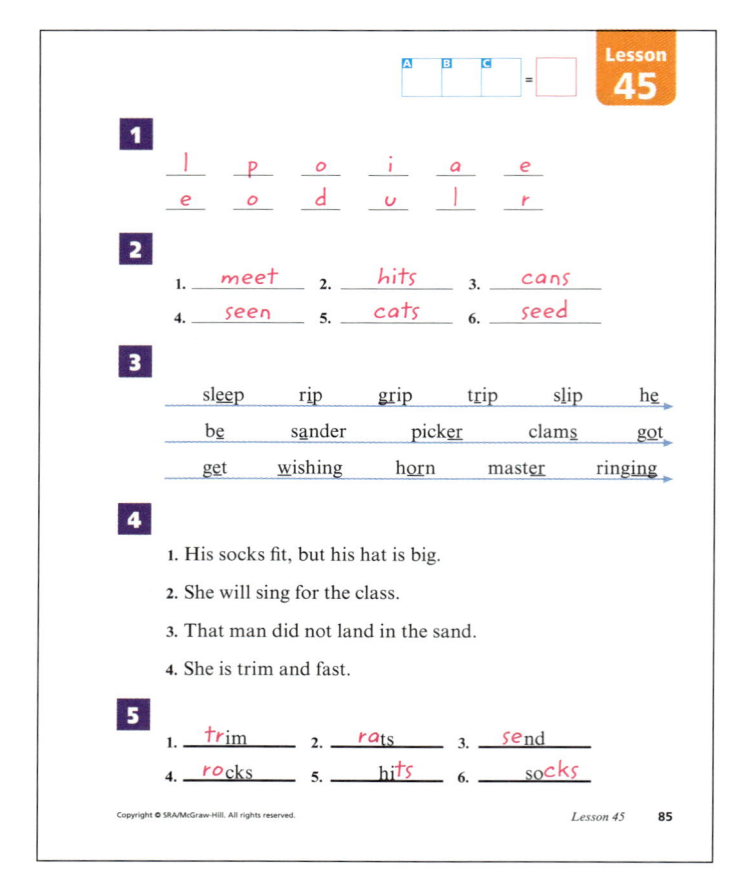

3. Next word. (Pause.) What sound? (Signal.) *ĭĭĭ.*
   - (Pause.) What word? (Signal.) *Rip.*
4. (Repeat step 3 for remaining words.)

EXERCISE 7
SENTENCE READING

1. Everybody, touch part 4. ✓
2. Touch under the first word in sentence 1. ✓
   - What word? (Signal.) *His.*
3. Next word. ✓
   - What word? (Signal.) *Socks.*
4. (Repeat step 3 for **fit, but, his, hat, is, big.**)

98   Lesson 45

Lesson 45

5. (Repeat steps 2–4 until the students can correctly identify all the words in the sentence in order.)
6. (Repeat steps 2–5 for each remaining sentence.)

> **Individual test**
> (Give each student a chance to read one of the sentences.)

EXERCISE 8
WORD COMPLETION

1. Touch the first word in part 5. ✓
- What word? (Signal.) *im.* Yes, **im.**
- Fix it up to say (pause) **trim.** What word? (Signal.) *Trim.*
- Fix it up.
  (Observe students and give feedback.)
2. Touch the next word. ✓
- Fix it up to say (pause) **rats.** What word? (Signal.) *Rats.*
- Fix it up.
  (Observe students and give feedback.)
3. (Repeat step 2 for **send, rocks, hits, socks.**)

EXERCISE 9
STORY READING

Task A

1. Everybody, touch part 6. ✓
- You're going to read the sentences the fast way.
2. Touch under the first word. ✓
- What word? (Signal.) *She.*
3. Next word. ✓
- What word? (Signal.) *Told.*
4. (Repeat step 3 for **him, to, sell, the, clock.**)
5. (Repeat steps 2–4 until the students correctly identify all the words in the sentence.)
6. (Repeat steps 2–5 for each remaining sentence.)
7. (If students miss more than four words, repeat the story reading from the beginning.)

Task B

1. Now I'll read the story and ask questions. Follow along.
2. **She told him to sell the clock. He went to a shop to sell the clock.** Everybody, when he sells the clock, what will he give to the person at the shop? (Signal) *The clock.*
- If he's selling the clock, what will the person at the shop give him? (Call on a student.) (Idea: *Money or cash.*)
3. **Now he has no clock and no cash. But he has 3 cats.** When he sold the clock, he got cash. You can figure out what he did with the cash. What did he do? (Call on a student.) (Idea: *Bought three cats.*)

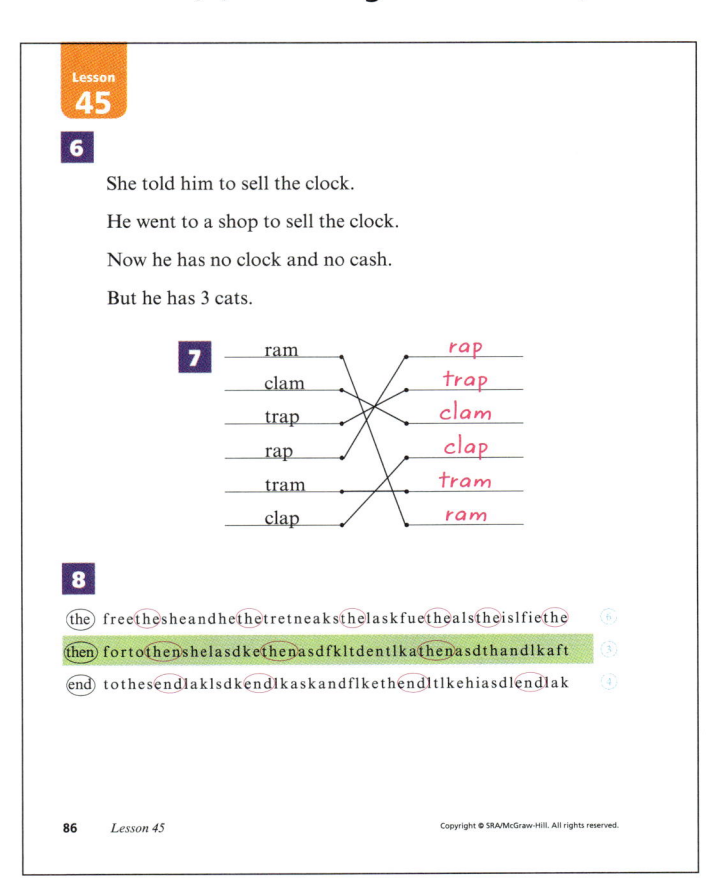

Lesson 45

6
She told him to sell the clock.
He went to a shop to sell the clock.
Now he has no clock and no cash.
But he has 3 cats.

7
ram — rap
clam — trap
trap — clam
rap — clap
tram — tram
clap — ram

8
(the) freetheshandhethetretneaksthelaskfuethealstheislfiethe
(then) fortothenshelasdkethenasdfkltdentlkathenasdthandlkaft
(end) tothesendlaklsdkendlkaskandflkethendltlkehiasdlendlak

Lesson 45   99

Lesson 45

EXERCISE 10
MATCHING COMPLETION

1. Everybody, touch part 7. ✓
- Read the words the fast way.
2. Touch under the first word. ✓
- What word? (Signal.) *Ram.*
3. Next word. ✓
- What word? (Signal.) *Clam.*
4. (Repeat step 3 for **trap, rap, tram, clap**.)
5. Later, you're going to write the words in the second column.

EXERCISE 11
CIRCLE GAME

1. Everybody, touch part 8. ✓
2. What word will you circle in the first line? (Signal.) *The.*
3. What word will you circle in the second line? (Signal.) *Then.*
4. What word will you circle in the third line? (Signal.) *End.*
5. Circle the words and finish the rest of your Workbook lesson.

EXERCISE 12
NEW WORKBOOK CHECK

1. (Check each student's Workbook.)
2. (Award points for Workbook performance.)
3. (Record the student's total points in Box B.)

0–3 errors	8 points
4–5 errors	4 points
6 errors	2 points
7 or more errors	0 points

INDIVIDUAL READING CHECKOUTS

EXERCISE 13
STORY-READING CHECKOUT

- Study the story. If you read all the sentences with no more than 1 error, you'll earn 6 points.
- (Check the students individually.)
- (Record either 6 or 0 points in Box C.)

Lesson point total

(Tell students to write the point total in the last box at the top of the Workbook page. Maximum = 20 points.)

Point Summary Chart

(Tell students to write this point total in the box for Lesson 45 in the Point Summary Chart.)

Five-lesson point summary

(Tell students to add the point totals for Lessons 41 through 45 in the Point Summary Chart and to write the total for Block 9. Maximum for Block 9 = 100 points.)

END OF LESSON 45

MASTERY TEST 10

— AFTER LESSON 45, BEFORE LESSON 46 —

> **Note:** Use students' performance on the Lesson 45 Story reading checkout for Mastery Test 10.

Scoring the test

1. (Count each student's errors on the Story reading checkout. Write these numbers in the Test 10 boxes on the *Decoding A* Mastery Test Student Profile form. Circle **P** or **F**.)
2. (When all students have been tested, circle **P** or **F** for each student on the *Decoding A* Mastery Test Group Summary form. Determine if more than 25 percent of the students failed the Story reading checkout by dividing the number of students who failed by the total number of students in the group.)

Remedies

(If more than 25 percent of the students made 2 or more errors on the Story reading checkout, [1] repeat the Story reading checkouts for Lessons 41 through 44, and [2] repeat all of Lesson 45. Permission is granted to reproduce the Workbook pages for Lesson 45 for classroom use.)

Lesson Objectives	LESSON 46 Exercise	LESSON 47 Exercise	LESSON 48 Exercise	LESSON 49 Exercise	LESSON 50 Exercise
Word Attack					
Phonemic Awareness					
Sound/Word Pronunciation	1, 2	1, 2	1–3	1–3	1, 2
Identify Sounds in Words	2	2	2, 3	2, 3	2
Decoding and Word Analysis					
Letter Sounds: y, ē, ĕ, ō, ŏ, b, n, p, u, ck, wh, th, g, l, d	1				
Letter Sounds: y, ē, ĕ, ō, ŏ, b, ol, p, d, or, x, a, i, er, h		1			
Letter Sounds: w, wh, x, h, u, sh, th, y, er, b, d			1		
Letter Sounds: ē, ĕ, y, b, u, th, or, ol, d				1	
Letter Sounds: ē, ĕ, ō, ŏ, sh, ck, p, u, ing, n, l, d, b, t, f					1
Word Recognition	3	3, 4	3, 4	3, 4	3
High-Frequency Words		3	3	3	
Assessment					
Ongoing: Individual Tests	1	1	1	1	1
Group Reading					
Decoding and Word Analysis					
Read Decodable Text	9	10	10	10	9
Comprehension					
Make Predictions	9				9
Access Prior Knowledge		10	10		9
Draw Inferences	9	10	10	10	9
Note Details			10	10	9
Assessment					
Ongoing: Comprehension Check	9	10	10	10	9
Ongoing: Decoding Accuracy	9	10	10	10	9
Formal: Mastery Test					MT 11
Workbook Exercises					
Decoding and Word Analysis					
Word Recognition	6	7			6
Sentence Reading	7	8	9	9	7
Sound Combinations	6	7			6
Spelling: Sound/Letter Relationships	4, 8, 10	5, 9, 11	5, 7, 8	5, 7, 8	4, 8, 10
Spelling: CVC, CCVVC, CVVCC		6			5
Spelling: CVC, CCVC, CVCC, CVVC	5		6		
Spelling: CVC, CCVC, CVCC, CVVC				6	
Visual Discrimination	10, 11	11, 12	8	8	10, 11
Assessment					
Ongoing: Individual Tests	7	8	9	9	7
Ongoing: Teacher-Monitored Accuracy	13	14	12	12	13
Ongoing: Teacher-Monitored Fluency	13	14	12	12	13
Ongoing: Workcheck	12	13	11	11	12

WORD-ATTACK SKILLS

EXERCISE 1
SOUND INTRODUCTION

1. (Point to **y:**) This letter usually makes the sound *yēēē*. What sound? (Touch.) *yēēē*.
2. (Point to **e:**) One sound you learned for this letter is the letter name. Everybody, what's that sound? (Touch.) *ēēē*. Yes, **ēēē**.
   - What's the other sound? (Touch.) *ĕĕĕ*. Yes, **ĕĕĕ**.
3. (Point to **o:**) One sound you learned for this letter is the letter name. Everybody, what's that sound? (Touch.) *ōōō*. Yes, **ōōō**.
   - What's the other sound? (Touch.) *ŏŏŏ*. Yes, **ŏŏŏ**.
4. Say each sound when I touch it.
5. (Point to **y:**) What sound? (Touch.) *yēēē*. Yes, **yēēē**.
6. (Repeat step 5 for **b, n, p, ŭ, ck, wh, th, g, l, d.**)

y e o
y b n
p u ck
wh th
g l d

> **Individual test**
> (Call on two or three students. Touch under each sound. Each student says all the sounds.)

EXERCISE 2
PRONUNCIATIONS

Task A

1. Listen: **clods.** Say it. (Signal.) *Clods.*
2. Next word: **trods.** Say it. (Signal.) *Trods.*
3. (Repeat step 2 for **trots, must, slugs, flips, flaps.**)
4. (Repeat all the words until firm.)

Task B **Trot, treat**

1. Listen: **trot** (pause) **treat.** Say those words. (Signal.) *Trot, treat.* (Repeat until firm.)
2. One of those words has the middle sound **ēēē**. I'll say the words again: **trot** (pause) **treat.**
3. Which word has the middle sound **ēēē**? (Signal.) *Treat.* Yes, **treat.**
   - Which word has the middle sound **ŏŏŏ**? (Signal.) *Trot.* Yes, **trot.**
4. Listen: **trŏŏŏt.** What's the middle sound in the word **trot**? (Signal.) *ŏŏŏ.* Yes, **ŏŏŏ**.
   - Listen: **trēēēt.** What's the middle sound in the word **treat**? (Signal.) *ēēē.* Yes, **ēēē**.
5. (Repeat step 4 until firm.) Good job.

Task C **Trick, track, truck**

1. Listen: **trick, track, truck.** Say those words. (Signal.) *Trick, track, truck.* (Repeat until firm.)
2. One of those words has the middle sound **ăăă**. I'll say the words again: **trick, track, truck.**
3. Which word has the middle sound **ăăă**? (Signal.) *Track.* Yes, **track.**
   - Which word has the middle sound **ŭŭŭ**? (Signal.) *Truck.* Yes, **truck.**
   - Which word has the middle sound **ĭĭĭ**? (Signal.) *Trick.* Yes, **trick.**

Lesson 46

Lesson 46

- 4. Listen: **trĭĭĭck.** What's the middle sound in the word **trick?** (Signal.) *ĭĭĭ.* Yes, **ĭĭĭ.**
- Listen: **trăăăck.** What's the middle sound in the word **track?** (Signal.) *ăăă.* Yes, **ăăă.**
- Listen: **trŭŭŭck.** What's the middle sound in the word **truck?** (Signal.) *ŭŭŭ.* Yes, **ŭŭŭ.**
- 5. (Repeat step 4 until firm.) Good job.

EXERCISE 3
WORD READING THE FAST WAY

1. You're going to read these words the fast way.
2. (For each word: Touch the ball of the arrow. Pause.) What word? (Slash right.)

> **To correct:**
> a. (Say the correct word.)
> b. What word? (Slash right.)
>   Yes, _____. Remember that word.
> c. (Return to the first word in the list and present the words in order.)

3. (Repeat each word list until firm.)

pills

but

bus

glad

seller

how

no

now

pinning

must

dust

bust

rust

crust

4. (For each word: Touch the ball of the arrow. Pause.) **What word?** (Slash right.)
5. (Repeat each word list until firm.)

clip

rip

drip

big

dig

bug

dug

rug

dents

with

went

us

Lesson 46

WORKBOOK EXERCISES

Note: Pass out the Workbooks. Direct the students to open to Lesson 46.

(Award 6 points if the group worked well during the word attack. Remind the students of the points they can earn in their Workbook.)

EXERCISE 4
SOUND DICTATION

1. I'll say the sounds. You write the letters in part 1 in your Workbook.
2. First sound. (Pause.) **ŏŏŏ.** What sound? (Signal.) ŏŏŏ.
- Write it in the first blank.
(Observe students and give feedback.)
3. Next sound. (Pause.) **ŭŭŭ.** What sound? (Signal.) ŭŭŭ.
- Write it.
(Observe students and give feedback.)
4. (Repeat step 3 for **ĕĕĕ, ĭĭĭ, ăăă, g, ōōō, ēēē, d, lll, p, fff.**)
5. (Repeat sounds students had trouble with.)

EXERCISE 5
SPELLING FROM DICTATION

1. Touch part 2. ✓
- You're going to write words that I dictate.
2. First word: **shots.** What word? (Signal.) *Shots.*
- Listen again: **shshsh . . . ŏŏŏ . . . t . . . sss.** Write it in the first blank.
(Observe students and give feedback.)
3. Next word: **hits.** What word? (Signal.) *Hits.*
- Listen again: **h . . . ĭĭĭ . . . t . . . sss.** Write it in the next blank.
(Observe students and give feedback.)
4. (Repeat step 3 for **red, hats, then, rods.**)

EXERCISE 6
WORD READING: Workbook

1. Touch the first word in part 3. ✓
2. Look at the underlined sound in the first word. (Pause.) What sound? (Signal.) *rrr.*
- (Pause.) What word? (Signal.) *Trim.*
3. Next word. (Pause.) What sound? (Signal.) *g.*
- (Pause.) What word? (Signal.) *Grim.*
4. (Repeat step 3 for remaining words.)

EXERCISE 7
SENTENCE READING

1. Everybody, touch part 4. ✓
2. Touch under the first word in sentence 1. ✓
- What word? (Signal.) *I.*
3. Next word. ✓
- What word? (Signal.) *Am.*
4. (Repeat step 3 for **not, a, big, winner.**)

106 Lesson 46

5. (Repeat steps 2–4 until the students can correctly identify all the words in the sentence in order.)
6. (Repeat steps 2–5 for each remaining sentence.)

> **Individual test**
> (Give each student a chance to read one of the sentences.)

EXERCISE 8
WORD COMPLETION

1. Touch the first word in part 5. ✓
- Fix it up to say (pause) **list.** What word? (Signal.) *List.*
- Fix it up.
  (Observe students and give feedback.)
2. Touch the next word. ✓
- Fix it up to say (pause) **fits.** What word? (Signal.) *Fits.*
- Fix it up.
  (Observe students and give feedback.)
3. Touch the next word. ✓
- Fix it up to say (pause) **hand.** What word? (Signal.) *Hand.*
- Fix it up.
  (Observe students and give feedback.)
4. (Repeat step 3 for **trot, sick, when.**)

EXERCISE 9
STORY READING

Task A

1. Everybody, touch part 6. ✓
- You're going to read the sentences the fast way.
2. Touch under first word. ✓
- What word? (Signal.) *That.*
3. Next word. ✓
- What word? (Signal.) *Clock.*
4. (Repeat step 3 for **is, running, fast.**)
5. (Repeat steps 2–4 until the students correctly identify all the words in the sentence.)
6. (Repeat steps 2–5 for each remaining sentence.)

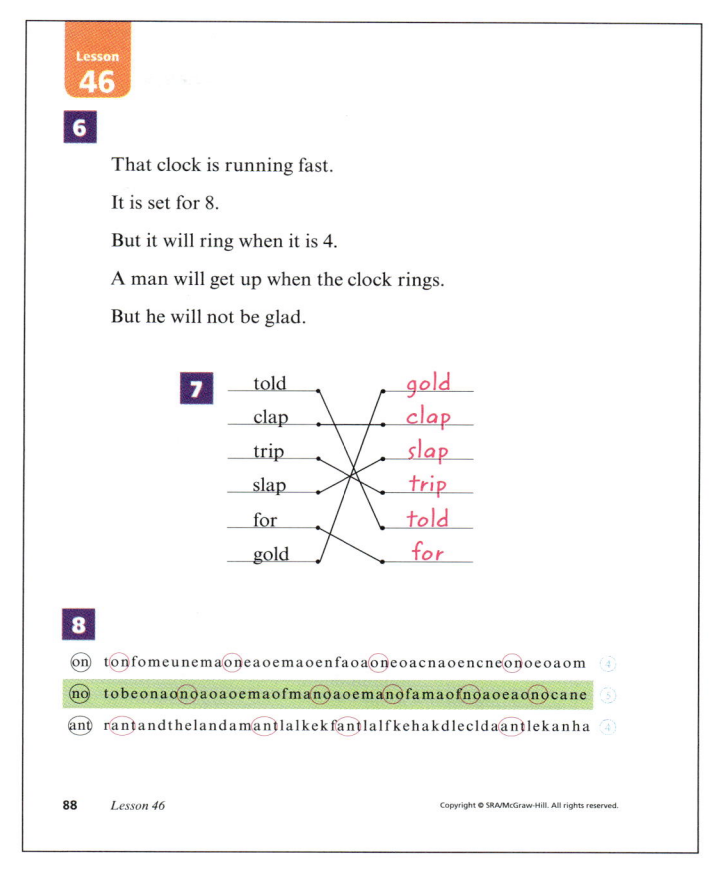

7. (If students miss more than four words, repeat the story reading from the beginning.)

Task B

1. Now I'll read the story and ask questions. Follow along.
2. **That clock is running fast.** (Call on a student.) **If a clock is running fast, what is it doing?** (Ideas: *Not keeping accurate time; showing a later time than the actual time.*)
3. **It is set for 8.** (Call on a student.) **If a clock is set for 8 in the morning, what will the clock do?** (Idea: *The alarm will go off at eight o'clock in the morning.*)
4. **But it will ring when it is 4.** (Call on a student.) **Why will it ring at 4 instead of at 8?** (Ideas: *The clock is running fast; it does not keep accurate time.*)
5. **A man will get up when the clock rings. But he will not be glad.** (Call on a student.) **How would you feel if your clock got you up at four in the morning?** (Ideas: *Mad; tired.*)

Lesson 46 107

Lesson 46

EXERCISE 10
MATCHING COMPLETION

1. Everybody, touch part 7. ✓
- Read the words the fast way.
2. Touch under the first word. ✓
- What word? (Signal.) *Told.*
3. Next word. ✓
- What word? (Signal.) *Clap.*
4. (Repeat step 3 for **trip, slap, for, gold.**)
5. Later, you're going to write the words in the second column.

EXERCISE 11
CIRCLE GAME

1. Everybody, touch part 8. ✓
2. What word will you circle in the first line? (Signal.) *On.*
3. What word will you circle in the second line? (Signal.) *No.*
4. What word will you circle in the third line? (Signal.) *Ant.*
5. Circle the words and finish the rest of your Workbook lesson.

EXERCISE 12
WORKBOOK CHECK

1. (Check each student's Workbook.)
2. (Award points for Workbook performance.)
3. (Record the student's total points in Box B.)

0–3 errors	8 points
4–5 errors	4 points
6 errors	2 points
7 or more errors	0 points

INDIVIDUAL READING CHECKOUTS

EXERCISE 13
NEW TIMED STORY-READING CHECKOUT

Note: For the timed checkouts, you will need a stopwatch.

- Study the story. Today you are going to be timed when you read the story.
- If you read the story with no more than 2 errors and read it in 45 seconds or less, you'll earn 6 points.
- If you make more than 2 errors, or if you take more than 45 seconds to read the story, you won't earn any points.
- If you don't earn points the first time you read the story, you can try again. If you succeed the second time you try, you'll earn 3 points.
- (Check the students individually.)
- (Record either 6, 3, or 0 points in Box C.)

Lesson point total

(Tell students to write the point total in the last box at the top of the Workbook page. Maximum = 20 points.)

Point Summary Chart

(Tell students to write this point total in the box for Lesson 46 in the Point Summary Chart.)

END OF LESSON 46

WORD-ATTACK SKILLS

EXERCISE 1
SOUND INTRODUCTION

1. (Point to **y:**) This letter usually makes the sound **yēēē**. What sound? (Touch.) *yēēē*.
2. (Point to **e:**) One sound you learned for this letter is the letter name. Everybody, what's that sound? (Touch.) *ēēē*. Yes, **ēēē**.
- What's the other sound? (Touch.) *ĕĕĕ*. Yes, **ĕĕĕ**.
3. (Point to **o:**) One sound you learned for this letter is the letter name. Everybody, what's that sound? (Touch.) *ōōō*. Yes, **ōōō**.
- What's the other sound? (Touch.) *ŏŏŏ*. Yes, **ŏŏŏ**.
4. Say each sound when I touch it.
5. (Point to **y:**) What sound? (Touch.) *yēēē*. Yes, **yēēē**.
6. (Repeat step 5 for **b, ol, p, d, or, x, ă, ĭ, er, h.**)

y   e   o
y   b   ol
p   d   or
x   a   i
er   h

Individual test
(Call on two or three students. Touch under each sound. Each student says all the sounds, including two sounds for **e** and two sounds for **o**.)

EXERCISE 2
PRONUNCIATIONS

Task A
1. Listen: **slack**. Say it. (Signal.) *Slack*.
2. Next word: **slick**. Say it. (Signal.) *Slick*.
3. (Repeat step 2 for **flack, track, trick, stack, smack**.)
4. (Repeat all the words until firm.)

Task B **Lick, luck, lock**
1. Listen: **lick, luck, lock**. Say those words. (Signal.) *Lick, luck, lock*. (Repeat until firm.)
2. One of those words has the middle sound **ŭŭŭ**. I'll say the words again: **lick, luck, lock**.
3. Which word has the middle sound **ŭŭŭ**? (Signal.) *Luck*. Yes, **luck**.
- Which word has the middle sound **ŏŏŏ**? (Signal.) *Lock*. Yes, **lock**.
- Which word has the middle sound **ĭĭĭ**? (Signal.) *Lick*. Yes, **lick**.
4. Listen: **lĭĭĭck**. What's the middle sound in the word **lick**? (Signal.) *ĭĭĭ*. Yes, **ĭĭĭ**.
- Listen: **lŭŭŭck**. What's the middle sound in the word **luck**? (Signal.) *ŭŭŭ*. Yes, **ŭŭŭ**.
- Listen: **lŏŏŏck**. What's the middle sound in the word **lock**? (Signal.) *ŏŏŏ*. Yes, **ŏŏŏ**.
5. (Repeat step 4 until firm.) Good job.

Task C **Must, mast, mist**
1. Listen: **must, mast, mist**. Say those words. (Signal.) *Must, mast, mist*. (Repeat until firm.)
2. One of those words has the middle sound **ăăă**. I'll say the words again: **must, mast, mist**.
3. Which word has the middle sound **ăăă**? (Signal.) *Mast*. Yes, **mast**.
- Which word has the middle sound **ĭĭĭ**? (Signal.) *Mist*. Yes, **mist**.
- Which word has the middle sound **ŭŭŭ**? (Signal.) *Must*. Yes, **must**.

Lesson 47

Lesson 47

4. Listen: **mŭŭŭst.** What's the middle sound in the word **must?** (Signal.) *ŭŭŭ.* Yes, *ŭŭŭ.*
- Listen: **măăăst.** What's the middle sound in the word **mast?** (Signal.) *ăăă.* Yes, *ăăă.*
- Listen: **mĭĭĭst.** What's the middle sound in the word **mist?** (Signal.) *ĭĭĭ.* Yes, *ĭĭĭ.*
5. (Repeat step 4 until firm.) Good job.

EXERCISE 3
NEW IRREGULAR WORDS

1. (Touch the ball of the arrow for **was:**) Sound out this word. Get ready. (Touch under **w, a, s:**) *wwwăăăsss.* (Repeat until the students say the sounds without pausing.)
2. That's how we sound out the word. But here's how we say the word: **wuz.** It's a funny word. How do we say the word? (Signal.) *Wuz.*
3. Sound it out. Get ready. (Touch under **w, a, s:**) *wwwăăăsss.* (Repeat until firm.)
4. Everybody, say the word. (Signal.) *Wuz.* Yes, **wuz.** Remember that word.

was

EXERCISE 4
WORD READING THE FAST WAY

1. You're going to read these words the fast way.
2. (For each word: Touch the ball of the arrow. Pause.) What word? (Slash right.)

> **To correct:**
> a. (Say the correct word.)
> b. What word? (Slash right.)
>   Yes, ____. Remember that word.
> c. (Return to the first word in each list and present the words in order.)

3. (Repeat each list until firm.)

yes

deep

yell

but

tub

crack

creek

bust

dust

pond

Lesson 47

4. (For each word: Touch the ball of the arrow. Pause.) **What word?** (Slash right.)
5. (Repeat each list until firm.)

rags

rugs

pop

stop

swimming

happy

silly

sold

better

pens

cut

slip

sleep

swim

or

fork

pets

greets

sending

Lesson 47 111

Lesson 47

WORKBOOK EXERCISES

Note: Pass out the Workbooks. Direct the students to open to Lesson 47.

(Award 6 points if the group worked well during the word attack. Remind the students of the points they can earn in their Workbook.)

EXERCISE 5
SOUND DICTATION

1. I'll say the sounds. You write the letters in part 1 in your Workbook.
2. First sound. (Pause.) **ŭŭŭ.** What sound? (Signal.) *ŭŭŭ.*
 - Write it in the first blank.
 (Observe students and give feedback.)
3. Next sound. (Pause.) **nnn.** What sound? (Signal.) *nnn.*
 - Write it.
 (Observe students and give feedback.)
4. (Repeat step 3 for **ththth, b, p, ēēē, ōōō, ĭĭĭ, g, shshsh, d, ēēē.**)
5. (Repeat sounds students had trouble with.)

EXERCISE 6
SPELLING FROM DICTATION

1. Touch part 2. ✓
 - You're going to write words that I dictate.
2. First word: **had.** What word? (Signal.) *Had.*
 - Listen again: **h . . . ăăă . . . d.** Write it in the first blank.
 (Observe students and give feedback.)
3. Next word: **this.** What word? (Signal.) *This.*
 - Listen again: **ththth . . . ĭĭĭ . . . sss.** Write it in the next blank.
 (Observe students and give feedback.)
4. (Repeat step 3 for **sit, red, sheet, seems.**)

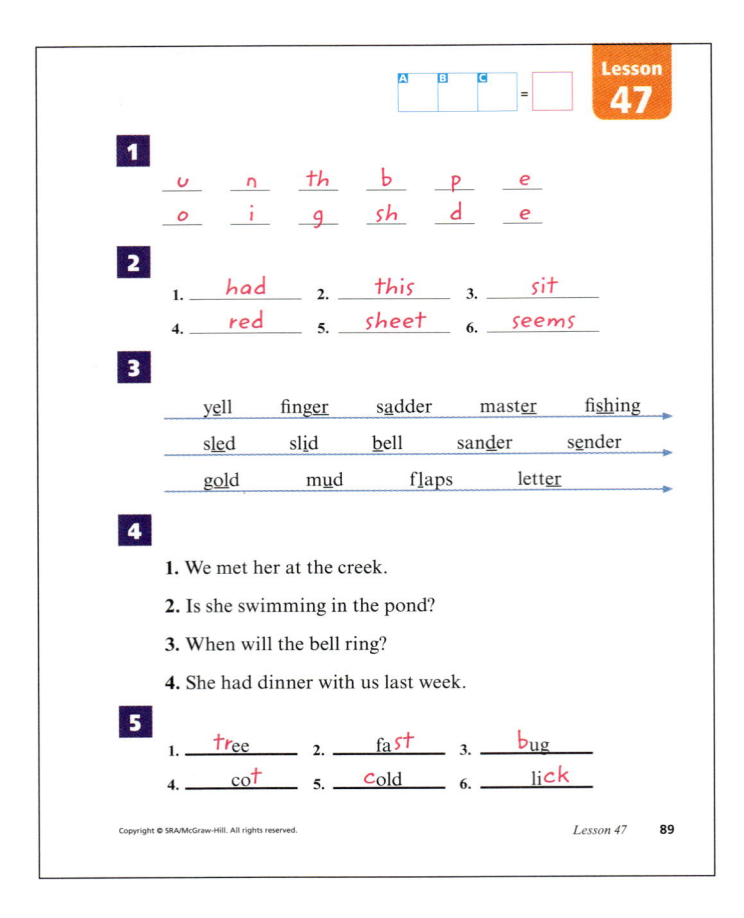

1
u n th b p e
o i g sh d e

2
1. had 2. this 3. sit
4. red 5. sheet 6. seems

3
y<u>e</u>ll   fi<u>n</u>ger   sa<u>dd</u>er   ma<u>s</u>ter   fi<u>sh</u>ing
s<u>l</u>ed   s<u>l</u>id   <u>b</u>ell   <u>s</u>ander   <u>s</u>ender
<u>g</u>old   m<u>u</u>d   f<u>l</u>aps   <u>l</u>etter

4
1. We met her at the creek.
2. Is she swimming in the pond?
3. When will the bell ring?
4. She had dinner with us last week.

5
1. tree 2. fast 3. bug
4. cot 5. cold 6. lick

EXERCISE 7
WORD READING: Workbook

1. Touch the first word in part 3. ✓
2. Look at the underlined sound in the first word. (Pause.) What sound? (Signal.) *ĕĕĕ.*
 - (Pause.) What word? (Signal.) *Yell.*
3. Next word. (Pause.) What sound? (Signal.) *er.*
 - (Pause.) What word? (Signal.) *Finger.*
4. (Repeat step 3 for remaining words.)

EXERCISE 8
SENTENCE READING

1. Everybody, touch part 4. ✓
2. Touch under the first word in sentence 1. ✓
- What word? (Signal.) *We.*
3. Next word. ✓
- What word? (Signal.) *Met.*
4. (Repeat step 3 for **her, at, the, creek.**)
5. (Repeat steps 2–4 until the students can correctly identify all the words in the sentence in order.)
6. (Repeat steps 2–5 for each remaining sentence:
- **2. Is she swimming in the pond?**
- **3. When will the bell ring?**
- **4. She had dinner with us last week.**)

> **Individual test**
> (Give each student a chance to read one of the sentences.)

EXERCISE 9
WORD COMPLETION

1. Touch the first word in part 5. ✓
- What sound? (Signal.) *ēēē.* Yes, **ēēē.**
- Fix it up to say (pause) **tree.** What word? (Signal.) *Tree.*
- Fix it up.
  (Observe students and give feedback.)
2. Touch the next word. ✓
- Fix it up to say (pause) **fast.** What word? (Signal.) *Fast.*
- Fix it up.
  (Observe students and give feedback.)
3. (Repeat step 2 for **bug, cot, cold, lick.**)

EXERCISE 10
STORY READING

Task A

1. Everybody, touch part 6. ✓
- You're going to read the sentences the fast way.
2. Touch under the first word. ✓
- What word? (Signal.) *We.*
3. Next word. ✓
- What word? (Signal.) *Will.*
4. (Repeat step 3 for **go, fishing.**)
5. (Repeat steps 2–4 until the students correctly identify all the words in the sentence.
6. (Repeat steps 2–5 for each remaining sentence:
- **A big fish is in the creek.**
- **If we get that fish, we will pop it in a pan.**
- **Then we will have a big fish for dinner.**)
7. (If students miss more than four words, repeat the story reading from the beginning.)

Task B

1. Now I'll read the story and ask questions. Follow along.
2. **We will go fishing. A big fish is in the creek.** (Call on a student.) What is a creek? (Idea: *A small stream.*)
3. **If we get that fish, we will pop it in a pan.** (Call on a student.) Why would you pop a fish in a pan? (Idea: *To cook it.*)
4. **Then we will have a big fish for dinner.** Does that sound like a good dinner? (Call on individual students to respond.)

EXERCISE 11
NEW MATCHING COMPLETION

1. Everybody, touch part 7. ✓
- This is a new type of matching exercise.
2. Touch the top word in the first column. ✓
- What word? (Signal.) *Ham.*
3. Touch the only part in the second column that can be fixed up to say **hăăămmm.** ✓
4. Draw a line from the word **ham** to the correct line in the second column. ✓
5. Now fix up the part in the second column so it says **hăăămmm.** ✓

Lesson 47

Lesson 47

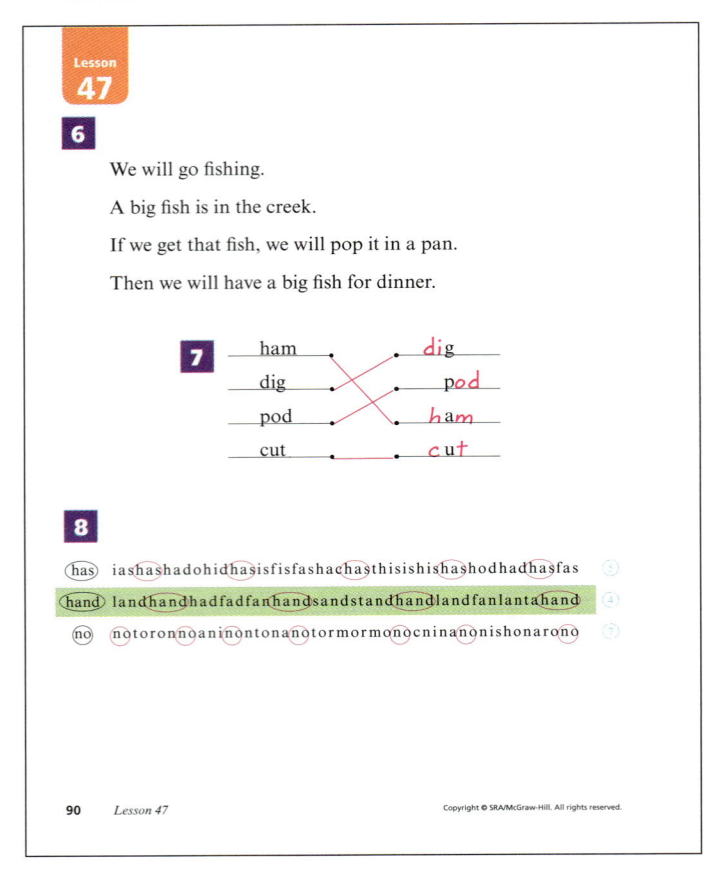

(Workbook page 90)

6
We will go fishing.
A big fish is in the creek.
If we get that fish, we will pop it in a pan.
Then we will have a big fish for dinner.

7
ham — di**g**
dig — p**od**
pod — **h**am
cut — c**u**t

8
(has) iashashadohidhasisfisfashachasthisishishashodhadhasfas
(hand) landhandhadfadfanhandsandstandhandlandfanlantahand
(no) notoronnoaninontonanotormormonocninanonishonarono

---

6. Touch the next word in the first column. ✓
• What word? (Signal.) *Dig.*
7. Touch the only part in the second column that can be fixed up to say **dīīg.** ✓
8. Draw a line from the word **dig** to the correct line in the second column. ✓
9. Now fix up the part in the second column so it says **dīīg.** ✓
10. Do the rest of the matching words. Remember, draw a line. Then complete the part in the second column.

EXERCISE 12
CIRCLE GAME

1. Everybody, touch part 8. ✓
2. What word will you circle in the first line? (Signal.) *Has.*
3. What word will you circle in the second line? (Signal.) *Hand.*
4. What word will you circle in the third line? (Signal.) *No.*
5. Circle the words and finish the rest of your Workbook lesson.

EXERCISE 13
WORKBOOK CHECK

1. (Check each student's Workbook.)
2. (Award points for Workbook performance.)
3. (Record the student's total points in Box B.)

0–3 errors	8 points
4–5 errors	4 points
6 errors	2 points
7 or more errors	0 points

INDIVIDUAL READING CHECKOUTS

EXERCISE 14
TIMED STORY-READING CHECKOUT

Note: For the timed checkouts, you will need a stopwatch.

• Study the story. If you read the story with no more than 2 errors and read it in 45 seconds or less, you'll earn 6 points.
• If you make more than 2 errors, or if you take more than 45 seconds to read the story, you won't earn any points.
• If you don't earn points the first time you read the story, you can try again. If you succeed the second time you try, you'll earn 3 points.
• (Check the students individually.)
• (Record either 6, 3, or 0 points in Box C.)

Lesson point total
(Tell students to write the point total in the last box at the top of the Workbook page. Maximum = 20 points.)

Point Summary Chart
(Tell students to write this point total in the box for Lesson 47 in the Point Summary Chart.)

END OF LESSON 47

Lesson 48

WORD-ATTACK SKILLS

EXERCISE 1
SOUND IDENTIFICATION

1. Say each sound when I touch it.
2. (Point to **w:**) What sound? (Touch.) *www.* Yes, **www.**
3. (Point to **wh:**) What sound? (Touch.) *www.* Yes, **www.**
4. (Repeat step 3 for **x, h, ŭ, sh, th, y, er, b, d.**)

w   wh   x
h   u   sh
th   y   er
b   d

Individual test
(Call on two or three students. Touch under each sound. Each student says all the sounds.)

EXERCISE 2
PRONUNCIATIONS

Task A Begs, bags, bugs

1. Listen: **begs, bags, bugs.** Say those words. (Signal.) *Begs, bags, bugs.* (Repeat until firm.)
2. One of those words has the middle sound **ăăă.** I'll say the words again: **begs, bags, bugs.**
3. Which word has the middle sound **ăăă?** (Signal.) *Bags.* Yes, **bags.**
- Which word has the middle sound **ŭŭŭ?** (Signal.) *Bugs.* Yes, **bugs.**
- Which word has the middle sound **ĕĕĕ?** (Signal.) *Begs.* Yes, **begs.**
4. Listen: **bĕĕĕgs.** What's the middle sound in the word **begs?** (Signal.) *ĕĕĕ.* Yes, **ĕĕĕ.**
- Listen: **băăăgs.** What's the middle sound in the word **bags?** (Signal.) *ăăă.* Yes, **ăăă.**
- Listen: **bŭŭŭgs.** What's the middle sound in the word **bugs?** (Signal.) *ŭŭŭ.* Yes, **ŭŭŭ.**
5. (Repeat step 4 until firm.) Good job.

Task B Slap, sleep, slip

1. Listen: **slap, sleep, slip.** Say those words. (Signal.) *Slap, sleep, slip.* (Repeat until firm.)
2. One of those words has the middle sound **ĭĭĭ.** I'll say the words again: **slap, sleep, slip.**
3. Which word has the middle sound **ĭĭĭ?** (Signal.) *Slip.* Yes, **slip.**
- Which word has the middle sound **ēēē?** (Signal.) *Sleep.* Yes, **sleep.**
- Which word has the middle sound **ăăă?** (Signal.) *Slap.* Yes, **slap.**
4. Listen: **slăăăp.** What's the middle sound in the word **slap?** (Signal.) *ăăă.* Yes, **ăăă.**
- Listen: **slēēēp.** What's the middle sound in the word **sleep?** (Signal.) *ēēē.* Yes, **ēēē.**
- Listen: **slĭĭĭp.** What's the middle sound in the word **slip?** (Signal.) *ĭĭĭ.* Yes, **ĭĭĭ.**
5. (Repeat step 4 until firm.) Good job.

Lesson 48

Lesson 48

EXERCISE 3
IRREGULAR WORDS

Task A Was

1. (Touch the ball of the arrow for **was:**) Sound out this word. Get ready. (Touch under **w, a, s:**) *wwwăăăsss.* (Repeat until the students say the sounds without pausing.)
2. That's how we sound out the word. But how do we say the word? (Signal.) *Wuz.*
3. Sound it out. Get ready. (Touch under **w, a, s:**) *wwwăăăsss.* (Repeat until firm.)
4. Everybody, say the word. (Signal.) *Wuz.* Yes, **wuz.** Remember that word.

was ⟶

Task B To

1. (Touch the ball of the arrow for **to:**) Sound out this word. Get ready. (Touch under **t, o:**) *tŏŏŏ.* (Repeat until the students say the sounds without pausing.)
2. That's how we sound out the word. But here's how we say the word: **too.** It's a funny word. How do we say the word? (Signal.) *Too.*
3. Sound it out. Get ready. (Touch under **t, o:**) *tŏŏŏ.* (Repeat until firm.)
4. Everybody, say the word. (Signal.) *Too.* Yes, **too.** Remember that word.

to ⟶

EXERCISE 4
WORD READING THE FAST WAY

1. You're going to read these words the fast way.
2. (For each word: Touch the ball of the arrow. Pause.) What word? (Slash right.)

To correct:
a. (Say the correct word.)
b. What word? (Slash right.) Yes, ____. Remember that word.
c. (Return to the first word and present the words in order.)

3. (Repeat the column until firm.)

still ⟶

mix ⟶

six ⟶

fix ⟶

fox ⟶

winning ⟶

but ⟶

happy ⟶

Lesson 48

4. (For each word: Touch the ball of the arrow. Pause.) **What word?** (Slash right.)
5. (Repeat each list until firm.)

wishing
flag
fits
wig
yell
bell
truck
dinner
short
born

dig
lack
slack
well
shed
down

pop
fist
test
bet
running

Lesson 48 117

Lesson 48

WORKBOOK EXERCISES

> **Note:** Pass out the Workbooks. Direct the students to open to Lesson 48.

(Award 6 points if the group worked well during the word attack. Remind the students of the points they can earn in their Workbook.)

EXERCISE 5
SOUND DICTATION

1. I'll say the sounds. You write the letters in part 1 in your Workbook.
2. First sound. (Pause.) **ĕĕĕ.** What sound? (Signal.) *ĕĕĕ.*
- Write it in the first blank.
   (Observe students and give feedback.)
3. Next sound. (Pause.) **b.** What sound? (Signal.) *b.*
- Write it.
   (Observe students and give feedback.)
4. (Repeat step 3 for **p, d, t, ĭĭĭ, shshsh, kss [x], h, sss, lll, ŭŭŭ.**)
5. (Repeat sounds students had trouble with.)

EXERCISE 6
SPELLING FROM DICTATION

1. Touch part 2. ✓
- You're going to write words that I dictate.
2. First word: **when.** What word? (Signal.) *When.*
- Listen again: **www . . . ĕĕĕ . . . nnn.** Write it in the first blank.
   (Observe students and give feedback.)
3. Next word: **than.** What word? (Signal.) *Than.*
- Listen again: **thththth . . . ăăă . . . nnn.** Write it in the next blank.
   (Observe students and give feedback.)
4. (Repeat step 3 for **got, red, cats, hit, seed, shop.**)

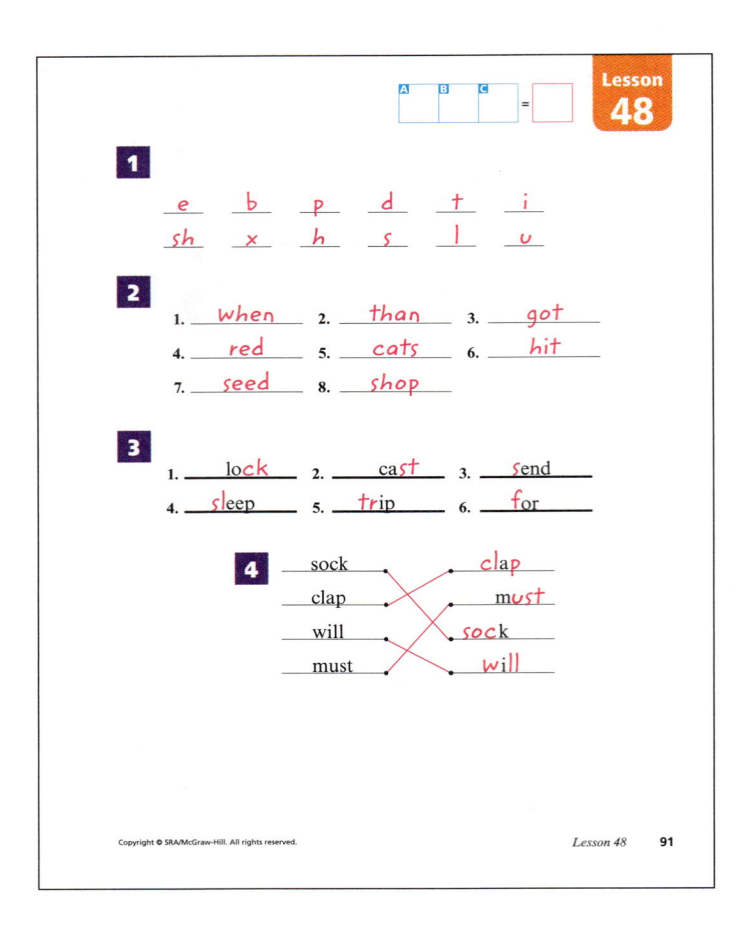

EXERCISE 7
WORD COMPLETION

1. Touch the first word in part 3. ✓
- Fix it up to say (pause) **lock.** What word? (Signal.) *Lock.*
- Fix it up.
   (Observe students and give feedback.)
2. Touch the next word. ✓
- What word? (Signal.) *ca.* Yes, **ca.**
- Fix it up to say (pause) **cast.** What word? (Signal.) *Cast.*
- Fix it up.
   (Observe students and give feedback.)
3. (Repeat step 2 for **end [send], eep [sleep], ip [trip], or [for].**)

118   Lesson 48

EXERCISE 8
MATCHING COMPLETION

1. Everybody, touch part 4. ✓
2. Touch the top word in the first column. ✓
   - What word? (Signal.) *Sock.*
3. Touch the only part in the second column that can be fixed up to say **sssŏŏŏck**. ✓
4. Draw a line from the word **sock** to the correct line in the second column. ✓
5. Now fix up the part in the second column so it says **sssŏŏŏck**. ✓
6. Touch the next word in the first column. ✓
   - What word? (Signal.) *Clap.*
7. Touch the only part in the second column that can be fixed up to say **clllăăăp**. ✓
8. Draw a line from the word **clap** to the correct line in the second column. ✓
9. Now fix up the part in the second column so it says **clllăăăp**. ✓
10. Do the rest of the matching words. Remember, draw a line. Then complete the part in the second column.

EXERCISE 9
NEW SENTENCE READING

1. Everybody, touch part 5. ✓
2. I'm going to read all the words in sentence 1 the fast way. I'll clap and read a word each time I clap. Here I go. (Clap for each word. Pause about 2 seconds between claps as you read:)
   The . . . black . . . colt . . . will . . . trot . . . on . . . the . . . track.
3. Your turn to read sentence 1 the fast way. Read a word each time I clap.
4. Touch under the first word. ✓
   - Get ready. (Clap for each word. Pause about 2 seconds between claps.) *The . . . black . . . colt . . . will . . . trot . . . on . . . the . . . track.*
5. (Repeat step 4 until the students correctly identify all the words in the sentence in order.)

Lesson 48

5
1. The black colt will trot on the track.
2. Her hat fits, but her wig is big.
3. The class will end with a test.
4. The bell will ring for dinner.
5. The flag is old and torn.
6. The fox is running up the steep hill.
7. Send him six green sheets.

6

She will lend us a big tent.
We will go on a trip.
We will swim in the pond.
Then we will set up the tent on a hill.

---

6. Touch under the first word of sentence 2. ✓
   - Get ready. (Clap for each word. Pause about 2 seconds between claps.) *Her . . . hat . . . fits, . . . but . . . her . . . wig . . . is . . . big.*
7. (Repeat step 6 until the students read the sentence without a mistake.)
8. (Repeat steps 6 and 7 for each remaining sentence.)

Individual test
(Give each student a chance to read one of the sentences. Praise students who read accurately without long pauses.)

Lesson 48

EXERCISE 10
NEW STORY READING

Task A

1. Everybody, touch part 6. ✓
2. You're going to read the sentences in this story the fast way. I'll clap for each word.
3. Touch under the first word. ✓
- Get ready. (Clap for each word. Pause about 2 seconds between claps.) *She . . . will . . . lend . . . us . . . a . . . big . . . tent.*
4. (Repeat step 3 until the students correctly identify all the words in the sentence in order.)
5. Next sentence. (Students touch under the first word of the next sentence.)
6. Get ready. (Clap for each word. Pause about 2 seconds between claps.) *We . . . will . . . go . . . on . . . a . . . trip.*
7. (Repeat step 6 until students correctly identify all the words in the sentence in order.)
8. (Repeat steps 5–7 for each remaining sentence:
- **We will swim in the pond.**
- **Then we will set up the tent on a hill.**)
9. (If the students miss more than four words, repeat the story reading from the beginning.)

Task B

1. Now I'll read the story and ask questions. Follow along.
2. **She will lend us a big tent.** (Call on a student.) What do you do when you lend somebody something? (Idea: *Let them borrow it for a while.*)
3. **We will go on a trip. We will swim in the pond. Then we will set up the tent on a hill.** (Call on a student.) Name all the things they will do. (Idea: *Go on a trip, swim in a pond, and set up the tent on a hill.*)
- Does that sound like fun? (Call on a student to respond.)

EXERCISE 11
WORKBOOK CHECK

1. (Check each student's Workbook.)
2. (Award points for Workbook performance.)
3. (Record the student's total points in Box B.)

0–3 errors	8 points
4–5 errors	4 points
6 errors	2 points
7 or more errors	0 points

INDIVIDUAL READING CHECKOUTS

EXERCISE 12
TIMED STORY-READING CHECKOUT

Note: For the timed checkouts, you will need a stopwatch.

- Study the story. If you read the story with no more than 2 errors and read it in 45 seconds or less, you'll earn 6 points.
- If you make more than 2 errors, or if you take more than 45 seconds to read the story, you won't earn any points.
- If you don't earn points the first time you read the story, you can try again. If you succeed the second time you try, you'll earn 3 points.
- (Check the students individually.)
- (Record either 6, 3, or 0 points in Box C.)

Lesson point total

(Tell students to write the point total in the last box at the top of the Workbook page. Maximum = 20 points.)

Point Summary Chart

(Tell students to write this point total in the box for Lesson 48 in the Point Summary Chart.)

END OF LESSON 48

Lesson 49

WORD-ATTACK SKILLS

EXERCISE 1
SOUND IDENTIFICATION

1. (Point to **e:**) One sound you learned for this letter is the letter name. Everybody, what's that sound? (Touch.) ēēē. Yes, ēēē.
- What's the other sound? (Touch.) ĕĕĕ. Yes, ĕĕĕ.
2. Say each sound when I touch it.
3. (Point to **y:**) What sound? (Touch.) yēēē. Yes, yēēē.
4. (Repeat step 3 for **b, ŭ, th, or, ol, d.**)

e y
b u
th or
ol d

Individual test
(Call on two or three students. Touch under each sound. Each student says all the sounds, including two sounds for **e.**)

EXERCISE 2
PRONUNCIATIONS

Task A Slim, slam

1. Listen: **slim** (pause) **slam.** Say those words. (Signal.) *Slim, slam.* (Repeat until firm.)
2. One of those words has the middle sound ăăă. I'll say the words again: **slim** (pause) **slam.**
3. Which word has the middle sound ăăă? (Signal.) *Slam.* Yes, **slam.**
- Which word has the middle sound ĭĭĭ? (Signal.) *Slim.* Yes, **slim.**
4. Listen: **slĭĭĭm.** What's the middle sound in the word **slim?** (Signal.) ĭĭĭ. Yes, ĭĭĭ.
- Listen: **slăăăm.** What's the middle sound in the word **slam?** (Signal.) ăăă. Yes, ăăă.
5. (Repeat step 4 until firm.)

Task B Truck, track, trick

1. Listen: **truck, track, trick.** Say those words. (Signal.) *Truck, track, trick.* (Repeat until firm.)
2. One of those words has the middle sound ĭĭĭ. I'll say the words again: **truck, track, trick.**
3. Which word has the middle sound ĭĭĭ? (Signal.) *Trick.* Yes, **trick.**
- Which word has the middle sound ăăă? (Signal.) *Track.* Yes, **track.**
- Which word has the middle sound ŭŭŭ? (Signal.) *Truck.* Yes, **truck.**
4. Listen: **trŭŭŭck.** What's the middle sound in the word **truck?** (Signal.) ŭŭŭ. Yes, ŭŭŭ.
- Listen: **trĭĭĭck.** What's the middle sound in the word **trick?** (Signal.) ĭĭĭ. Yes, ĭĭĭ.
- Listen: **trăăăck.** What's the middle sound in the word **track?** (Signal.) ăăă. Yes, ăăă.
5. (Repeat step 4 until firm.) Good job.

Lesson 49

EXERCISE 3
IRREGULAR WORDS

Task A Was

1. (Touch the ball of the arrow for **was:**) Sound out this word. Get ready. (Touch under **w, a, s:**) *wwwăăăsss*. (Repeat until the students say the sounds without pausing.)
2. That's how we sound out the word. But how do we say the word? (Signal.) *Wuz.*
3. Sound it out. Get ready. (Touch under **w, a, s:**) *wwwăăăsss*. (Repeat until firm.)
4. Everybody, say the word. (Signal.) *Wuz.* Yes, **wuz**. Remember that word.

was

Task B To

1. (Touch the ball of the arrow for **to:**) Sound out this word. Get ready. (Touch under **t, o:**) *tŏŏŏ*. (Repeat until the students say the sounds without pausing.)
2. That's how we sound out the word. But how do we say the word? (Signal.) *Too.*
3. Sound it out. Get ready. (Touch under **t, o:**) *tŏŏŏ*. (Repeat until firm.)
4. Everybody, say the word. (Signal.) *Too.* Yes, **too**. Remember that word.

to

EXERCISE 4
WORD READING THE FAST WAY

1. You're going to read these words the fast way.
2. (For each word: Touch the ball of the arrow. Pause.) What word? (Slash right.)
3. (Repeat each list until firm.)

pit

bit

bits

rub

cold

creek

fun

funny

big

gift

122   Lesson 49

Lesson 49

4. (For each word: Touch the ball of the arrow. Pause.) What word? (Slash right.)
5. (Repeat each list until firm.)

swim

dust

swimming

greeting

sent

rush

brush

fork

dig

short

better

bust

grip

drip

letter

last

lasting

bed

six

Lesson 49

WORKBOOK EXERCISES

Note: Pass out the Workbooks. Direct the students to open to Lesson 49.

(Award 6 points if the group worked well during the word attack. Remind the students of the points they can earn in their Workbook.)

EXERCISE 5
SOUND DICTATION

1. I'll say the sounds. You write the letters in part 1 in your Workbook.
2. First sound. (Pause.) ăăă. What sound? (Signal.) ăăă.
   - Write it in the first blank.
   (Observe students and give feedback.)
3. Next sound. (Pause.) ŏŏŏ. What sound? (Signal.) ŏŏŏ.
   - Write it.
   (Observe students and give feedback.)
4. (Repeat step 3 for ĕĕĕ, ĭĭĭ, ŭŭŭ, shshsh, rrr, b, d, p, nnn, mmm.)
5. (Repeat sounds students had trouble with.)

EXERCISE 6
SPELLING FROM DICTATION

1. Touch part 2. ✓
   - You're going to write words that I dictate.
2. First word: **or**. What word? (Signal.) *Or.*
   - Listen again: ōōō . . . rrr. Write it in the first blank.
   (Observe students and give feedback.)
3. Next word: **for**. What word? (Signal.) *For.*
   - Listen again: fff . . . ōōō . . . rrr. Write it in the next blank.
   (Observe students and give feedback.)
4. (Repeat step 3 for **than, send, rub, bud, bed, tent.**)

EXERCISE 7
WORD COMPLETION

1. Touch the first word in part 3. ✓
   - Fix it up to say (pause) **send**. What word? (Signal.) *Send.*
   - Fix it up.
   (Observe students and give feedback.)

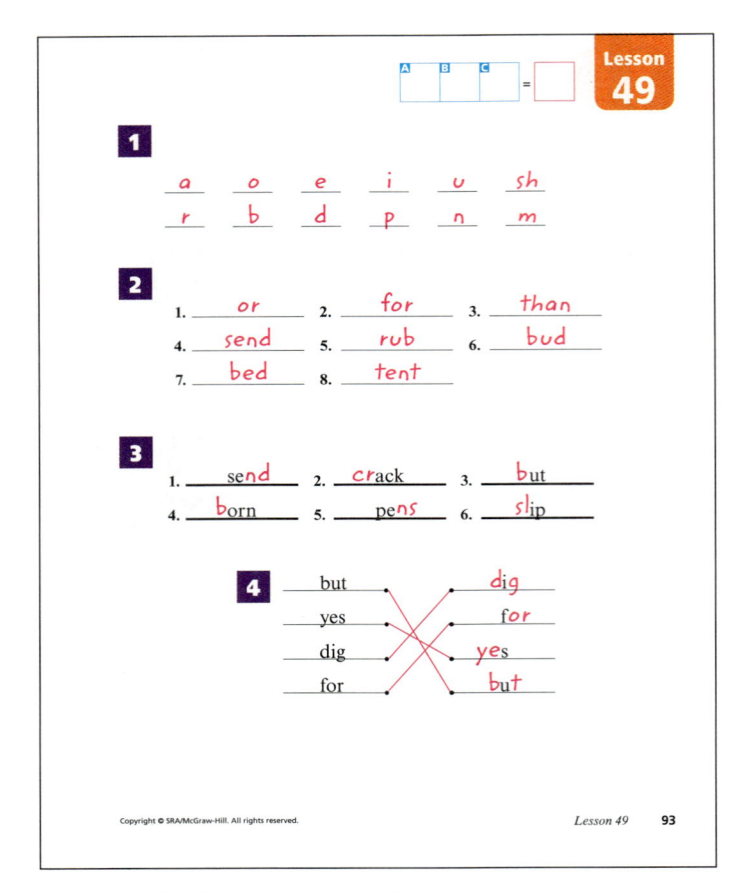

2. Touch the next word. ✓
   - What word? (Signal.) *ack.* Yes, **ack**.
   - Fix it up to say (pause) **crack**. What word? (Signal.) *Crack.*
   - Fix it up.
   (Observe students and give feedback.)
3. (Repeat step 2 for **ut [but], orn [born], pe [pens], ip [slip]**.)

EXERCISE 8
NEW MATCHING COMPLETION

1. Everybody, touch part 4. ✓
2. Touch the top word in the first column. ✓
   - What word? (Signal.) *But.*
3. Touch the only part in the second column that can be fixed up to say **bŭŭŭt**. ✓

124   Lesson 49

4. Draw a line from the word **but** to the correct line in the second column. ✓
5. Now fix up the line in the second column so it says **bŭŭŭt**. ✓
6. Do the rest of the matching words on your own.

EXERCISE 9
NEW SENTENCE READING

1. Everybody, touch sentence 1 in part 5. ✓
2. You're going to read the fast way. Read a word each time I clap.
3. First word. ✓
- Get ready. (Clap for each word. Pause about 2 seconds between claps.) *How . . . can . . . we . . . fix . . . the . . . truck?*
4. (Repeat step 3 until the students correctly identify all the words in the sentence in order.)
5. (Repeat steps 3 and 4 for each remaining sentence.)

> **Individual test**
> (Give each student a chance to read one of the sentences. Praise students who read accurately without long pauses.)

EXERCISE 10
NEW STORY READING

Task A

1. Everybody, touch part 6. ✓
- You're going to read this story.
2. First word. ✓
- Get ready. (Clap for each word. Pause about 2 seconds between claps.) *A . . . ram . . . was . . . sick.*
3. (Repeat step 2 until the students correctly identify all the words in the sentence in order.)
4. Next sentence. ✓
- Get ready. (Clap for each word:) *Six . . . sheep . . . sent . . . him . . . a . . . greeting.*
5. (Repeat step 4 until students correctly identify all the words in the sentence in order.)

6. (Repeat steps 4 and 5 for each remaining sentence.)
7. (If the students miss more than four words, repeat the story reading from the beginning.)

Lesson 49

5
1. How can we fix the truck?
2. Her cat is sleeping in her bed.
3. The swimming class went well.
4. See me sleep in the green grass.
5. Keep sending me happy letters.
6. Now I will cut down six trees.
7. When can we swim at the creek?
8. She left us and got on the bus.

6

A ram was sick.

Six sheep sent him a greeting.

The sheep sent him a big dinner and a gift.

Now he is happy, but he is still sick.

Task B

1. Now I'll read the story and ask questions. Follow along.
2. **A ram was sick. Six sheep sent him a greeting. The sheep sent him a big dinner and a gift.** The sheep sent him three things. (Call on a student.) **What were they?** (Idea: *A greeting, a big dinner, and a gift.*)
3. **Now he is happy, but he is still sick.** (Call on a student.) **Why is he happy?** (Idea: *His friends sent him things.*)

Lesson 49   125

Lesson 49

EXERCISE 11
WORKBOOK CHECK

1. (Check each student's Workbook.)
2. (Award points for Workbook performance.)
3. (Record the student's total points in Box B.)

0–3 errors	8 points
4–5 errors	4 points
6 errors	2 points
7 or more errors	0 points

INDIVIDUAL READING CHECKOUTS

EXERCISE 12
TIMED STORY-READING CHECKOUT

Note: For the timed checkouts, you will need a stopwatch.

- Study the story. If you read the story with no more than 2 errors and read it in 45 seconds or less, you'll earn 6 points.
- If you make more than 2 errors, or if you take more than 45 seconds to read the story, you won't earn any points.
- If you don't earn points the first time you read the story, you can try again. If you succeed the second time you try, you'll earn 3 points.
- (Check the students individually.)
- (Record either 6, 3, or 0 points in Box C.)

Lesson point total
(Tell students to write the point total in the last box at the top of the Workbook page. Maximum = 20 points.)

Point Summary Chart
(Tell students to write this point total in the box for Lesson 49 in the Point Summary Chart.)

END OF LESSON 49

WORD-ATTACK SKILLS

EXERCISE 1
SOUND IDENTIFICATION

1. (Point to **e:**) One sound you learned for this letter is the letter name. Everybody, what's that sound? (Touch.) *ēēē.* Yes, **ēēē.**
   - What's the other sound? (Touch.) *ĕĕĕ.* Yes, **ĕĕĕ.**
2. (Point to **o:**) One sound you learned for this letter is the letter name. Everybody, what's that sound? (Touch.) *ōōō.* Yes, **ōōō.**
   - What's the other sound? (Touch.) *ŏŏŏ.* Yes, **ŏŏŏ.**
3. Say each sound when I touch it.
4. (Point to **sh:**) What sound? (Touch.) *shshsh.* Yes, **shshsh.**
5. (Repeat step 4 for **ck, p, ŭ, ing, n, l, d, b, t, f.**)

e o sh
ck p
u ing
n l d
b t f

Individual test
(Call on two or three students. Touch under each sound. Each student says all the sounds, including two sounds for **e** and two sounds for **o.**)

EXERCISE 2
NEW PRONUNCIATIONS

Task A Trip, trick

1. Listen: **trip** (pause) **trick.** Say those words. (Signal.) *Trip, trick.* (Repeat until firm.)
2. Listen: **trip** (pause) **trick.** One of those words means **a journey or a voyage.** (Pause.) Which word? (Signal.) *Trip.* Yes, **trip.**

To correct:
   a. (Tell the students the word.)
   b. (Repeat step 2.)

3. One of those words means **something you do when you fool someone.** (Pause.) Which word? (Signal.) *Trick.* Yes, **trick.**
4. (Repeat steps 2 and 3 until firm.)

Task B Thorns, rusts

1. Listen: **thorns.** Say it. (Signal.) *Thorns.*
2. Next word: **rusts.** Say it. (Signal.) *Rusts.*
3. (Repeat the words until firm.)

Task C Creek, crack, crock

1. Listen: **creek, crack, crock.** Say those words. (Signal.) *Creek, crack, crock.* (Repeat until firm.)
2. One of those words has the middle sound **ŏŏŏ.** I'll say the words again: **creek, crack, crock.**
3. Which word has the middle sound **ŏŏŏ?** (Signal.) *Crock.* Yes, **crock.**
   - Which word has the middle sound **ăăă?** (Signal.) *Crack.* Yes, **crack.**
   - Which word has the middle sound **ēēē?** (Signal.) *Creek.* Yes, **creek.**
4. Listen: **crēēēk.** What's the middle sound in the word **creek?** (Signal.) *ēēē.* Yes, **ēēē.**
   - Listen: **crăăăck.** What's the middle sound in the word **crack?** (Signal.) *ăăă.* Yes, **ăăă.**
   - Listen: **crŏŏŏck.** What's the middle sound in the word **crock?** (Signal.) *ŏŏŏ.* Yes, **ŏŏŏ.**
5. (Repeat step 4 until firm.) Good job.

Lesson 50

Lesson 50

EXERCISE 3
WORD READING THE FAST WAY

1. You're going to read these words the fast way.
2. (For each word: Touch the ball of the arrow. Pause.) What word? (Slash right.)
3. (Repeat each list until firm.)

was

to

or

short

tub

drip

best

fells

but

feels

WORKBOOK EXERCISES

Note: Pass out the Workbooks. Direct the students to open to Lesson 50.

(Award 6 points if the group worked well during the word attack. Remind the students of the points they can earn in their Workbook.)

EXERCISE 4
SOUND DICTATION

1. I'll say the sounds. You write the letters in part 1 in your Workbook.
2. First sound. (Pause.) **rrr.** What sound? (Signal.) *rrr.*
- Write it in the first blank.
  (Observe students and give feedback.)
3. Next sound. (Pause.) **mmm.** What sound? (Signal.) *mmm.*
- Write it.
  (Observe students and give feedback.)
4. (Repeat step 3 for **ĕĕĕ, kss [x], lll, ăăă, t, ēēē, ōōō, b, ĭĭĭ, d.**)
5. (Repeat sounds students had trouble with.)

EXERCISE 5
SPELLING FROM DICTATION

1. Touch part 2. ✓
- You're going to write words that I dictate.
2. First word: **then.** What word? (Signal.) *Then.*
- Listen again: **thththth . . . ĕĕĕ . . . nnn.** Write it in the first blank.
  (Observe students and give feedback.)
3. Next word: **when.** What word? (Signal.) *When.*
- Listen again: **www . . . ĕĕĕ . . . nnn.** Write it in the next blank.
  (Observe students and give feedback.)
4. (Repeat step 3 for **sheets, get, sits, rob.**)

EXERCISE 6
WORD READING: Workbook

1. Touch the first word in part 3. ✓
2. Look at the underlined sound in the first word. (Pause.) What sound? (Signal.) *t.*
- (Pause.) What word? (Signal.) *Pits.*
3. Next word. (Pause.) What sound? (Signal.) *er.*
- (Pause.) What word? (Signal.) *Under.*
4. (Repeat step 3 for remaining words.)

EXERCISE 7
SENTENCE READING

1. Everybody, touch sentence 1 in part 4. ✓
2. You're going to read the fast way.
3. First word. ✓
- Get ready. (Clap for each word. Pause about 2 seconds between claps.)
  How . . . can . . . he . . . sleep . . . when . . . we . . . sing?

Lesson 50

4. (Repeat step 3 until the students correctly identify all the words in the sentence in order.)
5. (Repeat steps 3 and 4 for each remaining sentence.)

> **Individual test**
> (Give each student a chance to read one of the sentences. Praise students who read accurately without long pauses.)

EXERCISE 8
WORD COMPLETION

1. Touch the first word in part 5. ✓
- Fix it up to say (pause) **bug.** What word? (Signal.) *Bug.*
- Fix it up.
  (Observe students and give feedback.)
2. Touch the next word. ✓
- Fix it up to say (pause) **must.** What word? (Signal.) *Must.*
- Fix it up.
  (Observe students and give feedback.)
3. (Repeat step 2 for **fold, trip, send, shag.**)

EXERCISE 9
STORY READING

Task A

1. Everybody, touch part 6. ✓
- You're going to read this story.
2. First word. ✓
- Get ready. (Clap for each word. Pause about 2 seconds between claps.) *An . . . ant . . . sat . . . in . . . wet . . . sand.*
3. (Repeat step 2 until the students correctly identify all the words in the sentence in order.)
4. Next sentence. ✓
- Get ready. (Clap for each word:) *A . . . man . . . dug . . . in . . . that . . . sand . . . for . . . clams.*
5. (Repeat step 4 until students correctly identify all the words in the sentence in order.)
6. (Repeat steps 4 and 5 for each remaining sentence.)

7. (If the students miss more than four words, repeat the story reading from the beginning.)

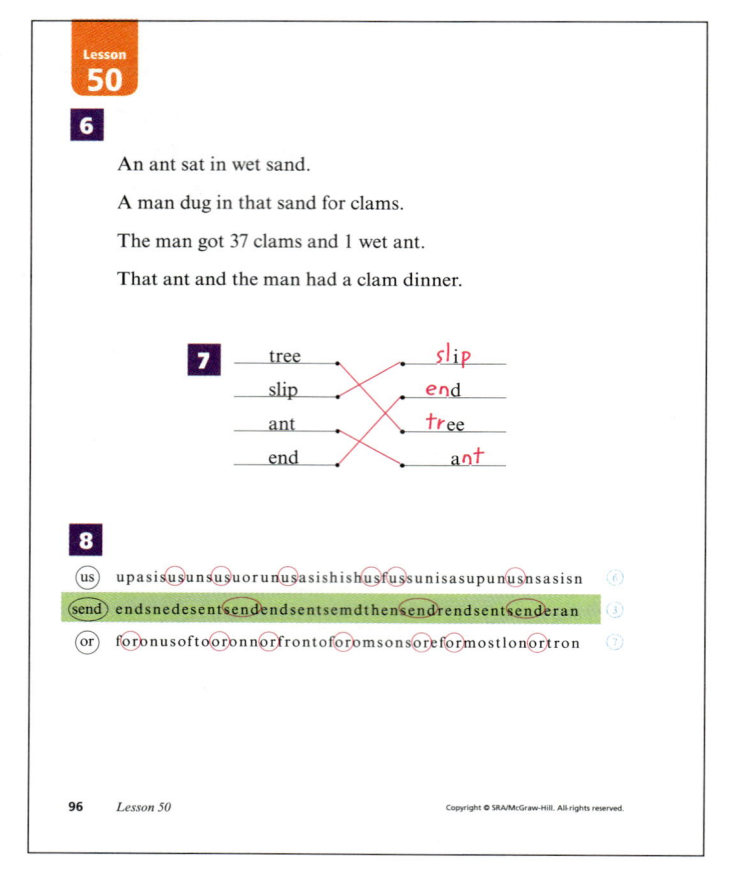

An ant sat in wet sand.
A man dug in that sand for clams.
The man got 37 clams and 1 wet ant.
That ant and the man had a clam dinner.

tree — slip
slip — end
ant — tree
end — ant

Task B

1. Now I'll read the story and ask questions. Follow along.
2. **An ant sat in wet sand. A man dug in that sand for clams.** (Call on a student.) What is a clam? (Idea: *A small animal that lives in the sea and has a shell.*)
3. **The man got 37 clams and 1 wet ant. That ant and the man had a clam dinner.** (Call on a student.) How did the ant get in the clams? (Idea: *The ant was in the wet sand.*)
4. Everybody, did the ant get cooked with the clams? (Signal.) *No.*
- (Call on a student.) Who ate a clam dinner? (Idea: *The ant and the man.*)

Lesson 50

EXERCISE 10
MATCHING COMPLETION

1. Everybody, touch part 7. ✓
2. Touch the top word in the first column. ✓
- What word? (Signal.) *Tree.*
3. Touch the only part in the second column that can be fixed up to say **trrrēēē**. ✓
4. Draw a line from the word **tree** to the correct line in the second column. ✓
5. Now fix up the part in the second column so it says **trrrēēē**. ✓
6. Do the rest of the matching words on your own.

EXERCISE 11
CIRCLE GAME

1. Everybody, touch part 8. ✓
2. What word will you circle in the first line? (Signal.) *Us.*
3. What word will you circle in the second line? (Signal.) *Send.*
4. What word will you circle in the third line? (Signal.) *Or.*
5. Circle the words and finish the rest of your Workbook lesson.

EXERCISE 12
WORKBOOK CHECK

1. (Check each student's Workbook.)
2. (Award points for Workbook performance.)
3. (Record the student's total points in Box B.)

0–3 errors	8 points
4–5 errors	4 points
6 errors	2 points
7 or more errors	0 points

INDIVIDUAL READING CHECKOUTS

EXERCISE 13
TIMED STORY-READING CHECKOUT

Note: For the timed checkouts, you will need a stopwatch.

- Study the story. If you read the story with no more than 2 errors and read it in 45 seconds or less, you'll earn 6 points.
- If you make more than 2 errors, or if you take more than 45 seconds to read the story, you won't earn any points.
- If you don't earn points the first time you read the story, you can try again. If you succeed the second time you try, you'll earn 3 points.
- (Check the students individually.)
- (Record either 6, 3, or 0 points in Box C.)

Lesson point total
(Tell students to write the point total in the last box at the top of the Workbook page. Maximum = 20 points.)

Point Summary Chart
(Tell students to write this point total in the box for Lesson 50 in the Point Summary Chart.)

Five-lesson point summary
(Tell students to add the point totals for Lessons 46 through 50 in the Point Summary Chart and to write the total for Block 10. Maximum for Block 10 = 100 points.)

END OF LESSON 50

Mastery Test 11

MASTERY TEST 11
— AFTER LESSON 50, BEFORE LESSON 51 —

> **Note:** Use students' performance on the Lesson 50 Story reading checkout for Mastery Test 11.

Scoring the test

1. (Count each student's errors on the Story reading checkout. Write these numbers in the Test 11 boxes on the appropriate *Decoding A* Mastery Test Student Profile form. Circle **P** or **F**.)
2. (When all students have been tested, circle **P** or **F** for each student on the *Decoding A* Mastery Test Group Summary form. Determine if more than 25 percent of the students failed the Story reading checkout by dividing the number of students who failed by the total number of students in the group.)

Remedies

(If more than 25 percent of the students fail to earn 6 points for their Story reading checkout, [1] repeat the Story reading checkouts for Lessons 46 through 49, and [2] repeat all of Lesson 50. Permission is granted to reproduce the Workbook pages for Lesson 50 for classroom use.)

Lesson Objectives	LESSON 51 Exercise	LESSON 52 Exercise	LESSON 53 Exercise	LESSON 54 Exercise	LESSON 55 Exercise
Word Attack					
Phonemic Awareness					
Sound/Word Pronunciation	1–3	1, 3	1, 2	1–3	1, 2
Identify Sounds in Words	2, 3	2–4	2, 3	2, 3	2
Decoding and Word Analysis					
Letter Sounds: *ch, ō, ŏ, ē, ĕ, y, b, sh, wh, w, s, n, h, i, c*	1				
Letter Sounds: *ch, ō, ŏ, ē, ĕ, ch, sh, b, g, i, h, k, d, a, r, ing*		1			
Letter Sounds: *ē, ĕ, u, sh, or, ol, ch, y, b, i, d*			1		
Letter Sounds: *j, ē, ĕ, ō, ŏ, f, m, g, i, ing, x, b, p, u, ch*				1	
Letter Sounds: *j, ō, ŏ, ē, ĕ, f, ch, u, y, c, sh, er, l, g*					1
Sound Combination: *or*	3	4			
Word Recognition	3, 4	2, 4, 5	3, 4	3, 4	3
High-Frequency Words		2	3	3	
Assessment					
Ongoing: Individual Tests	1	1	1	1	1
Group Reading					
Decoding and Word Analysis					
Read Decodable Text	10	11	11	10	9
Comprehension					
Make Predictions		11			
Access Prior Knowledge	10	11	11		
Draw Inferences	10		11	10	9
Note Details		11	11	10	9
Assessment					
Ongoing: Comprehension Check	10	11	11	10	9
Ongoing: Decoding Accuracy	10	11	11	10	9
Formal: Mastery Test					MT 12
Workbook Exercises					
Decoding and Word Analysis					
Word Recognition	7	8		7	6
Sentence Reading	8	9	9, 10	8	7
Sound Combinations	7	8		7	6
Spelling: Sound/Letter Relationships	5, 9, 11	6, 10, 12	5, 7, 8	5, 9	4, 8, 10
Spelling: CVC, CVV, CCVC, CVCC	6			6	
Spelling: CVC, VCC, CCVC, CVCC, CCVCC		7			
Spelling: CVC, CVCC			6		
Spelling: CVC, VCC, CCVC, CCVCC					5
Visual Discrimination	11, 12	12, 13	8	11, 12	10, 11
Study Skills					
Punctuation			9	8	
Assessment					
Ongoing: Individual Tests	8	9	10	8	7
Ongoing: Teacher-Monitored Accuracy	14	15	13	14	13
Ongoing: Teacher-Monitored Fluency	14	15	13	14	13
Ongoing: Workcheck	13	14	12	13	12

Lesson 51

WORD-ATTACK SKILLS

EXERCISE 1
SOUND INTRODUCTION

1. (Point to **ch:**) These letters make the sound **ch.** What sound? (Touch.) *ch.*
2. (Point to **o:**) One sound you learned for this letter is the letter name. Everybody, what's that sound? (Touch.) *ōōō.* Yes, **ōōō.**
- What's the other sound? (Touch.) *ŏŏŏ.* Yes, **ŏŏŏ.**
3. (Point to **e:**) One sound you learned for this letter is the letter name. Everybody, what's that sound? (Touch.) *ēēē.* Yes, **ēēē.**
- What's the other sound? (Touch.) *ĕĕĕ.* Yes, **ĕĕĕ.**
4. (Point to **ch:**) What sound? (Touch.) *ch.* Yes, **ch.**
5. (Repeat step 4 for **y, b, sh, wh, w, s, n, h, ĭ, c.**)

```
ch    o    e
ch    y    b
sh    wh
w     s    n
h     i    c
```

Individual test
(Call on two or three students. Touch under each sound. Each student says all the sounds, including two sounds for **o** and two sounds for **e.**)

EXERCISE 2
PRONUNCIATIONS

Note: Do not write the words on the board. This is an oral exercise.

Task A Clot, clock

1. Listen: **clot** (pause) **clock.** Say those words. (Signal.) *Clot, clock.* (Repeat until firm.)
2. Listen: **clot** (pause) **clock.** One of those words means **something that shows time.**
- (Pause.) Which word? (Signal.) *Clock.* Yes, **clock.**

To correct:
a. (Tell the students the word.)
b. (Repeat step 2.)

3. One of those words means **a gummy mass.**
- (Pause.) Which word? (Signal.) *Clot.* Yes, **clot.**
4. (Repeat steps 2 and 3 until firm.)

Task B Rests, vests, splash

1. Say these words. Listen: **rests.** Say it. (Signal.) *Rests.*
2. Next word: **vests.** Say it. (Signal.) *Vests.*
3. Next word: **splash.** Say it. (Signal.) *Splash.*
4. (Repeat the words until firm.)

Task C Lip, lap, leap

1. Listen: **lip, lap, leap.** Say those words. (Signal.) *Lip, lap, leap.*
2. One of those words has the middle sound **ēēē.** I'll say the words again: **lip, lap, leap.**
3. Which word has the middle sound **ēēē?** (Signal.) *Leap.* Yes, **leap.**
- Which word has the middle sound **ăăă?** (Signal.) *Lap.* Yes, **lap.**
- Which word has the middle sound **ĭĭĭ?** (Signal.) *Lip.* Yes, **lip.**

Lesson 51

4. Listen: lĭĭĭp. What's the middle sound in the word **lip**? (Signal.) ĭĭĭ. Yes, ĭĭĭ.
- Listen: lăăăp. What's the middle sound in the word **lap**? (Signal.) ăăă. Yes, ăăă.
- Listen: lēēēp. What's the middle sound in the word **leap**? (Signal.) ēēē. Yes, ēēē.
5. (Repeat step 4 until firm.) Good job.

EXERCISE 3
NEW SOUND COMBINATION: or

1. (Point to **ore**:) This word is **ore**. The **e** at the end of the word does not make a sound. What word? (Signal.) *Ore.*
2. (Point to the underlined part of **more**:) What sound? (Signal.) *Or.*
- What word? (Signal.) *More.*
3. (Repeat step 2 for **sore, store, short, horse**.)

ore

more

sore

store

short

horse

EXERCISE 4
WORD READING THE FAST WAY

1. You're going to read these words the fast way.
2. (For each word: Touch the ball of the arrow. Pause.) What word? (Slash right.)
3. (Repeat the column until firm.)

to

fold

bust

creek

steep

Lesson 51

Lesson 51

4. (For each word: Touch the ball of the arrow. Pause.) What word? (Slash right.)
5. (Repeat each list until firm.)

smell

dust

dusty

they

yelling

sunny

was

mats

cuts

hands

class

well

green

funny

yes

WORKBOOK EXERCISES

Note: Pass out the Workbooks. Direct the students to open to Lesson 51.

(Award 6 points if the group worked well during the word attack. Remind the students of the points they can earn in their Workbook.)

EXERCISE 5
SOUND DICTATION

1. **I'll say the sounds. You write the letters in part 1 in your Workbook.**
2. **First sound. Write a letter that says k in the first blank.**
   (Observe students and give feedback.)
3. **Next sound. Write another letter that says k.**
   (Observe students and give feedback.)
4. **Next sound. Write two letters that go together and say k.**
   (Observe students and give feedback.)
5. **Next sound. (Pause.) d. What sound?** (Signal.) *d.*
   - **Write it.**
   (Observe students and give feedback.)
6. (Repeat step 5 for **b, fff, ĕĕĕ, ĭĭĭ, lll, sss, rrr, ŏŏŏ**.)
7. (Repeat sounds students had trouble with.)

EXERCISE 6
SPELLING FROM DICTATION

1. **Touch part 2.** ✓
   - **You're going to write words that I dictate.**
2. **First word: when. What word?** (Signal.) *When.*
   - **Listen again: www . . . ĕĕĕ . . . nnn. Write it in the first blank.**
   (Observe students and give feedback.)
3. **Next word: that. What word?** (Signal.) *That.*
   - **Listen again: thththth . . . ăăă . . . t. Write it in the next blank.**
   (Observe students and give feedback.)
4. (Repeat step 3 for **see, hits, rugs, bet, them.**)

Lesson 51

1
(c k) ck d b f
e i l s r o

2
1. when   2. that   3. see
4. hits   5. rugs   6. bet
7. them

3
best   west   path   felt
cold   corn   drop   drip   black
greets   club   box   happy

4
1. She trots faster than the sheep.
2. How can ten men fit in that tent?
3. When they met, they felt happy.
4. When will they stop sending me letters?

EXERCISE 7
WORD READING: Workbook

1. **Touch the first word in part 3.** ✓
2. **Look at the underlined sound in the first word. (Pause.) What sound?** (Signal.) *ĕĕĕ.*
   - **(Pause.) What word?** (Signal.) *Best.*
3. **Next word. (Pause.) What sound?** (Signal.) *sss.*
   - **(Pause.) What word?** (Signal.) *West.*
4. (Repeat step 3 for remaining words.)

EXERCISE 8
SENTENCE READING

1. **Everybody, touch sentence 1 in part 4.** ✓
2. **You're going to read the fast way.**
3. **First word.** ✓
   - **Get ready.** (Clap for each word. Pause about 2 seconds between claps.) *She . . . trots . . . faster . . . than . . . the . . . sheep.*
4. (Repeat step 3 until the students correctly identify all the words in the sentence in order.)
5. (Repeat steps 3 and 4 for each remaining sentence.)

Lesson 51

> **Individual test: Part 4**
> (Give each student a chance to read one of the sentences. Praise students who read accurately without long pauses.)

EXERCISE 9
WORD COMPLETION

1. Touch the first word in part 5. ✓
- Fix it up to say (pause) **slip.** What word? (Signal.) *Slip.*
- Fix it up.
  (Observe students and give feedback.)
2. Touch the next word. ✓
- Fix it up to say (pause) **when.** What word? (Signal.) *When.*
- Fix it up.
  (Observe students and give feedback.)
3. (Repeat step 2 for **la [land], ru [rugs], an [than], eep [sleep].**)

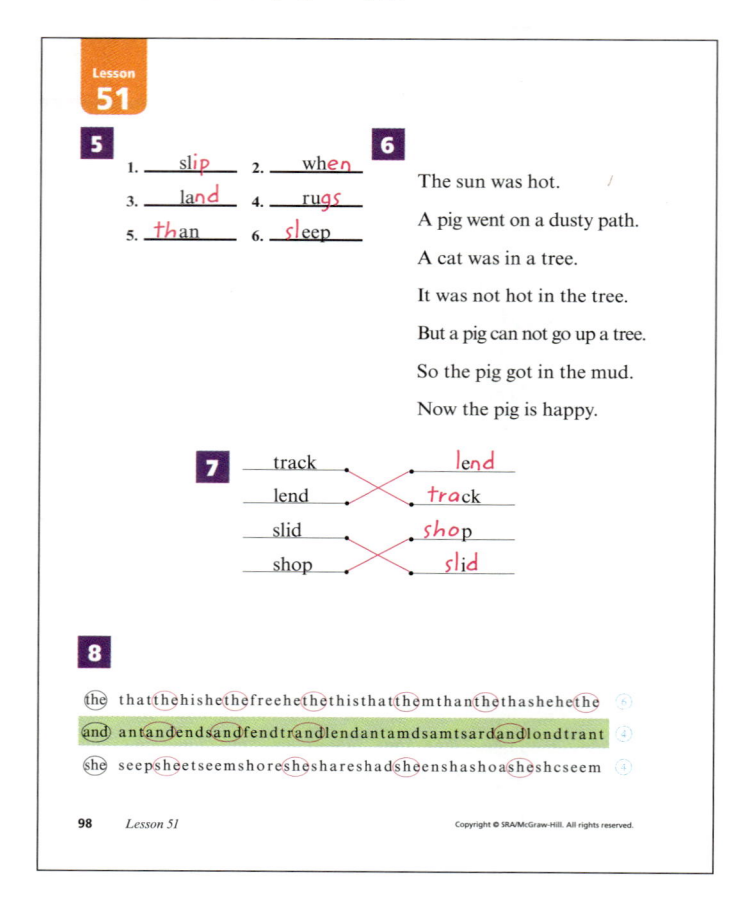

EXERCISE 10
STORY READING

Task A
1. Everybody, touch part 6. ✓
- You're going to read this story.
2. First word. ✓
- Get ready. (Clap for each word. Pause about 2 seconds between claps.) *The . . . sun . . . was . . . hot.*
3. (Repeat step 2 until the students correctly identify all the words in the sentence in order.)
4. Next sentence. ✓
- Get ready. (Clap for each word:) *A . . . pig . . . went . . . on . . . a . . . dusty . . . path.*
5. (Repeat step 4 until students correctly identify all the words in the sentence in order.)
6. (Repeat steps 4 and 5 for each remaining sentence.)
7. (If the students miss more than four words, repeat the story reading from the beginning.)

Task B
1. Now I'll read the story and ask questions. Follow along.
2. **The sun was hot. A pig went on a dusty path. A cat was in a tree.** Everybody, what was the weather like in this story? (Signal.) *Hot.*
3. (Call on a student.) Where was the pig? (Idea: *On a dusty path.*)
- (Call on a student.) Where was the cat? (Idea: *In a tree.*)
4. **It was not hot in the tree. But a pig can not go up a tree.** (Call on a student.) Why can't a pig go up a tree? (Ideas: *A pig has no claws; it has the wrong kind of feet for climbing.*)
- (Call on a student.) How did the cat get up the tree? (Idea: *It climbed up.*)
5. **So the pig got in the mud. Now the pig is happy.** (Call on a student.) Why is the pig happy? (Idea: *Because it is cool.*)

5
1. slip 2. when
3. land 4. rugs
5. than 6. sleep

6
The sun was hot.
A pig went on a dusty path.
A cat was in a tree.
It was not hot in the tree.
But a pig can not go up a tree.
So the pig got in the mud.
Now the pig is happy.

7
track — lend
lend — track
slid — shop
shop — slid

8
the — that the his he the free he the this that the m than the thas he he the
and — an t an d en ds an d f en d tr an d l en d an t am ds am ts ar d an d l on d tr an t
she — sees sh ee t s ee m sh or e sh e sh ar e sh ad sh ee n sh a sh o a sh e sh c s ee m

EXERCISE 11
MATCHING COMPLETION

1. Everybody, touch part 7. ✓
2. Touch the top word in the first column. ✓
   - What word? (Signal.) *Track.*
3. Touch the only part in the second column that can be fixed up to say **trrrăăăck**. ✓
4. Draw a line from the word **track** to the correct line in the second column. ✓
5. Now fix up the part in the second column so it says **trrrăăăck**. ✓
6. Do the rest of the matching words on your own.

EXERCISE 12
CIRCLE GAME

1. Everybody, touch part 8. ✓
2. What word will you circle in the first line? (Signal.) *The.*
3. What word will you circle in the second line? (Signal.) *And.*
4. What word will you circle in the third line? (Signal.) *She.*
5. Circle the words and finish the rest of your Workbook lesson.

EXERCISE 13
WORKBOOK CHECK

1. (Check each student's Workbook.)
2. (Award points for Workbook performance.)
3. (Record the student's total points in Box B.)

0–3 errors	8 points
4–5 errors	4 points
6 errors	2 points
7 or more errors	0 points

Lesson 51

INDIVIDUAL READING CHECKOUTS

EXERCISE 14
NEW ▶ TIMED STORY-READING CHECKOUT

> **Note:** For the timed checkouts, you will need a stopwatch.

- Study the story. If you read the story with no more than 2 errors and read it in **1 minute or less,** you'll earn 6 points.
- If you make more than 2 errors, or if you take more than **1 minute** to read the story, you won't earn any points.
- If you don't earn points the first time you read the story, you can try again. If you succeed the second time you try, you'll earn 3 points.
- (Check the students individually.)
- (Record either 6, 3, or 0 points in Box C.)

Lesson point total

(Tell students to write the point total in the last box at the top of the Workbook page. Maximum = 20 points.)

Point Summary Chart

(Tell students to write this point total in the box for Lesson 51 in the Point Summary Chart.)

END OF LESSON 51

Lesson 52

WORD-ATTACK SKILLS

EXERCISE 1
SOUND INTRODUCTION

1. (Point to **ch:**) These letters make the sound **ch.** What sound? (Touch.) *ch.*
2. (Point to **o:**) One sound you learned for this letter is the letter name. Everybody, what's that sound? (Touch.) *ōōō.* Yes, *ōōō.*
   - What's the other sound? (Touch.) *ŏŏŏ.* Yes, *ŏŏŏ.*
3. (Point to **e:**) One sound you learned for this letter is the letter name. Everybody, what's that sound? (Touch.) *ēēē.* Yes, *ēēē.*
   - What's the other sound? (Touch.) *ĕĕĕ.* Yes, *ĕĕĕ.*
4. (Point to **ch:**) What sound? (Touch.) *ch.* Yes, **ch.**
5. (Repeat step 4 for **sh, b, g, ĭ, h, k, d, ă, r, ing.**)

ch   o   e

ch   sh

b   g   i

h   k   d

a   r   ing

Individual test
(Call on two or three students. Touch under each sound. Each student says all the sounds, including two sounds for **o** and two sounds for **e.**)

EXERCISE 2
IRREGULAR WORDS

Task A Do

1. (Touch the ball of the arrow for **do:**) Sound out this word. Get ready. (Touch under **d, o:**) *dŏŏŏ.* (Repeat until the students say the sounds without pausing.)
2. That's how we sound out the word. But here's how we say the word: **doo.** It's a funny word. How do we say the word? (Signal.) *Doo.*
3. Sound it out. Get ready. (Touch under **d, o:**) *dŏŏŏ.* (Repeat until firm.)
4. Everybody, say the word. (Signal.) *Doo.* Yes, **doo.** Remember that word.

do

Task B Said

1. (Touch the ball of the arrow for **said**:) Sound out this word. Get ready. (Touch under **s, a, i, d:**) *sssăăăĭĭĭd.* (Repeat until the students say the sounds without pausing.)
2. That's how we sound out the word. But here's how we say the word: **sed.** It's a funny word. How do we say the word? (Signal.) *Sed.*
3. Sound it out. Get ready. (Touch under **s, a, i, d:**) *sssăăăĭĭĭd.* (Repeat until firm.)
4. Everybody, say the word. (Signal.) *Sed.* Yes, **sed.** Remember that word.

said

Lesson 52

EXERCISE 3
PRONUNCIATIONS

Note: Do not write the words on the board. This is an oral exercise.

Task A Trick, trip

1. Listen: **trick** (pause) **trip.** Say those words. (Signal.) *Trick, trip.* (Repeat until firm.)
2. Listen: **trick** (pause) **trip.** One of those words means **a journey or voyage.**
- (Pause.) Which word? (Signal.) *Trip.* Yes, **trip.**

To correct:
  a. (Tell the students the word.)
  b. (Repeat step 2.)

3. One of those words means **something you do when you fool someone.**
- (Pause.) Which word? (Signal.) *Trick.* Yes, **trick.**
4. (Repeat steps 2 and 3 until firm.)

Task B Churches, noses

1. Listen: **churches.** Say it. (Signal.) *Churches.*
2. Next word: **noses.** Say it. (Signal.) *Noses.*
3. (Repeat the words until firm.)

Task C Spring, sprang, sprung

1. Listen: **spring, sprang, sprung.** Say those words. (Signal.) *Spring, sprang, sprung.* (Repeat until firm.)
2. One of those words has the middle sound **ăăă.** I'll say the words again: **spring, sprang, sprung.**
3. Which word has the middle sound **ăăă**? (Signal.) *Sprang.* Yes, **sprang.**
- Which word has the middle sound **ŭŭŭ**? (Signal.) *Sprung.* Yes, **sprung.**
- Which word has the middle sound **ĭĭĭ**? (Signal.) *Spring.* Yes, **spring.**

4. Listen: **sprĭĭĭng.** What's the middle sound in the word **spring**? (Signal.) *ĭĭĭ.* Yes, **ĭĭĭ.**
- Listen: **sprăăăng.** What's the middle sound in the word **sprang**? (Signal.) *ăăă.* Yes, **ăăă.**
- Listen: **sprŭŭŭng.** What's the middle sound in the word **sprung**? (Signal.) *ŭŭŭ.* Yes, **ŭŭŭ.**
5. (Repeat step 4 until firm.) Good job.

EXERCISE 4
NEW SOUND COMBINATION: or

1. You're going to say the sound for the underlined part and then read the word.
2. (Point to **ore:**) This word is **ore.** The **e** at the end of the word does not make a sound. What word? (Signal.) *Ore.*
3. (Point to the underlined part of **more:**) What sound? (Touch.) *Or.*
- What word? (Signal.) *More.*
4. (Repeat step 3 for **st<u>or</u>e, h<u>or</u>se.**)

<u>or</u>e

m<u>o</u>re

st<u>or</u>e

h<u>or</u>se

Lesson 52

EXERCISE 5
WORD READING THE FAST WAY

1. You're going to read these words the fast way.
2. (For each word: Touch the ball of the arrow. Pause.) What word? (Slash right.)
3. (Repeat each list until firm.)

yet

gold

when

silly

lasting

was

crust

wheel

luck

chip

to

ship

chop

much

sends

slams

dropping

4. (For each word: Touch the ball of the arrow. Pause.) What word? (Slash right.)
5. (Repeat the list until firm.)

- cod
- sling
- camp
- champ
- lags
- bent
- black
- winning

Lesson 52

WORKBOOK EXERCISES

Note: Pass out the Workbooks. Direct the students to open to Lesson 52.

(Award 6 points if the group worked well during the word attack. Remind the students of the points they can earn in their Workbook.)

EXERCISE 6
SOUND DICTATION

1. I'll say the sounds. You write the letters in part 1 in your Workbook.
2. First sound. (Pause.) **ch.** What sound? (Signal.) *ch.*
- Write it in the first blank.
  (Observe students and give feedback.)
3. Next sound. (Pause.) **ththth.** What sound? (Signal.) *ththth.*
- Write it.
  (Observe students and give feedback.)
4. Next sound. (Pause.) **g.** What sound? (Signal.) *g.*
- Write it.
  (Observe students and give feedback.)
5. (Repeat step 4 for **b, ōōō, lll, ăăă, ŏŏŏ, h, nnn, ĕĕĕ, ĭĭĭ.**)
6. (Repeat sounds students had trouble with.)

Lesson 52   143

Lesson 52

EXERCISE 7
SPELLING FROM DICTATION

1. Touch part 2. ✓
   - You're going to write words that I dictate.
2. First word: **dad.** What word? (Signal.) *Dad.*
   - Listen again: **d . . . ăăă . . . d.** Write it in the first blank.
   (Observe students and give feedback.)
3. Next word: **bad.** What word? (Signal.) *Bad.*
   - Listen again: **b . . . ăăă . . . d.** Write it in the next blank.
   (Observe students and give feedback.)
4. (Repeat step 3 for **shots, and, when, mats, then.**)

EXERCISE 8
WORD READING: Workbook

1. Touch the first word in part 3. ✓
2. Look at the underlined sound in the first word. (Pause.) What sound? (Signal.) *ing.*
   - (Pause.) What word? (Signal.) *Gripping.*
3. Next word. (Pause.) What sound? (Signal.) *shshsh.*
   - (Pause.) What word? (Signal.) *Shops.*
4. (Repeat step 3 for remaining words.)

EXERCISE 9
SENTENCE READING

1. Everybody, touch sentence 1 in part 4. ✓
2. You're going to read the fast way.
3. First word. ✓
   - Get ready. (Clap for each word. Pause about 2 seconds between claps.) They . . . will . . . lock . . . the . . . shed . . . in . . . the . . . morning.

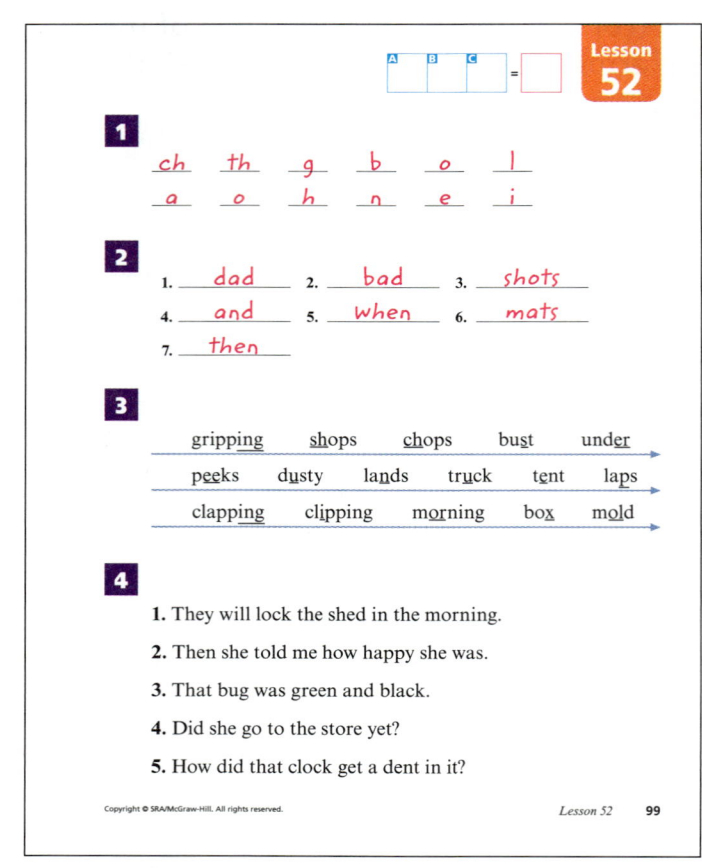

1

ch	th	g	b	o	l
a	o	h	n	e	i

2

1. dad   2. bad   3. shots
4. and   5. when   6. mats
7. then

3

gripping   shops   chops   bust   under
peeks   dusty   lands   truck   tent   laps
clapping   clipping   morning   box   mold

4

1. They will lock the shed in the morning.
2. Then she told me how happy she was.
3. That bug was green and black.
4. Did she go to the store yet?
5. How did that clock get a dent in it?

---

4. (Repeat step 3 until the students correctly identify all the words in the sentence in order.)
5. (Repeat steps 3 and 4 for each remaining sentence.)

Individual test
(Give each student a chance to read one of the sentences. Praise students who read accurately without long pauses.)

EXERCISE 10
WORD COMPLETION

1. Touch the first word in part 5. ✓
   - Fix it up to say (pause) **slam.** What word? (Signal.) *Slam.*
   - Fix it up.
   (Observe students and give feedback.)
2. Touch the second word. ✓
   - What word? (Signal.) *mu.* Yes, **mu.**
   - Fix it up to say (pause) **must.** What word? (Signal.) *Must.*
   - Fix it up.
   (Observe students and give feedback.)
3. (Repeat step 2 for **co** [cold], **im** [trim], **la** [last], **eep** [sleep].)

Lesson 52

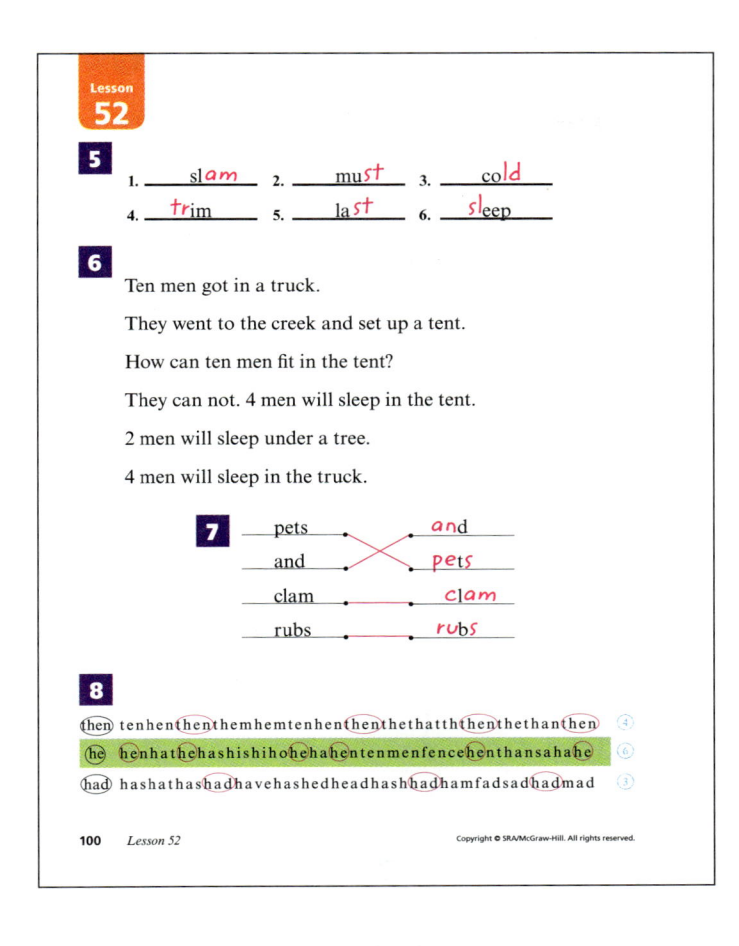

5.
1. sl**am**
2. mu**st**
3. co**ld**
4. **tr**im
5. la**st**
6. **sl**eep

6.
Ten men got in a truck.
They went to the creek and set up a tent.
How can ten men fit in the tent?
They can not. 4 men will sleep in the tent.
2 men will sleep under a tree.
4 men will sleep in the truck.

7.
pets — and
and — pets
clam — clam
rubs — rubs

8.
(then) tenhen(then)themhemten hen(then)thethatth(then)thethan(then) (4)
(he) henhathehashishihohehahentenmenfence(hen)thansahahe (6)
(had) hashathas(had)havehashedheadhash(had)(had)hamfadsad(had)mad (3)

100 Lesson 52

EXERCISE 11
STORY READING

Task A

1. Everybody, touch part 6. ✓
- You're going to read this story.
2. First word. ✓
- Get ready. (Clap for each word. Pause about 2 seconds between claps.) Ten . . . men . . . got . . . in . . . a . . . truck.
3. (Repeat step 2 until the students correctly identify all the words in the sentence in order.)
4. Next sentence. ✓
- Get ready. (Clap for each word:) They . . . went . . . to . . . the . . . creek . . . and . . . set . . . up . . . a . . . tent.
5. (Repeat step 4 until students correctly identify all the words in the sentence in order.)

6. (Repeat steps 4 and 5 for each remaining sentence:
- How can ten men fit in the tent?
- They can not. 4 men will sleep in the tent.
- 2 men will sleep under a tree.
- 4 men will sleep in the truck.)
7. (If the students miss more than four words, repeat the story reading from the beginning.)

Task B

1. Now I'll read the story and ask questions. Follow along.
2. **Ten men got in a truck. They went to the creek and set up a tent.** (Call on a student.) How do you set up a tent? (Accept a reasonable response.)
3. (Call on a student.) What do you think those ten men are going to do by the creek? (Idea: *Go fishing.*)
4. **How can ten men fit in the tent? They can not. 4 men will sleep in the tent. 2 men will sleep under a tree. 4 men will sleep in the truck.** Everybody, how many men are there? (Signal.) *Ten.*
- How many men will sleep in the tent? (Signal.) *Four.*
- How many men will sleep under a tree? (Signal.) *Two.*
- How many men will sleep in the truck? (Signal.) *Four.* Yes, four.

EXERCISE 12
MATCHING COMPLETION

1. Everybody, touch part 7. ✓
2. Touch the top word in the first column. ✓
- What word? (Signal.) *Pets.*
3. Touch the only part in the second column that can be fixed up to say **pĕĕĕtsss**. ✓
4. Draw a line from the word **pets** to the correct line in the second column. ✓
5. Now fix up the part in the second column so it says **pĕĕĕtsss**. ✓
6. Do the rest of the matching words on your own.

Lesson 52

EXERCISE 13
CIRCLE GAME

1. Everybody, touch part 8. ✓
2. What word will you circle in the first line? (Signal.) *Then.*
3. What word will you circle in the second line? (Signal.) *He.*
4. What word will you circle in the third line? (Signal.) *Had.*
5. Circle the words and finish the rest of your Workbook lesson.

EXERCISE 14
WORKBOOK CHECK

1. (Check each student's Workbook.)
2. (Award points for Workbook performance.)
3. (Record the student's total points in Box B.)

0–3 errors	8 points
4–5 errors	4 points
6 errors	2 points
7 or more errors	0 points

INDIVIDUAL READING CHECKOUTS

EXERCISE 15
TIMED STORY-READING CHECKOUT

Note: For the timed checkouts, you will need a stopwatch.

- Study the story. If you read the story with no more than 2 errors and read it in 1 minute or less, you'll earn 6 points.
- If you make more than 2 errors, or if you take more than 1 minute to read the story, you won't earn any points.
- If you don't earn points the first time you read the story, you can try again. If you succeed the second time you try, you'll earn 3 points.
- (Check the students individually.)
- (Record either 6, 3, or 0 points in Box C.)

Lesson point total

(Tell students to write the point total in the last box at the top of the Workbook page. Maximum = 20 points.)

Point Summary Chart

(Tell students to write this point total in the box for Lesson 52 in the Point Summary Chart.)

END OF LESSON 52

Lesson 53

WORD-ATTACK SKILLS

EXERCISE 1
SOUND IDENTIFICATION

1. (Point to **e**:) One sound you learned for this letter is the letter name. Everybody, what's that sound? (Touch.) *ēēē*. Yes, **ēēē**.
   - What's the other sound? (Touch.) *ĕĕĕ*. Yes, **ĕĕĕ**.
2. Say each sound when I touch it.
3. (Point to **u**:) What sound? (Touch.) *ŭŭŭ*. Yes, **ŭŭŭ**.
4. (Repeat step 3 for **sh, or, ol, ch, y, b, ĭ, d.**)

e u sh
or ol
ch y
b i d

Individual test
(Call on two or three students. Touch under each sound. Each student says all the sounds, including two sounds for **e**.)

EXERCISE 2
PRONUNCIATIONS

Task A

1. Listen: **cheap.** Say it. (Signal.) *Cheap.*
2. Next word: **sheep.** Say it. (Signal.) *Sheep.*
3. (Repeat step 2 for **ship, chip**.)
4. (Repeat the words until firm.)

Task B Chump, chimp, champ

1. Listen: **chump, chimp, champ.** Say those words. (Signal.) *Chump, chimp, champ.* (Repeat until firm.)
2. One of those words has the middle sound **ăăă**. I'll say the words again: **chump, chimp, champ.**
3. Which word has the middle sound **ăăă**? (Signal.) *Champ.* Yes, **champ.**
   - Which word has the middle sound **ŭŭŭ**? (Signal.) *Chump.* Yes, **chump.**
   - Which word has the middle sound **ĭĭĭ**? (Signal.) *Chimp.* Yes, **chimp.**
4. Listen: **chŭŭŭmp.** What's the middle sound in the word **chump**? (Signal.) *ŭŭŭ.* Yes, **ŭŭŭ.**
   - Listen: **chĭĭĭmp.** What's the middle sound in the word **chimp**? (Signal.) *ĭĭĭ.* Yes, **ĭĭĭ.**
   - Listen: **chăăămp.** What's the middle sound in the word **champ**? (Signal.) *ăăă.* Yes, **ăăă.**
5. (Repeat step 4 until firm.) Good job.

EXERCISE 3
IRREGULAR WORDS

Task A Said

1. (Touch the ball of the arrow for **said**:) Sound out this word. Get ready. (Touch under **s, a, i, d**:) *sssăăăĭĭĭd.* (Repeat until the students say the sounds without pausing.)
2. That's how we sound out the word. But how do we say the word? (Signal.) *Sed.*
3. Sound it out. Get ready. (Touch under **s, a, i, d**:) *sssăăăĭĭĭd.* (Repeat until firm.)
4. Everybody, say the word. (Signal.) *Sed.* Yes, **sed**. Remember that word.

said

Lesson 53

Lesson 53

Task B Do

1. (Touch the ball of the arrow for **do**:) Sound out this word. Get ready. (Touch under **d, o**:) *dŏŏŏ*. (Repeat until the students say the sounds without pausing.)
2. That's how we sound out the word. But how we do say the word? (Signal.) *Doo*.
3. Sound it out. Get ready. (Touch under **d, o**:) *dŏŏŏ*. (Repeat until firm.)
4. Everybody, say the word. (Signal.) *Doo*. Yes, **doo**. Remember that word.

do

EXERCISE 4
WORD READING THE FAST WAY

1. You're going to read these words the fast way.
2. (For each word: Touch the ball of the arrow. Pause.) What word? (Slash right.)
3. (Repeat each list until firm.)

chip

lunch

mixer

next

lamp

clamp

funny

told

yet

mister

sore

store

shore

swimming

148   Lesson 53

Lesson 53

4. (For each word: Touch the ball of the arrow. Pause.) **What word?** (Slash right.)
5. (Repeat each list until firm.)

pan

ship

was

colder

smell

left

to

bold

clipper

still

plant

WORKBOOK EXERCISES

Note: Pass out the Workbooks. Direct the students to open to Lesson 53.

(Award 6 points if the group worked well during the word attack. Remind the students of the points they can earn in their Workbook.)

EXERCISE 5
SOUND DICTATION

1. I'll say the sounds. You write the letters in part 1 in your Workbook.
2. First sound. Write a letter that says **k** in the first blank.
   (Observe students and give feedback.)
3. Next sound. Write another letter that says **k**.
   (Observe students and give feedback.)
4. Next sound. Write two letters that go together and say **k**.
   (Observe students and give feedback.)

Lesson 53   **149**

Lesson 53

Worksheet (Part 1)

1. (c k) ck ch b x
      u p d i th sh

2. 1. for 2. big 3. must
      4. send 5. ship 6. yes
      7. bad

3. 1. **ch**amp 2. **b**olt 3. **s**ing
      4. **sl**ip 5. **th**ey 6. **y**et

4. short — much
      sold — bath
      much — short
      bath — sold

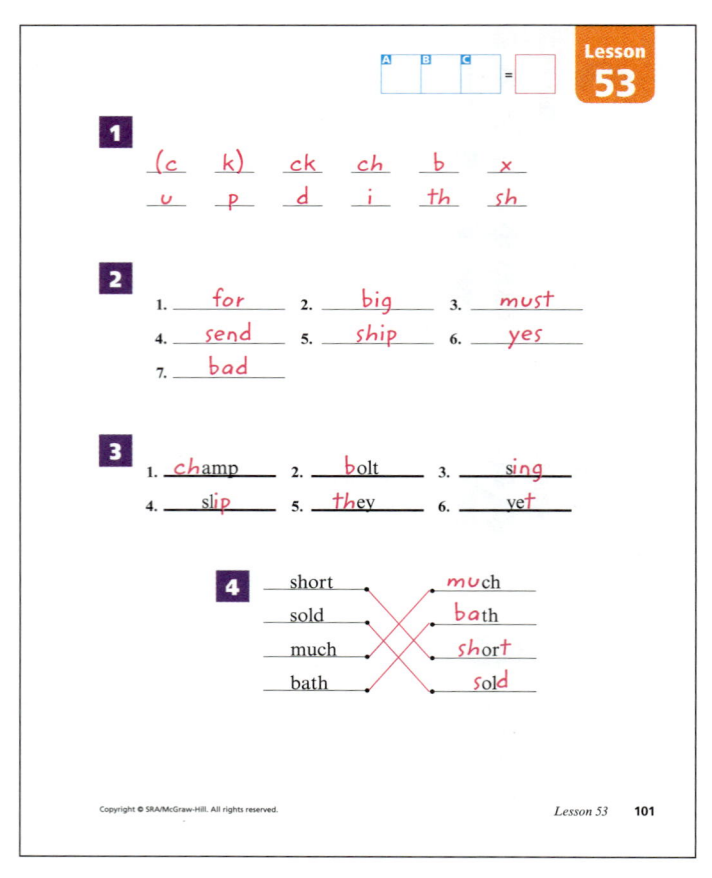

5. Next sound. (Pause.) **ch.** What sound? (Signal.) *ch.*
   - Write it.
     (Observe students and give feedback.)
6. (Repeat step 5 for **b, kss [x], ŭŭŭ, p, d, ĭĭĭ, ththth, shshsh.**)
7. (Repeat sounds students had trouble with.)

EXERCISE 6
SPELLING FROM DICTATION

1. Touch part 2. ✓
   - You're going to write words that I dictate.
2. First word: **for.** What word? (Signal.) *For.*
   - Listen again: **fff . . . or.** Write it in the first blank.
     (Observe students and give feedback.)
3. Next word: **big.** What word? (Signal.) *Big.*
   - Listen again: **b . . . ĭĭĭ . . . g.** Write it in the next blank.
     (Observe students and give feedback.)
4. (Repeat step 3 for **must, send, ship, yes, bad.**)

EXERCISE 7
WORD COMPLETION

1. Touch the first word in part 3. ✓
   - What word? (Signal.) *amp.* Yes, **amp.**
   - Fix it up to say (pause) **champ.** What word? (Signal.) *Champ.*
   - Fix it up.
     (Observe students and give feedback.)
2. Touch the second word. ✓
   - Fix it up to say (pause) **bolt.** What word? (Signal.) *Bolt.* Yes, **bolt.**
   - Fix it up.
     (Observe students and give feedback.)
3. (Repeat step 2 for **sing, slip, they, yet.**)

EXERCISE 8
MATCHING COMPLETION

1. Everybody, touch part 4. ✓
2. Touch the top word in the first column. ✓
   - What word? (Signal.) *Short.*
3. Touch the only part in the second column that can be fixed up to say **shshshōrt.** ✓
4. Draw a line from the word **short** to the correct line in the second column. ✓
5. Now fix up the part in the second column so it says **shshshōrt.** ✓
6. Do the rest of the matching words on your own.

Lesson 53

5

1. He said, "I will go to the store."
2. She told him, "Go rent a truck."
3. They said, "We had fun on the trip."

6

1. Next week, we will plant six seeds.
2. Send me a better letter.
3. On the trip, I got sick.
4. For lunch, they had fish and chips.

7

She told him, "Let us go on a clipper ship."
But he had no cash. And she had no cash.
He said, "We will pan for gold."
So they went to the hills. They got gold.
Then they went on that clipper ship.

EXERCISE 9
NEW SENTENCE READING: Quotations

Task A

1. (Print on the board:)

   > She said, "I am happy."

2. Here's a sentence with quote marks. (Touch both quotation marks.) The words inside the quote marks tell what the person said.
3. (Underline the words between the quotation marks: **She said, "I am happy."**)
   - I'll read the sentence. **She said, "I am happy."** That's the whole sentence.
4. Here's what she said. (Pause.) **I am happy.**
5. Your turn to say the whole sentence. Get ready. (Signal.) *She said, "I am happy."*
6. Now say the words that she said. Get ready. (Signal.) *I am happy.*
7. (Repeat steps 5 and 6 until firm.)

Task B

1. Everybody, find part 5. ✓
2. Each sentence has quote marks. You're going to read each sentence and then tell the words the person said.

3. Touch sentence 1. ✓
   - Read the sentence. Get ready. (Clap for each word. Pause about 2 seconds between claps.) *He . . . said . . . "I . . . will . . . go . . . to . . . the . . . store."*
4. I'll say the whole sentence. **He said, "I will go to the store."**
5. (Call on a student.) Say the words he said. *I will go to the store.*
6. Everybody, touch sentence 2. ✓
   - Read the sentence. Get ready. (Clap for each word. Pause about 2 seconds between claps.) *She . . . told . . . him, . . . "Go . . . rent . . . a . . . truck."*
7. I'll say the whole sentence. **She told him, "Go rent a truck."**
8. (Call on a student.) Say the words she said. *Go rent a truck.*
9. Everybody, touch sentence 3. ✓
   - Read the sentence. Get ready. (Clap for each word. Pause about 2 seconds between claps.) *They . . . said, . . . "We . . . had . . . fun . . . on . . . the . . . trip."*
10. I'll say the whole sentence. **They said, "We had fun on the trip."**
11. (Call on a student.) Say the words they said. *We had fun on the trip.*

EXERCISE 10
SENTENCE READING

1. Everybody, touch sentence 1 in part 6. ✓
2. You're going to read the fast way. Read a word each time I clap.
3. First word. ✓
   - Get ready. (Clap for each word. Pause about 2 seconds between claps.) *Next . . . week, . . . we . . . will . . . plant . . . six . . . seeds.*
4. (Repeat step 3 until the students correctly identify all the words in the sentence in order.)
5. (Repeat steps 3 and 4 for each remaining sentence:
   - **2. Send me a better letter.**
   - **3. On the trip, I got sick.**
   - **4. For lunch, they had fish and chips.**)

Lesson 53

> **Individual test : Part 6**
> (Give each student a chance to read one of the sentences. Praise students who read accurately without long pauses.)

EXERCISE 11
STORY READING

Task A

1. Everybody, touch part 7. ✓
- You're going to read this story.
2. First word. ✓
- Get ready. (Clap for each word. Pause about 2 seconds between claps.) *She . . . told . . . him, . . . "Let . . . us . . . go . . . on . . . a . . . clipper . . . ship."*
3. (Repeat step 2 until the students correctly identify all the words in the sentence in order.)
4. Next sentence. ✓
- Get ready. (Clap for each word:) *But . . . he . . . had . . . no . . . cash.*
5. (Repeat step 4 until students correctly identify all the words in the sentence in order.)
6. (Repeat steps 4 and 5 for each remaining sentence:
- **And she had no cash.**
- **He said, "We will pan for gold."**
- **So they went to the hills. They got gold.**
- **Then they went on that clipper ship.**)
7. (If the students miss more than four words, repeat the story reading from the beginning.)

Task B

1. Now I'll read the story and ask questions. Follow along.
2. **She told him, "Let us go on a clipper ship."** Everybody, what did she say? (Signal.) *Let us go on a clipper ship.*
- (Call on a student.) What is a clipper ship? (Idea: *A large ship with sails.*)
3. **But he had no cash. And she had no cash.** (Call on a student.) Can you go on a ship if you have no cash? (Idea: *No.*)
4. **He said, "We will pan for gold."** Everybody, what did he say? (Signal.) *We will pan for gold.*
- (Call on a student.) What does this mean: **pan for gold**? (Idea: *Sift stones in a metal pan in order to find gold.*)
5. **So they went to the hills.** (Call on a student.) Why did they go to the hills? (Idea: *To pan for gold.*)
6. **They got gold. Then they went on that clipper ship.** Everybody, if they went on the clipper ship, did they have cash? (Signal.) *Yes.*
- (Call on a student.) How did they get cash? (Idea: *Sold the gold they found.*)
- So they must have found some gold when they went panning.

Lesson 53

EXERCISE 12
WORKBOOK CHECK

1. (Check each student's Workbook.)
2. (Award points for Workbook performance.)
3. (Record the student's total points in Box B.)

0–3 errors	8 points
4–5 errors	4 points
6 errors	2 points
7 or more errors	0 points

INDIVIDUAL READING CHECKOUTS

EXERCISE 13
TIMED STORY-READING CHECKOUT

Note: For the timed checkouts, you will need a stopwatch.

- Study the story. If you read the story with no more than 2 errors and read it in 1 minute or less, you'll earn 6 points.
- If you make more than 2 errors, or if you take more than 1 minute to read the story, you won't earn any points.
- If you don't earn points the first time you read the story, you can try again. If you succeed the second time you try, you'll earn 3 points.
- (Check the students individually.)
- (Record either 6, 3, or 0 points in Box C.)

Lesson point total

(Tell students to write the point total in the last box at the top of the Workbook page. Maximum = 20 points.)

Point Summary Chart

(Tell students to write this point total in the box for Lesson 53 in the Point Summary Chart.)

END OF LESSON 53

Lesson 54

WORD-ATTACK SKILLS

EXERCISE 1
SOUND INTRODUCTION

1. (Point to **j**:) This letter makes the sound **j**. What sound? (Touch.) *j*.
2. (Point to **e**:) One sound you learned for this letter is the letter name. Everybody, what's that sound? (Touch.) *ēēē*. Yes, **ēēē**.
- What's the other sound? (Touch.) *ĕĕĕ*. Yes, **ĕĕĕ**.
3. (Point to **o**:) One sound you learned for this letter is the letter name. Everybody, what's that sound? (Touch.) *ōōō*. Yes, **ōōō**.
- What's the other sound? (Touch.) *ŏŏŏ*. Yes, **ŏŏŏ**.
4. (Point to **j**:) What sound? (Touch.) *j*. Yes, **j**.
5. (Repeat step 4 for **f, m, g, ĭ, ing, x, b, p, ŭ, ch**.)

j   e   o

j   f   m   g

i   ing

x   b   p

u   ch

Individual test
(Call on two or three students. Touch under each sound. Each student says all the sounds, including two sounds for **o** and two sounds for **e**.)

EXERCISE 2
PRONUNCIATIONS

Note: Do not write the words on the board. This is an oral exercise.

Task A Clock, clot

1. Listen: **clock** (pause) **clot**. Say those words. (Signal.) *Clock, clot*. (Repeat until firm.)
2. Listen: **clock** (pause) **clot**. One of those words means **something that shows the time**.
- (Pause.) Which word? (Signal.) *Clock*. Yes, **clock**.

To correct:
 a. (Tell the students the word.)
 b. (Repeat step 2.)

3. One of those words means **a gummy mass**.
- (Pause.) Which word? (Signal.) *Clot*. Yes, **clot**.
4. (Repeat steps 2 and 3 until firm.)

Task B

1. Listen: **benches**. Say it. (Signal.) *Benches*.
2. Next word: **rests**. Say it. (Signal.) *Rests*.
3. Next word: **flaps**. Say it. (Signal.) *Flaps*.
4. (Repeat the words until firm.)

Task C Bust, beast, best

1. Listen: **bust, beast, best**. Say those words. (Signal.) *Bust, beast, best*. (Repeat until firm.)
2. One of those words has the middle sound **ēēē**. I'll say the words again: **bust, beast, best**.
3. Which word has the middle sound **ēēē**? (Signal.) *Beast*. Yes, **beast**.
- Which word has the middle sound **ŭŭŭ**? (Signal.) *Bust*. Yes, **bust**.
- Which word has the middle sound **ĕĕĕ**? (Signal.) *Best*. Yes, **best**.

- 4. Listen: **bŭŭŭst**. What's the middle sound in the word **bust**? (Signal.) *ŭŭŭ*. Yes, *ŭŭŭ*.
- Listen: **bēēēst**. What's the middle sound in the word **beast**? (Signal.) *ēēē*. Yes, *ēēē*.
- Listen: **bĕĕĕst**. What's the middle sound in the word **best**? (Signal.) *ĕĕĕ*. Yes, *ĕĕĕ*.
- 5. (Repeat step 4 until firm.) Good job.

EXERCISE 3
IRREGULAR WORDS

Task A Do

1. (Touch the ball of the arrow for **do**:) Sound out this word. Get ready. (Touch under **d, o**:) *dŏŏŏ*. (Repeat until the students say the sounds without pausing.)
2. That's how we sound out the word. But how do we say the word? (Signal.) *Doo*.
3. Sound it out. Get ready. (Touch under **d, o**:) *dŏŏŏ*. (Repeat until firm.)
4. Everybody, say the word. (Signal.) *Doo*. Yes, **doo**. Remember that word.

do

Task B Said

1. (Touch the ball of the arrow for **said**:) Sound out this word. Get ready. (Touch under **s, a, i, d**:) *sssăăăĭĭĭd*. (Repeat until the students say the sounds without pausing.)
2. That's how we sound out the word. But how do we say the word? (Signal.) *Sed*.
3. Sound it out. Get ready. (Touch under **s, a, i, d**:) *sssăăăĭĭĭd*. (Repeat until firm.)
4. Everybody, say the word. (Signal.) *Sed*. Yes, **sed**. Remember that word.

said

EXERCISE 4
WORD READING THE FAST WAY

1. You're going to read these words the fast way.
2. (For each word: Touch the ball of the arrow. Pause.) What word? (Slash right.)
3. (Repeat the column until firm.)

chimp
champ
chump
was
stump
strip

Lesson 54

4. (For each word: Touch the ball of the arrow. Pause.) What word? (Slash right.)
5. (Repeat each list until firm.)

creek

bath

happy

muddy

dog

frog

pens

block

dust

bust

short

yelling

pills

fix

left

self

things

6. (For each word: Touch the ball of the arrow. Pause.) What word? (Slash right.)
7. (Repeat the column until firm.)

store

to

such

much

form

fold

Lesson 54

WORKBOOK EXERCISES

Note: Pass out the Workbooks. Direct the students to open to Lesson 54.

(Award 6 points if the group worked well during the word attack. Remind the students of the points they can earn in their Workbook.)

EXERCISE 5
SOUND DICTATION

1. I'll say the sounds. You write the letters in part 1 in your Workbook.
2. First sound. Write a letter that says **www** in the first blank.
   (Observe students and give feedback.)
3. Next sound. Write two letters that go together and say **www**.
   (Observe students and give feedback.)
4. Next sound. (Pause.) **ththth.** What sound? (Signal.) *ththth.*
- Write it.
   (Observe students and give feedback.)
5. (Repeat step 4 for **shshsh, ch, fff, sss, kss [x], nnn, ĕĕĕ, ŭŭŭ, ŏŏŏ.**)
6. (Repeat sounds students had trouble with.)

EXERCISE 6
SPELLING FROM DICTATION

1. Touch part 2. ✓
- You're going to write words that I dictate.
2. First word: **sits.** What word? (Signal.) *Sits.*
- Listen again: **sss . . . ĭĭĭ . . . t . . . sss.** Write it on the first line.
   (Observe students and give feedback.)
3. Next word: **ship.** What word? (Signal.) *Ship.*
- Listen again: **shshsh . . . ĭĭĭ . . . p.** Write it on the next line.
   (Observe students and give feedback.)
4. (Repeat step 3 for **and, rust, ram, red, bad.**)

Lesson 54 157

Lesson 54

Workbook Page (Lesson 54, p. 103)

1.
w wh th sh ch f
s x n e u o

2.
1. sits   2. ship   3. and
4. rust   5. ram   6. red
7. bad

3.
chip   sand   bent   rents   big
bug   gripping   help   need   they
silly for   now   mats   slug   rag

4.
1. He said, "I will win the meet."
2. She said, "Fix the casters on that bed."
3. The clock was running faster.
4. We went and sat under the tree.
5. If we rent a truck, we can go on a trip.

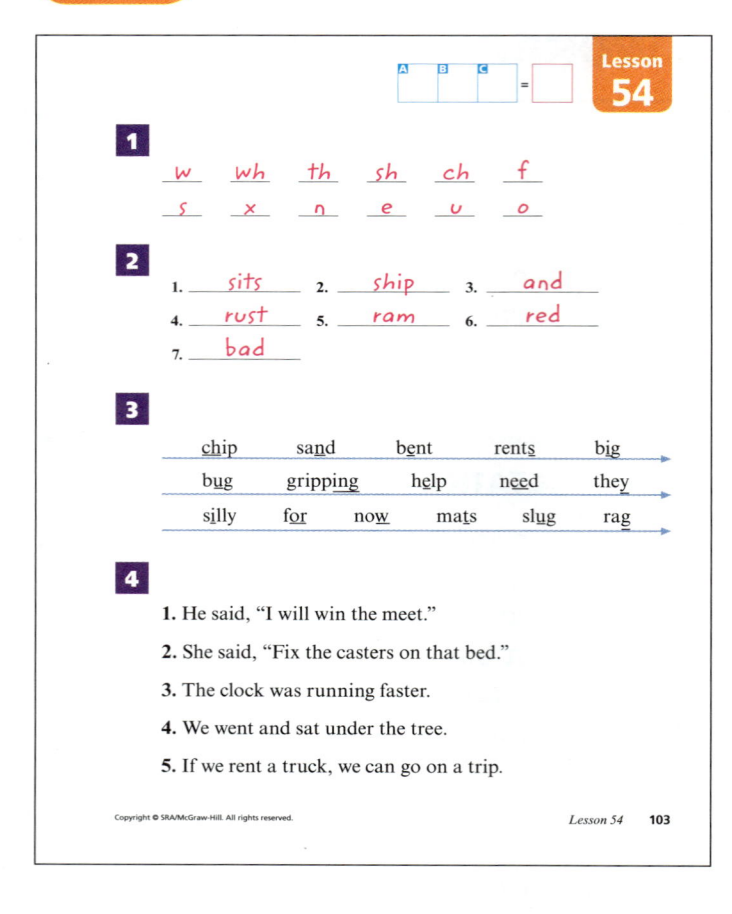

EXERCISE 7
WORD READING: Workbook

1. Touch the first word in part 3. ✓
2. Look at the underlined sound in the first word. (Pause.) What sound? (Signal.) *ch*.
   - (Pause.) What word? (Signal.) *Chip*.
3. Next word. (Pause.) What sound? (Signal.) *nnn*.
   - (Pause.) What word? (Signal.) *Sand*.
4. (Repeat step 3 for remaining words.)

EXERCISE 8
NEW SENTENCE READING: Quotations

1. Everybody, touch sentence 1 in part 4. ✓
2. Read the sentence. Get ready. (Clap for each word. Pause about 2 seconds between claps.) He . . . said, . . . "I . . . will . . . win . . . the . . . meet."
3. I'll say the whole sentence. **He said, "I will win the meet."**
4. (Call on a student.) Say the words he said. *I will win the meet.*
5. Everybody, touch sentence 2. ✓
   - Read the sentence. Get ready. (Clap for each word. Pause about 2 seconds between claps.) She . . . said, . . . "Fix . . . the . . . casters . . . on . . . that . . . bed."
6. I'll say the whole sentence. **She said, "Fix the casters on that bed."**
7. (Call on a student.) Say the words she said. *Fix the casters on that bed.*
8. Everybody, touch sentence 3. ✓
   - Read the sentence. Get ready. (Clap for each word.) The . . . clock . . . was . . . running . . . faster.
9. (Repeat step 8 for each remaining sentence.)

EXERCISE 9
WORD COMPLETION

1. Touch the first word in part 5. ✓
   - Fix it up to say (pause) **corn**. What word? (Signal.) *Corn*.
   - Fix it up.
     (Observe students and give feedback.)
2. Touch the second word. ✓
   - What word? (Signal.) *im*. Yes, **im**.
   - Fix it up to say (pause) **slim**. What word? (Signal.) *Slim*.
   - Fix it up.
     (Observe students and give feedback.)
3. (Repeat step 2 for **sa [sacks]**.)
4. Touch the fourth word. ✓
   - Fix it up to say (pause) **pet**. What word? (Signal.) *Pet*.
   - Fix it up.
     (Observe students and give feedback.)
5. (Repeat step 4 for **land, dug**.)

EXERCISE 10
STORY READING

Task A

1. Everybody, touch part 6. ✓
   - You're going to read this story.
2. First word. ✓
   - Get ready. (Clap for each word. Pause about 2 seconds between claps.) *The . . . dog . . . was . . . wet . . . and . . . muddy.*
3. (Repeat step 2 until the students correctly identify all the words in the sentence in order.)
4. Next sentence. ✓
   - Get ready. (Clap for each word:) *Ted . . . said, . . . "That . . . dog . . . needs . . . a . . . bath."*
5. (Repeat step 4 until students correctly identify all the words in the sentence in order.)
6. (Repeat steps 4 and 5 for each remaining sentence.)
7. (If the students miss more than four words, repeat the story reading from the beginning.)

Task B

1. Now I'll read the story and ask questions. Follow along.
2. **The dog was wet and muddy. Ted said, "That dog needs a bath."** (Call on a student.) **What did Ted say?** *That dog needs a bath.*
3. **Ann said, "Get a rag."** (Call on a student.) **What did Ann say?** *Get a rag.*
   - (Call on a student.) **Why would you need a rag to give a dog a bath?** (Idea: *To wash the dog.*)
4. **Ted did that. Then he said, "I will fill the tub."** (Call on a student.) **What did Ted do?** (Idea: *He got a rag and filled the tub.*)
5. **So the dog got a bath. But Ann and Ted got wet and muddy.** Everybody, who was wet and muddy at the beginning of the story? (Signal.) *The dog.*
   - (Call on a student.) **How did Ann and Ted get muddy?** (Idea: *By giving the dog a bath.*)
   - Did you ever get wet trying to give a dog a bath? (Call on individual students.)

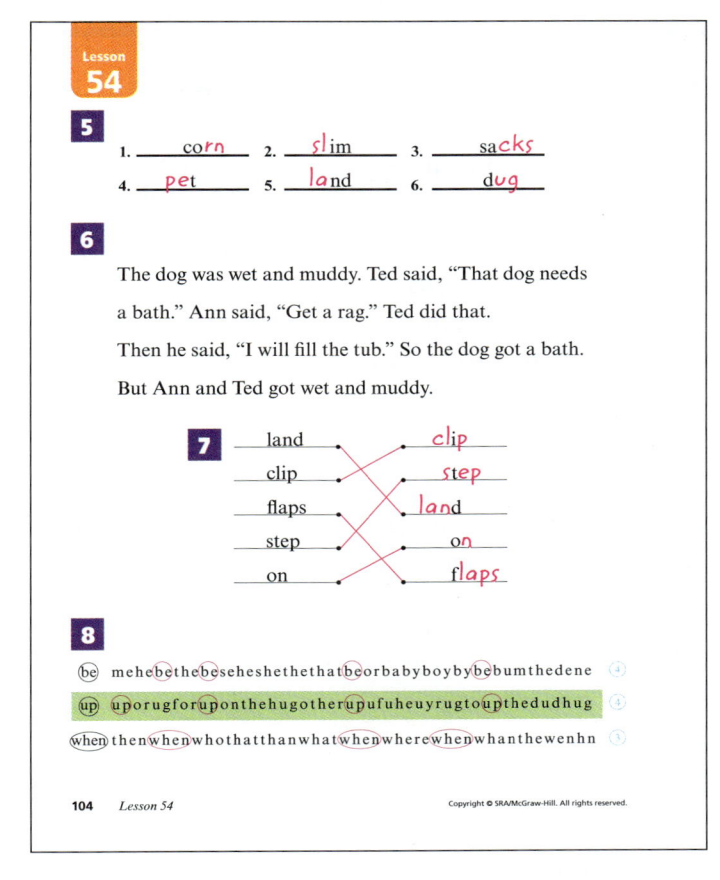

EXERCISE 11
MATCHING COMPLETION

1. Everybody, touch part 7. ✓
2. Touch the top word in the first column. ✓
   - What word? (Signal.) *Land.*
3. Touch the only part in the second column that can be fixed up to say **lllăăănnnd**. ✓
4. Draw a line from the word **land** to the correct line in the second column. ✓
5. Now fix up the part in the second column so it says **lllăăănnnd**. ✓
6. Do the rest of the matching words on your own.
   (Observe students and give feedback.)

Lesson 54

Lesson 54

EXERCISE 12
CIRCLE GAME

1. Everybody, touch part 8. ✓
2. What word will you circle in the first line? (Signal.) *Be.*
3. What word will you circle in the second line? (Signal.) *Up.*
4. What word will you circle in the third line? (Signal.) *When.*
5. Circle the words and finish the rest of your Workbook lesson.

EXERCISE 13
WORKBOOK CHECK

1. (Check each student's Workbook.)
2. (Award points for Workbook performance.)
3. (Record the student's total points in Box B.)

0–3 errors	8 points
4–5 errors	4 points
6 errors	2 points
7 or more errors	0 points

INDIVIDUAL READING CHECKOUTS

EXERCISE 14
TIMED STORY-READING CHECKOUT

Note: For the timed checkouts, you will need a stopwatch.

- Study the story. If you read the story with no more than 2 errors and read it in 1 minute or less, you'll earn 6 points.
- If you make more than 2 errors, or if you take more than 1 minute to read the story, you won't earn any points.
- If you don't earn points the first time you read the story, you can try again. If you succeed the second time you try, you'll earn 3 points.
- (Check the students individually.)
- (Record either 6, 3, or 0 points in Box C.)

Lesson point total

(Tell students to write the point total in the last box at the top of the Workbook page. Maximum = 20 points.)

Point Summary Chart

(Tell students to write this point total in the box for Lesson 54 in the Point Summary Chart.)

END OF LESSON 54

Lesson 55

WORD-ATTACK SKILLS

EXERCISE 1
SOUND INTRODUCTION

1. (Point to **j**:) This letter makes the sound **j**. What sound? (Touch.) *j*.
2. (Point to **o**:) One sound you learned for this letter is the letter name. Everybody, what's that sound? (Touch.) *ōōō*. Yes, **ōōō**.
   - What's the other sound? (Touch.) *ŏŏŏ*. Yes, **ŏŏŏ**.
3. (Point to **e**:) One sound you learned for this letter is the letter name. Everybody, what's that sound? (Touch.) *ēēē*. Yes, **ēēē**.
   - What's the other sound? (Touch.) *ěěě*. Yes, **ěěě**.
4. (Point to **j**:) What sound? (Touch.) *j*. Yes, **j**.
5. (Repeat step 4 for **f, ch, ŭ, y, c, sh, er, l, g**.)

j o e
j f ch
u y
c sh
er l g

Individual test
(Call on two or three students. Touch under each sound. Each student says all the sounds, including two sounds for **o** and two sounds for **e**.)

EXERCISE 2
PRONUNCIATIONS

Task A Sleek, sleet

1. Listen: **sleek** (pause) **sleet**. Say those words. (Signal.) *Sleek, sleet.* (Repeat until firm.)
2. Listen: **sleek** (pause) **sleet**. One of those words means **something that is very smooth**.
   - (Pause.) Which word? (Signal.) *Sleek.* Yes, **sleek**.

To correct:
   a. (Tell the students the word.)
   b. (Repeat step 2.)

3. One of those words means **frozen rain**.
   - (Pause.) Which word? (Signal.) *Sleet.* Yes, **sleet**.
4. (Repeat steps 2 and 3 until firm.)

Task B

1. Listen: **munches**. Say it. (Signal.) *Munches.*
2. Next word: **churned**. Say it. (Signal.) *Churned.*
3. Next word: **dropped**. Say it. (Signal.) *Dropped.*
4. (Repeat the words until firm.)

Task C Cloak, cluck, clack

1. Listen: **cloak, cluck, clack**. Say those words. (Signal.) *Cloak, cluck, clack.* (Repeat until firm.)
2. One of those words has the middle sound **ăăă**. I'll say the words again: **cloak, cluck, clack**.
3. Which word has the middle sound **ăăă**? (Signal.) *Clack.* Yes, **clack**.
   - Which word has the middle sound **ōōō**? (Signal.) *Cloak.* Yes, **cloak**.
   - Which word has the middle sound **ŭŭŭ**? (Signal.) *Cluck.* Yes, **cluck**.

Lesson 55   161

Lesson 55

4. Listen: **clōōōk.** What's the middle sound in the word **cloak?** (Signal.) ōōō. Yes, ōōō.
• Listen: **clŭŭŭck.** What's the middle sound in the word **cluck?** (Signal.) ŭŭŭ. Yes, ŭŭŭ.
• Listen: **clăăăck.** What's the middle sound in the word **clack?** (Signal.) ăăă. Yes, ăăă.
5. (Repeat step 4 until firm.) Good job.

EXERCISE 3
WORD READING THE FAST WAY

1. You're going to read these words the fast way.
2. (For each word: Touch the ball of the arrow. Pause.) What word? (Slash right.)
3. (Repeat each list until firm.)

to

do

better

glad

was

short

help

wishing

letters

lift

list

north

4. (For each word: Touch the ball of the arrow. Pause.) **What word?** (Slash right.)
5. (Repeat each list until firm.)

bolt

drips

frog

said

clipping

stops

black

blush

cold

block

steep

west

her

cats

Lesson 55

Lesson 55

WORKBOOK EXERCISES

Note: Pass out the Workbooks. Direct the students to open to Lesson 55.

(Award 6 points if the group worked well during the word attack. Remind the students of the points they can earn in their Workbook.)

EXERCISE 4
SOUND DICTATION

1. I'll say the sounds. You write the letters in part 1 in your Workbook.
2. First sound. (Pause.) **j.** What sound? (Signal.) *j.*
- Write it in the first blank.
  (Observe students and give feedback.)
3. Next sound. (Pause.) **ēēē.** What sound? (Signal.) *ēēē.*
- Write it.
  (Observe students and give feedback.)
4. (Repeat step 3 for **ĭĭĭ, shshsh, ch, g, b, ŭŭŭ, ōōō, ĭĭĭ, ŏŏŏ, ĕĕĕ.**)
5. (Repeat sounds students had trouble with.)

EXERCISE 5
SPELLING FROM DICTATION

1. Touch part 2. ✓
- You're going to write words that I dictate.
2. First word: **this.** What word? (Signal.) *This.*
- Listen again: **ththth . . . ĭĭĭ . . . sss.** Write it in the first blank.
  (Observe students and give feedback.)
3. Next word: **the.** What word? (Signal.) *The.*
- Listen again: **ththth . . . ēēē.** Write it in the next blank.
  (Observe students and give feedback.)
4. (Repeat step 3 for **when, his, then, ships.**)

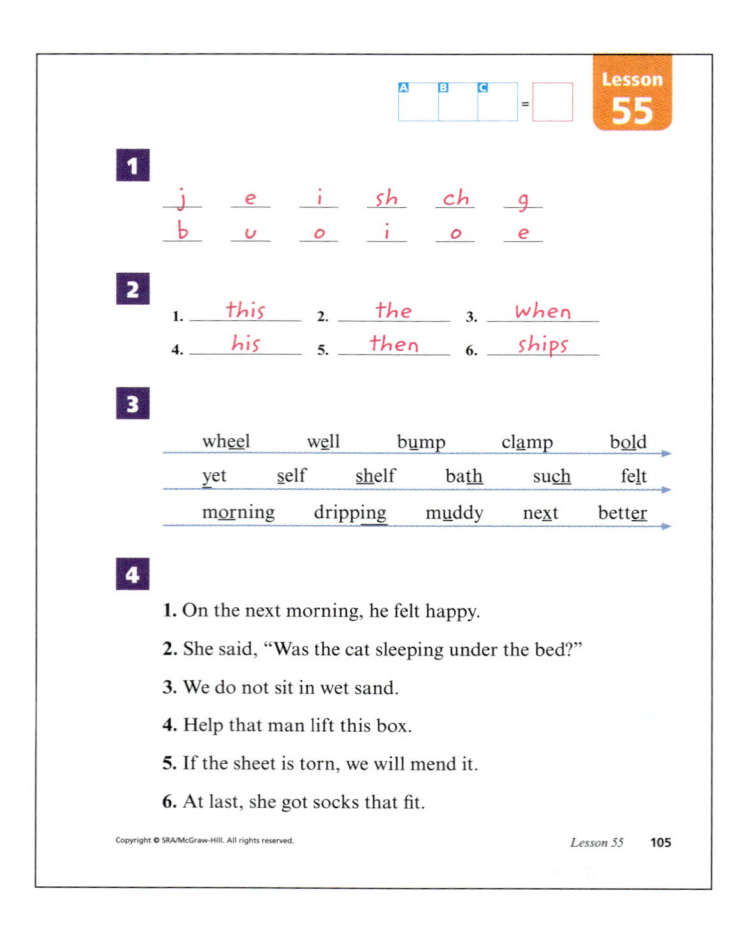

EXERCISE 6
WORD READING: Workbook

1. Touch the first word in part 3. ✓
2. Look at the underlined sound in the first word. (Pause.) What sound? (Signal.) *ēēē.*
- (Pause.) What word? (Signal.) *Wheel.*
3. Next word. (Pause.) What sound? (Signal.) *ĕĕĕ.*
- (Pause.) What word? (Signal.) *Well.*
4. (Repeat step 3 for remaining words.)

164 Lesson 55

Lesson 55

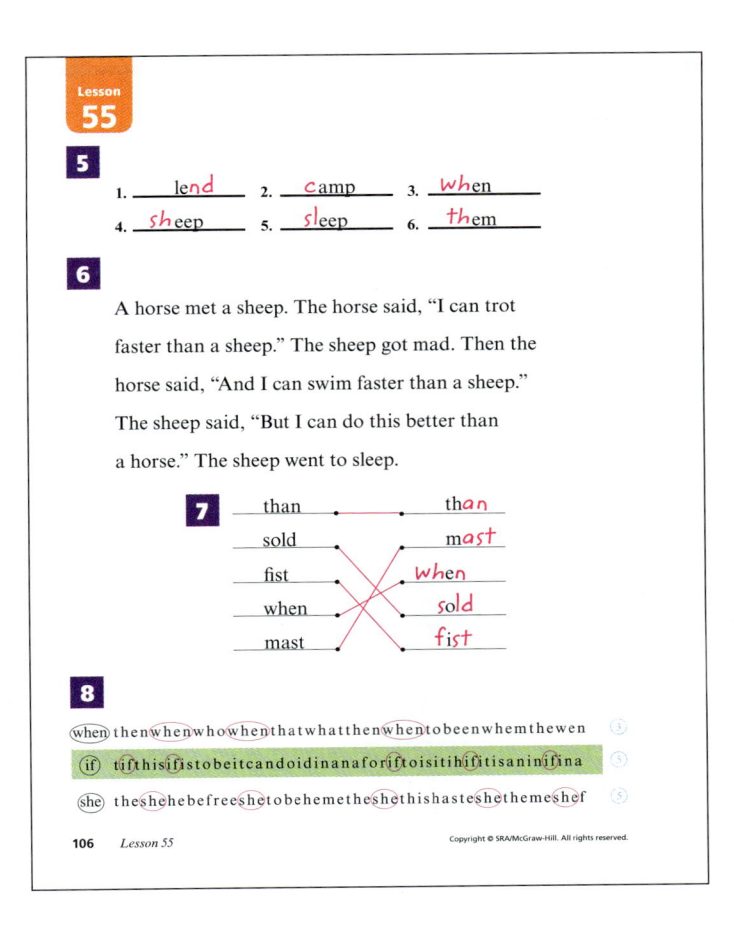

Individual test
(Give each student a chance to read one of the sentences. Praise students who read accurately without long pauses.)

EXERCISE 8
WORD COMPLETION

1. **Touch the first word in part 5.** ✓
   - **Fix it up to say** (pause) **lend. What word?** (Signal.) *Lend.*
   - **Fix it up.**
     (Observe students and give feedback.)
2. **Touch the second word.** ✓
   - **What word?** (Signal.) *amp.* Yes, **amp.**
   - **Fix it up to say** (pause) **camp. What word?** (Signal.) *Camp.*
   - **Fix it up.**
     (Observe students and give feedback.)
3. (Repeat step 2 for **en [when], eep [sheep], eep [sleep], em [them].**)

EXERCISE 7
SENTENCE READING

1. **Everybody, touch sentence 1 in part 4.** ✓
2. **You're going to read the fast way. Read a word each time I clap.**
3. **First word.** ✓
   - **Get ready.** (Clap for each word. Pause about 2 seconds between claps.) *On . . . the . . . next . . . morning, . . . he . . . felt . . . happy.*
4. (Repeat step 3 until the students correctly identify all the words in the sentence in order.)
5. (Repeat steps 3 and 4 for each remaining sentence:
   - **2. She said, "Was the cat sleeping under the bed?"**
   - **3. We do not sit in wet sand.**
   - **4. Help that man lift this box.**
   - **5. If the sheet is torn, we will mend it.**
   - **6. At last, she got socks that fit.**)

EXERCISE 9
STORY READING

Task A

1. **Everybody, touch part 6.** ✓
   - **You're going to read this story.**
2. **First word.** ✓
   - **Get ready.** (Clap for each word. Pause about 2 seconds between claps.) *A . . . horse . . . met . . . a . . . sheep.*
3. (Repeat step 2 until the students correctly identify all the words in the sentence in order.)
4. **Next sentence.** ✓
   - **Get ready.** (Clap for each word:) *The . . . horse . . . said, . . . "I . . . can . . . trot . . . faster . . . than . . . a . . . sheep."*
5. (Repeat step 4 until students correctly identify all the words in the sentence in order.)
6. (Repeat steps 4 and 5 for each remaining sentence.)
7. (If the students miss more than four words, repeat the story reading from the beginning.)

Lesson 55   165

Lesson 55

Task B

1. Now I'll read the story and ask questions. Follow along.
2. **A horse met a sheep. The horse said, "I can trot faster than a sheep."** (Call on a student.) **What did the horse say?** *I can trot faster than a sheep.*
   - **When a horse trots, it runs with its front legs hitting the ground one at a time.**
3. **The sheep got mad.** (Call on a student.) **Why did the sheep get mad?** (Idea: *Because the horse said it could trot faster.*)
4. **Then the horse said, "And I can swim faster than a sheep."** (Call on a student.) **What did the horse say?** *And I can swim faster than a sheep.*
5. **The sheep said, "But I can do this better than a horse." The sheep went to sleep.** (Call on a student.) **What did the sheep say?** *But I can do this better than a horse.*
   - (Call on a student.) **What could the sheep do better than a horse?** (Idea: *Sleep.*)

EXERCISE 10
NEW MATCHING COMPLETION

1. **Everybody, touch part 7.** ✓
2. **First word. What word?** (Signal.) *Than.*
3. **Next word. What word?** (Signal.) *Sold.*
4. (Repeat step 3 for **fist, when, mast.**)
5. **Later, you'll complete the matching words.**

EXERCISE 11
CIRCLE GAME

1. **Everybody, touch part 8.** ✓
2. **What word will you circle in the first line?** (Signal.) *When.*
3. **What word will you circle in the second line?** (Signal.) *If.*
4. **What word will you circle in the third line?** (Signal.) *She.*
5. **Circle the words and finish the rest of your Workbook lesson.**

EXERCISE 12
WORKBOOK CHECK

1. (Check each student's Workbook.)
2. (Award points for Workbook performance.)
3. (Record the student's total points in Box B.)

0–3 errors	8 points
4–5 errors	4 points
6 errors	2 points
7 or more errors	0 points

INDIVIDUAL READING CHECKOUTS

EXERCISE 13
NEW TIMED STORY-READING CHECKOUT

- **Study the story. If you read the story with no more than 3 errors and read it in 1 minute or less, you'll earn 6 points.**
- **If you make more than 3 errors, or if you take more than 1 minute to read the story, you won't earn any points.**
- **If you don't earn points the first time you read the story, you can try again. If you succeed the second time you try, you'll earn 3 points.**
- (Check the students individually.)
- (Record either 6, 3, or 0 points in Box C.)

Lesson point total

(Tell students to write the point total in the last box at the top of the Workbook page. Maximum = 20 points.)

Point Summary Chart

(Tell students to write this point total in the box for Lesson 55 in the Point Summary Chart.)

Five-lesson point summary

(Tell students to add the point totals for Lessons 51 through 55 in the Point Summary Chart and to write the total for Block 11. Maximum for Block 11 = 100 points.)

END OF LESSON 55

MASTERY TEST 12
AFTER LESSON 55, BEFORE LESSON 56

> **Note:** Use students' performance on the Lesson 55 Story reading checkout for Mastery Test 12.

Scoring the test

1. (Count each student's errors on the Story reading checkout. Write these numbers in the Test 12 boxes on the appropriate *Decoding A* Mastery Test Student Profile form. Circle **P** or **F**.)
2. (When all students have been tested, circle **P** or **F** for each student on the *Decoding A* Mastery Test Group Summary form. Determine if more than 25 percent of the students failed the Story reading checkout by dividing the number of students who failed by the total number of students in the group.)

Remedies

(If more than 25 percent of the students fail to earn 6 points for their Story reading checkout, [1] repeat the Story reading checkouts for Lessons 51 through 54, and [2] repeat all of Lesson 55. Permission is granted to reproduce the Workbook pages for Lesson 55 for classroom use.)

Mastery Test 12

Lesson Objectives	LESSON 56 Exercise	LESSON 57 Exercise	LESSON 58 Exercise	LESSON 59 Exercise	LESSON 60 Exercise
Word Attack					
Phonemic Awareness					
Sound/Word Pronunciation	1, 3	1–3	1–3	1, 2	1, 2
Identify Sounds in Words	2, 3	2, 3	2, 3	2	2
Decoding and Word Analysis					
Letter Sounds: v, ē, ĕ, ō, ŏ, s, r, a, f, w, j, b, p, g, th, d	1				
Letter Sounds: v, ō, ŏ, ē, ĕ, x, wh, er, i, d, b, ing, y, f, ch		1			
Letter Sounds: ō, ŏ, ē, ĕ, t, j, s, ch, ck, sh, u, p, d, a			1		
Letter Sounds: z, ō, ŏ, ē, ĕ, wh, er, j, v, c, b, l, d, u				1	
Letter Sounds: z, ē, ĕ, ō, ŏ, th, m, n, h, v, z, x, u, i, y					1
Word Recognition	2, 4	2, 4	3, 4	3	3
High-Frequency Words	2	2	3		
Assessment					
Ongoing: Individual Tests	1	1	1	1	1
Group Reading					
Decoding and Word Analysis					
Read Decodable Text	10	10	10	9	9
Comprehension					
Make Predictions		10			
Access Prior Knowledge		10			
Draw Inferences	10	10	10	9	9
Note Details	10	10	10	9	9
Assessment					
Ongoing: Comprehension Check	10	10	10	9	9
Ongoing: Decoding Accuracy	10	10	10	9	9
Formal: Mastery Test					MT 13
Workbook Exercises					
Decoding and Word Analysis					
Word Recognition	7	7	7	6	6
Sentence Reading	8	8	8	7	7
Sound Combinations	7	7	7	6	6
Spelling: Sound/Letter Relationships	5, 9, 11	5, 9, 11	5, 9, 11	4, 8, 10	4, 8, 10
Spelling: CV, CVC, CVCC, CVVC	6				
Spelling: CVC, CCVC, CVVC		6			
Spelling: CVC, CCVC			6		
Spelling: VC, CVC, CVCC, CCVC, CVVCC				5	
Spelling: VC, CVC, CVV, CCVC					5
Visual Discrimination	11, 12	11, 12	11, 12	10, 11	10, 11
Assessment					
Ongoing: Individual Tests	8, 14	8, 14	8, 14	7, 13	7, 13
Ongoing: Teacher-Monitored Accuracy	14	14	14	13	13
Ongoing: Teacher-Monitored Fluency	14	14	14	13	13
Ongoing: Workcheck	13	13	13	12	12

Lessons 56–60

Objectives

Lesson 56

WORD-ATTACK SKILLS

EXERCISE 1
SOUND INTRODUCTION

1. (Point to **v**:) This letter makes the sound **vvv**. What sound? (Touch.) *vvv*.
2. (Point to **e**:) One sound you learned for this letter is the letter name. Everybody, what's that sound? (Touch.) *ēēē*. Yes, *ēēē*.
   - What's the other sound? (Touch.) *ĕĕĕ*. Yes, *ĕĕĕ*.
3. (Point to **o**:) One sound you learned for this letter is the letter name. Everybody, what's that sound? (Touch.) *ōōō*. Yes, *ōōō*.
   - What's the other sound? (Touch.) *ŏŏŏ*. Yes, *ŏŏŏ*.
4. (Point to **s**:) What sound? (Touch.) *sss*. Yes, *sss*.
5. (Repeat step 4 for **r, ă, f, w, j, b, p, g, th, d**.)

v e o
s r a
f w j
b p g
th d

Individual test
(Call on two or three students. Touch under each sound. Each student says all the sounds, including two sounds for **e** and two sounds for **o**.)

EXERCISE 2
IRREGULAR WORDS

Task A Of

1. (Touch the ball of the arrow for **of**:) Sound out this word. Get ready. (Touch under **o, f**:) *ŏŏŏfff*. (Repeat until the students say the sounds without pausing.)
2. That's how we sound out the word. But here's how we say the word: **uv**. It's a funny word. How do we say the word? (Signal.) *Uv*.
3. Sound it out. Get ready. (Touch under **o, f**:) *ŏŏŏfff*. (Repeat until firm.)
4. Everybody, say the word. (Signal.) *Uv*. Yes, **uv**. Remember that word.

of

Task B You

1. (Touch the ball of the arrow for **you**:) Sound out this word. Get ready. (Touch under **y, o, u**:) *yēēēŏŏŏŭŭŭ*. (Repeat until the students say the sounds without pausing.)
2. That's how we sound out the word. But here's how we say the word: **yue**. It's a funny word. How do we say the word? (Signal.) *Yue*.
3. Sound it out. Get ready. (Touch under **y, o, u**:) *yēēēŏŏŏŭŭŭ*. (Repeat until firm.)
4. Everybody, say the word. (Signal.) *Yue*. Yes, **yue**. Remember that word.

you

Lesson 56

Task C What

1. (Touch the ball of the arrow for **what:**) Sound out this word. Get ready. (Touch under **wh, a, t:**) *wwwăăăt*. (Repeat until the students say the sounds without pausing.)
2. That's how we sound out the word. But here's how we say the word: **wut.** It's a funny word. How do we say the word? (Signal.) *Wut.*
3. Sound it out. Get ready. (Touch under **wh, a, t:**) *wwwăăăt*. (Repeat until firm.)
4. Everybody, say the word. (Signal.) *Wut.* Yes, **wut.** Remember that word.

what

Task C Fell, fill, feel

1. Listen: **fell, fill, feel.** Say those words. (Signal.) *Fell, fill, feel.* (Repeat until firm.)
2. One of those words has the middle sound **ĕĕĕ.** I'll say the words again: **fell, fill, feel.**
3. Which word has the middle sound **ĕĕĕ?** (Signal.) *Fell.* Yes, **fell.**
- Which word has the middle sound **ēēē?** (Signal.) *Feel.* Yes, **feel.**
- Which word has the middle sound **ĭĭĭ?** (Signal.) *Fill.* Yes, **fill.**
4. Listen: **fĕĕĕll.** What's the middle sound in the word **fell?** (Signal.) *ĕĕĕ.* Yes, **ĕĕĕ.**
- Listen: **fĭĭĭll.** What's the middle sound in the word **fill?** (Signal.) *ĭĭĭ.* Yes, **ĭĭĭ.**
- Listen: **fēēēl.** What's the middle sound in the word **feel?** (Signal.) *ēēē.* Yes, **ēēē.**
5. (Repeat step 4 until firm.) Good job.

EXERCISE 3
PRONUNCIATIONS

> **Note:** Do not write the words on the board. This is an oral exercise.

Task A Sack, sap

1. Listen: **sack** (pause) **sap.** Say those words. (Signal.) *Sack, sap.* (Repeat until firm.)
2. Listen: **sack** (pause) **sap.** One of those words means **sticky stuff that comes from trees.**
- (Pause.) Which word? (Signal.) *Sap.* Yes, **sap.**
3. One of those words means **a bag.**
- (Pause.) Which word? (Signal.) *Sack.* Yes, **sack.**
4. (Repeat steps 2 and 3 until firm.)

Task B

1. Listen: **masts.** Say it. (Signal.) *Masts.*
2. Next word: **lunches.** Say it. (Signal.) *Lunches.*
3. (Repeat step 2 for **feasts, stopped.**)
4. (Repeat the words until firm.)

170 Lesson 56

EXERCISE 4
WORD READING THE FAST WAY

1. You're going to read these words the fast way.
2. (For each word: Touch the ball of the arrow. Pause.) What word? (Slash right.)
3. (Repeat the column until firm.)

flag

to

shelf

do

flips

not

stand

said

sold

fell

was

such

tax

job

Lesson 56

4. (For each word: Touch the ball of the arrow. Pause.) **What word?** (Slash right.)
5. (Repeat each list until firm.)

jump

down

fix

jam

feel

town

plants

jumping

north

WORKBOOK EXERCISES

Note: Pass out the Workbooks. Direct the students to open to Lesson 56.

(Award 6 points if the group worked well during the word attack. Remind the students of the points they can earn in their Workbook.)

EXERCISE 5
SOUND DICTATION

1. **I'll say the sounds. You write the letters in part 1 in your Workbook.**
2. **First sound.** (Pause.) **lll. What sound?** (Signal.) *lll.*
   - **Write it in the first blank.**
     (Observe students and give feedback.)
3. **Next sound.** (Pause.) **j. What sound?** (Signal.) *j.*
   - **Write it.**
     (Observe students and give feedback.)
4. (Repeat step 3 for **kss [x], ch, ēēē, ŭŭŭ, rrr, shshsh, ĕĕĕ, ŏŏŏ, ĭĭĭ, ch.**)
5. (Repeat sounds students had trouble with.)

EXERCISE 6
SPELLING FROM DICTATION

1. **Touch part 2.** ✓
   - **You're going to write words that I dictate.**
2. **First word: rims. What word?** (Signal.) *Rims.*
   - **Listen again: rrr . . . ĭĭĭ . . . mmm . . . sss. Write it in the first blank.**
     (Observe students and give feedback.)
3. **Next word: seen. What word?** (Signal.) *Seen.*
   - **Listen again: sss . . . ēēē . . . nnn. Write it in the next blank.**
     (Observe students and give feedback.)
4. (Repeat step 3 for **dad, cans, he, bad, his.**)

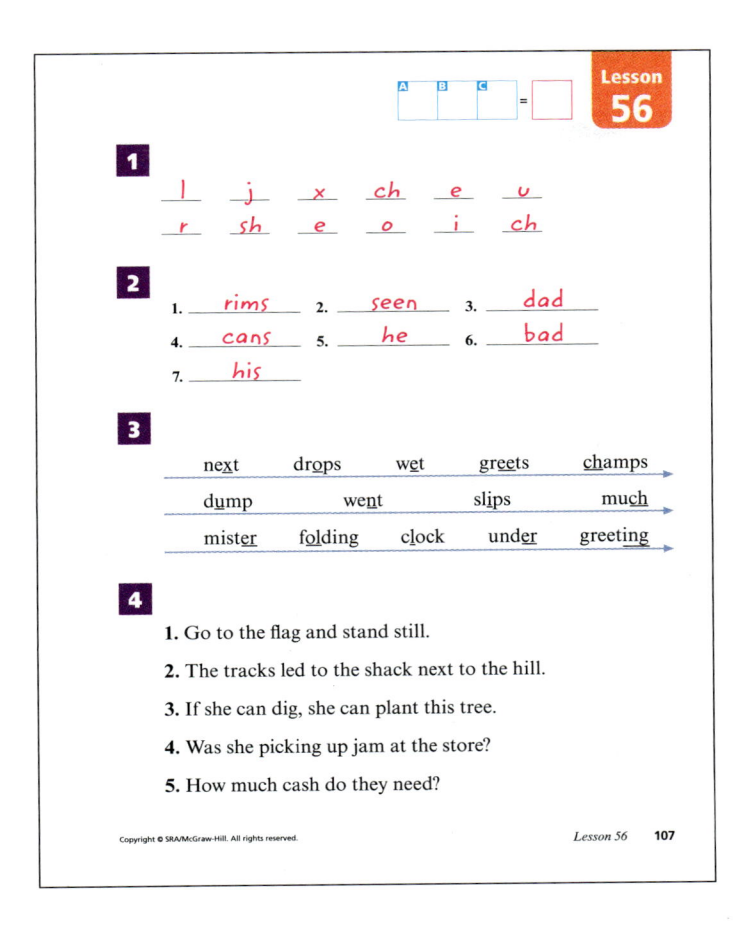

Lesson 56

Workbook Page (Lesson 56, p. 107)

1.
l j x ch e u
r sh e o i ch

2.
1. rims   2. seen   3. dad
4. cans   5. he   6. bad
7. his

3.
ne<u>x</u>t   dr<u>o</u>ps   w<u>e</u>t   gr<u>ee</u>ts   <u>ch</u>amps
d<u>u</u>mp   we<u>n</u>t   sli<u>p</u>s   mu<u>ch</u>
mist<u>er</u>   f<u>o</u>lding   <u>cl</u>ock   und<u>er</u>   greet<u>ing</u>

4.
1. Go to the flag and stand still.
2. The tracks led to the shack next to the hill.
3. If she can dig, she can plant this tree.
4. Was she picking up jam at the store?
5. How much cash do they need?

EXERCISE 7
WORD READING: Workbook

1. Touch the first word in part 3. ✓
2. Look at the underlined sound in the first word. (Pause.) What sound? (Signal.) *kss.*
- (Pause.) What word? (Signal.) *Next.*
3. Next word. (Pause.) What sound? (Signal.) *ŏŏŏ.*
- (Pause.) What word? (Signal.) *Drops.*
4. (Repeat step 3 for remaining words.)

EXERCISE 8
SENTENCE READING

1. Everybody, touch sentence 1 in part 4. ✓
2. You're going to read the fast way. Read a word each time I clap.
3. First word. ✓
- Get ready. (Clap for each word. Pause about 2 seconds between claps.) *Go . . . to . . . the . . . flag . . . and . . . stand . . . still.*
4. (Repeat step 3 until the students correctly identify all the words in the sentence in order.)
5. (Repeat steps 3 and 4 for each remaining sentence.)

Individual test
(Give each student a chance to read one of the sentences. Praise students who read accurately without long pauses.)

EXERCISE 9
WORD COMPLETION

1. Touch the first word in part 5. ✓
- Fix it up to say (pause) **fills.** What word? (Signal.) *Fills.*
- Fix it up.
(Observe students and give feedback.)
2. Touch the second word. ✓
- What word? (Signal.) *eep.* Yes, **eep.**
- Fix it up to say (pause) **sleep.** What word? (Signal.) *Sleep.*
- Fix it up.
(Observe students and give feedback.)
3. (Repeat step 2 for **ap [trap], en [when], fee [feels], la [lash].**)

Lesson 56

EXERCISE 10
STORY READING

Task A

1. Everybody, touch part 6. ✓
   - You're going to read this story.
2. First word. ✓
   - Get ready. (Clap for each word. Pause about 2 seconds between claps.) *Ann . . . was . . . a . . . winner . . . on . . . the . . . track.*
3. (Repeat step 2 until the students correctly identify all the words in the sentence in order.)
4. Next sentence. ✓
   - Get ready. (Clap for each word:) *And . . . she . . . was . . . the . . . best . . . singer . . . in . . . town.*
5. (Repeat step 4 until students correctly identify all the words in the sentence in order.)
6. (Repeat steps 4 and 5 for each remaining sentence.)
7. (If the students miss more than four words, repeat the story reading from the beginning.)

Task B

1. Now I'll read the story and ask questions. Follow along.
2. **Ann was a winner on the track. And she was the best singer in town.** (Call on a student.) What are the two things that Ann could do well? (Idea: *Win on the track and sing.*)
3. **She said to her self, "I need cash. I can get a job running or a job singing."** Listen again: **She said to her self, "I need cash. I can get a job running or a job singing."** (Call on a student.) Tell me everything Ann said to herself. *I need cash. I can get a job running or a job singing.*
4. **She got the best job. She is the singer at track meets, and she is glad.** (Call on a student.) What does she do? (Idea: *Sings at track meets.*)
   - (Call on a student.) Why is that the best job for her? (Idea: *She likes track and singing.*)

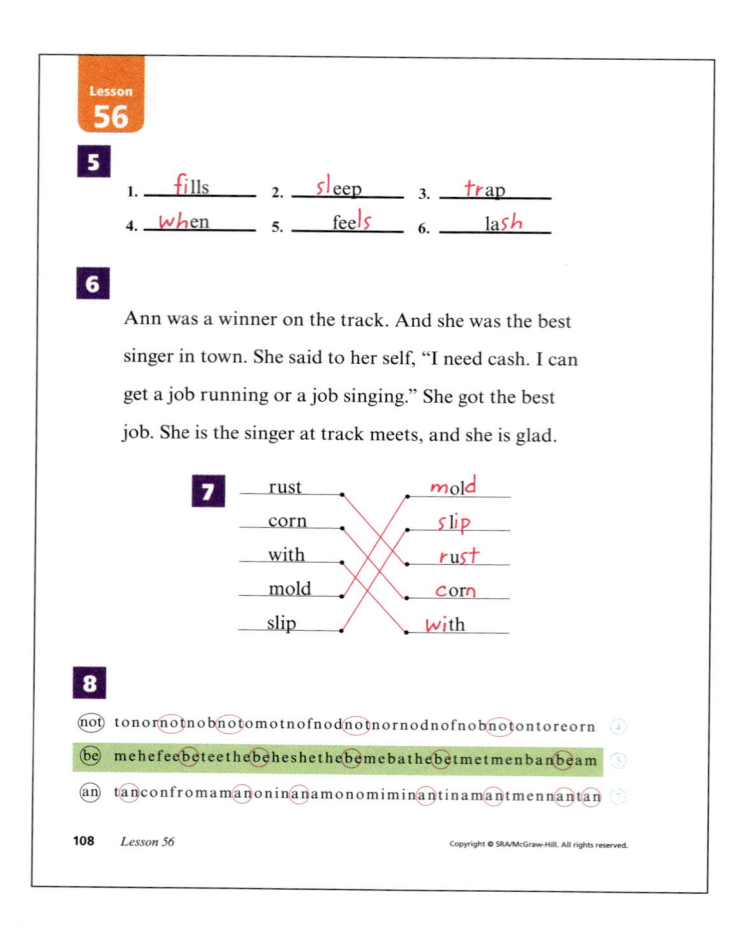

EXERCISE 11
MATCHING COMPLETION

1. Everybody, touch part 7. ✓
2. First word. What word? (Signal.) *Rust.*
3. Next word. What word? (Signal.) *Corn.*
4. (Repeat step 3 for **with, mold, slip.**)
5. Later, you'll complete the matching words.

174   Lesson 56

Lesson 56

EXERCISE 12
CIRCLE GAME

1. Everybody, touch part 8. ✓
2. What word will you circle in the first line? (Signal.) *Not.*
3. What word will you circle in the second line? (Signal.) *Be.*
4. What word will you circle in the third line? (Signal.) *An.*
5. Circle the words and finish the rest of your Workbook lesson.

EXERCISE 13
WORKBOOK CHECK

1. (Check each student's Workbook.)
2. (Award points for Workbook performance.)
3. (Record the student's total points in Box B.)

0–3 errors	8 points
4–5 errors	4 points
6 errors	2 points
7 or more errors	0 points

INDIVIDUAL READING CHECKOUTS

EXERCISE 14
TIMED STORY-READING CHECKOUT

- Study the story. If you read the story with no more than 3 errors and read it in 1 minute or less, you'll earn 6 points.
- If you make more than 3 errors, or if you take more than 1 minute to read the story, you won't earn any points.
- If you don't earn points the first time you read the story, you can try again. If you succeed the second time you try, you'll earn 3 points.
- (Check the students individually.)
- (Record either 6, 3, or 0 points in Box C.)

Lesson point total
(Tell students to write the point total in the last box at the top of the Workbook page. Maximum = 20 points.)

Point Summary Chart
(Tell students to write this point total in the box for Lesson 56 in the Point Summary Chart.)

END OF LESSON 56

Lesson 57

WORD-ATTACK SKILLS

EXERCISE 1
SOUND INTRODUCTION

1. (Point to **v**:) This letter makes the sound **vvv**. What sound? (Touch.) *vvv*.
2. (Point to **o**:) One sound you learned for this letter is the letter name. Everybody, what's that sound? (Touch.) *ōōō*. Yes, *ōōō*.
- What's the other sound? (Touch.) *ŏŏŏ*. Yes, *ŏŏŏ*.
3. (Point to **e**:) One sound you learned for this letter is the letter name. Everybody, what's that sound? (Touch.) *ēēē*. Yes, *ēēē*.
- What's the other sound? (Touch.) *ĕĕĕ*. Yes, *ĕĕĕ*.
4. (Point to **v**:) What sound? (Touch.) *vvv*. Yes, **vvv**.
5. (Repeat step 4 for **x, wh, er, ĭ, d, b, ing, y, f, ch**.)

v o e

v x wh

er i d

b ing

y f ch

Individual test
(Call on two or three students. Touch under each sound. Each student says all the sounds, including two sounds for **o** and two sounds for **e**.)

EXERCISE 2
IRREGULAR WORDS

Task A You

1. (Touch the ball of the arrow for **you**:) Sound out this word. Get ready. (Touch under **y, o, u**:) *yēēēŏŏŏŭŭŭ*. (Repeat until the students say the sounds without pausing.)
2. That's how we sound out the word. But how do we say the word? (Signal.) *Yue*.
3. Sound it out. Get ready. (Touch under **y, o, u**:) *yēēēŏŏŏŭŭŭ*. (Repeat until firm.)
4. Everybody, say the word. (Signal.) *Yue*. Yes, **yue**. Remember that word.

you

Task B Of

1. (Touch the ball of the arrow for **of**:) Sound out this word. Get ready. (Touch under **o, f**:) *ŏŏŏfff*. (Repeat until the students say the sounds without pausing.)
2. That's how we sound out the word. But how do we say the word? (Signal.) *Uv*.
3. Sound it out. Get ready. (Touch under **o, f**:) *ŏŏŏfff*. (Repeat until firm.)
4. Everybody, say the word. (Signal.) *Uv*. Yes, **uv**. Remember that word.

of

Lesson 57

Task C What

1. (Touch the ball of the arrow for **what:**) Sound out this word. Get ready. (Touch under **wh, a, t:**) *wwwăăăt.* (Repeat until the students say the sounds without pausing.)
2. That's how we sound out the word. But how do we say the word? (Signal.) *Wut.*
3. Sound it out. Get ready. (Touch under **wh, a, t:**) *wwwăăăt.* (Repeat until firm.)
4. Everybody, say the word. (Signal.) *Wut.* Yes, **wut.** Remember that word.

what

EXERCISE 3
PRONUNCIATIONS

Task A Sleep, sleet, sleek

1. Listen: **sleep, sleet, sleek.** Say those words. (Signal.) *Sleep, sleet, sleek.* (Repeat until firm.)
2. Listen: **sleep, sleet, sleek.** One of those words means **something that is very smooth.**
- (Pause.) Which word? (Signal.) *Sleek.* Yes, **sleek.**
3. One of those words means **something you do when you're tired.**
- (Pause.) Which word? (Signal.) *Sleep.* Yes, **sleep.**
4. One of those words means **frozen rain.**
- (Pause.) Which word? (Signal.) *Sleet.* Yes, **sleet.**
5. (Repeat steps 2–4 until firm.)

Task B

1. Listen: **lasted.** Say it. (Signal.) *Lasted.*
2. Next word: **didn't.** Say it. (Signal.) *Didn't.*
3. (Repeat step 2 for **beasts, every.**)
4. (Repeat the words until firm.)

Task C Must, mist, mast

1. Listen: **must, mist, mast.** Say those words. (Signal.) *Must, mist, mast.* (Repeat until firm.)
2. One of those words has the middle sound **ĭĭĭ.** I'll say the words again: **must, mist, mast.**
3. Which word has the middle sound **ĭĭĭ**? (Signal.) *Mist.* Yes, **mist.**
- Which word has the middle sound **ŭŭŭ**? (Signal.) *Must.* Yes, **must.**
- Which word has the middle sound **ăăă**? (Signal.) *Mast.* Yes, **mast.**
4. Listen: **mŭŭŭst.** What's the middle sound in the word **must**? (Signal.) *ŭŭŭ.* Yes, **ŭŭŭ.**
- Listen: **mĭĭĭst.** What's the middle sound in the word **mist**? (Signal.) *ĭĭĭ.* Yes, **ĭĭĭ.**
- Listen: **măăăst.** What's the middle sound in the word **mast**? (Signal.) *ăăă.* Yes, **ăăă.**
5. (Repeat step 4 until firm.) Good job.

EXERCISE 4
WORD READING THE FAST WAY

1. You're going to read these words the fast way.
2. (For each word: Touch the ball of the arrow. Pause.) What word? (Slash right.)
3. (Repeat the column until firm.)

class

horn

was

Lesson 57

4. (For each word: Touch the ball of the arrow. Pause.) What word? (Slash right.)
5. (Repeat each list until firm.)

glad

pants

desk

do

said

jelly

grins

next

help

cuts

tops

sending

grab

letter

much

chips

WORKBOOK EXERCISES

Note: Pass out the Workbooks. Direct the students to open to Lesson 57.

(Award 6 points if the group worked well during the word attack. Remind the students of the points they can earn in their Workbook.)

EXERCISE 5
SOUND DICTATION

1. I'll say the sounds. You write the letters in part 1 in your Workbook.
2. First sound. (Pause.) **vvv.** What sound? (Signal.) *vvv.*
- Write it in the first blank.
 (Observe students and give feedback.)
3. Next sound. Write a letter that says **www.**
 (Observe students and give feedback.)
4. Next sound. Write two letters that go together and say **www.**
 (Observe students and give feedback.)
5. Next sound. (Pause.) **ŭŭŭ.** What sound? (Signal.) *ŭŭŭ.*
- Write it.
 (Observe students and give feedback.)
6. (Repeat step 5 for **ch, ōōō, ăăă, ĭĭĭ, shshsh, sss, h, ĕĕĕ.**)
7. (Repeat sounds students had trouble with.)

EXERCISE 6
SPELLING FROM DICTATION

1. Touch part 2. ✓
- You're going to write words that I dictate.
2. First word: **red.** What word? (Signal.) *Red.*
- Listen again: **rrr . . . ĕĕĕ . . . d.** Write it in the first blank.
 (Observe students and give feedback.)
3. Next word: **met.** What word? (Signal.) *Met.*
- Listen again: **mmm . . . ĕĕĕ . . . t.** Write it in the next blank.
 (Observe students and give feedback.)
4. (Repeat step 3 for **meet, that, his, when, this.**)

Lesson 57

Lesson 57 Workbook

1
v	w	wh	u	ch	o
a	i	sh	s	h	e

2
1. red 2. met 3. meet
4. that 5. his 6. when
7. this

3
clash	lift	west	lunch	singer
flip	slipping	rust	crust	north
licks	winning	jumps	champ	clamp

4
1. He told me, "Do not go to class."
2. How steep is that hill?
3. We must plant more corn seeds.
4. Do they need help with that horse?
5. How fast can she cut the grass?
6. She said, "Do not set that pen on the desk."

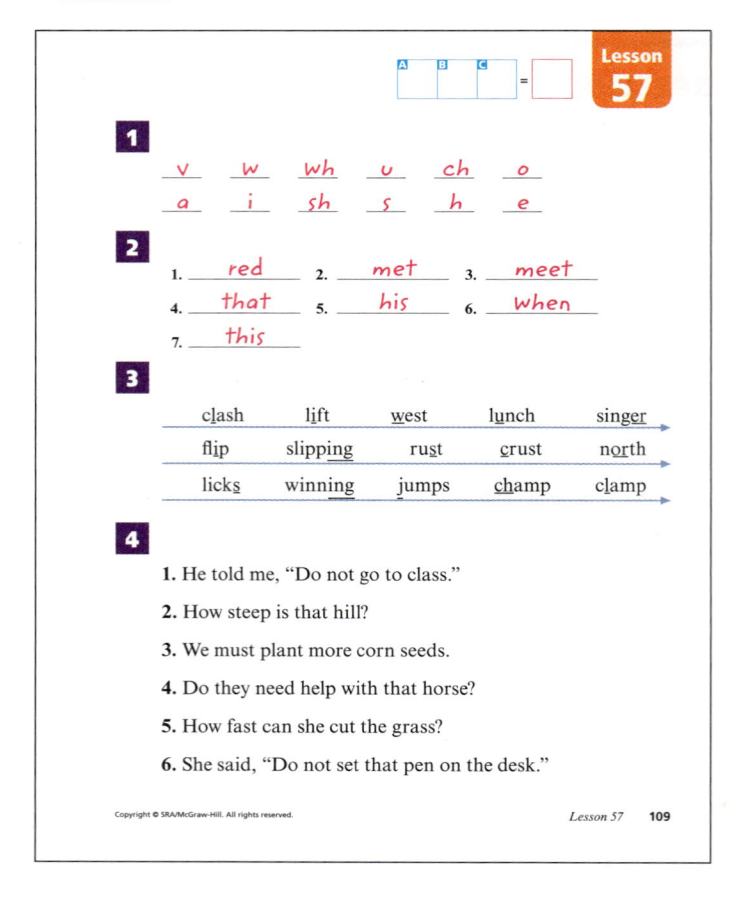

EXERCISE 7
WORD READING: Workbook

1. Touch the first word in part 3. ✓
2. Look at the underlined sound in the first word. (Pause.) What sound? (Signal.) *lll.*
• (Pause.) What word? (Signal.) *Clash.*
3. Next word. (Pause.) What sound? (Signal.) *ĭĭĭ.*
• (Pause.) What word? (Signal.) *Lift.*
4. (Repeat step 3 for remaining words.)

EXERCISE 8
SENTENCE READING

1. Everybody, touch sentence 1 in part 4. ✓
2. You're going to read the fast way. Read a word each time I clap.
3. First word. ✓
• Get ready. (Clap for each word. Pause about 2 seconds between claps.) *He . . . told . . . me, . . . "Do . . . not . . . go . . . to . . . class."*
4. (Repeat step 3 until the students correctly identify all the words in the sentence in order.)
5. (Repeat steps 3 and 4 for each remaining sentence:
• **2. How steep is that hill?**
• **3. We must plant more corn seeds.**
• **4. Do they need help with that horse?**
• **5. How fast can she cut the grass?**
• **6. She said, "Do not set that pen on the desk."**)

Individual test
(Give each student a chance to read one of the sentences. Praise students who read accurately without long pauses.)

EXERCISE 9
WORD COMPLETION

1. Touch the first word in part 5. ✓
- Fix it up to say (pause) **fist.** What word? (Signal.) *Fist.*
- Fix it up.
  (Observe students and give feedback.)
2. Touch the second word. ✓
- Fix it up to say (pause) **with.** What word? (Signal.) *With.*
- Fix it up.
  (Observe students and give feedback.)
3. (Repeat step 2 for **then, cats, went, slip.**)

EXERCISE 10
STORY READING

Task A

1. Everybody, touch part 6. ✓
- You're going to read this story.
2. First word. ✓
- Get ready. (Clap for each word. Pause about 2 seconds between claps.) *Bud . . . and . . . Al . . . went . . . on . . . a . . . trip.*
3. (Repeat step 2 until the students correctly identify all the words in the sentence in order.)
4. Next sentence. ✓
- Get ready. (Clap for each word:) *Al . . . said, . . . "We . . . will . . . stop . . . for . . . lunch."*
5. (Repeat step 4 until students correctly identify all the words in the sentence in order.)
6. (Repeat steps 4 and 5 for each remaining sentence.)
7. (If the students miss more than four words, repeat the story reading from the beginning.)

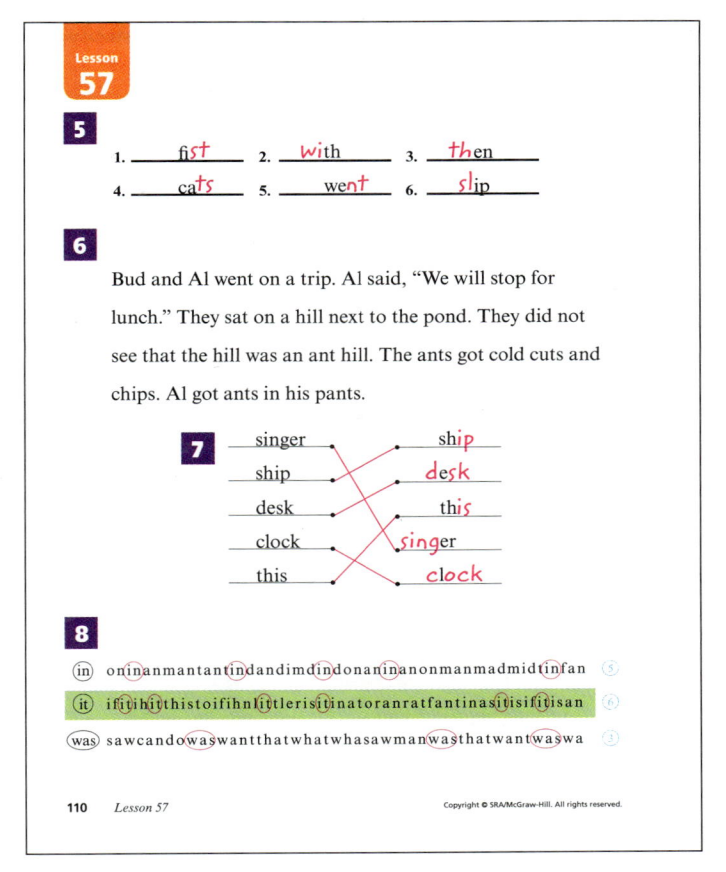

Task B

1. Now I'll read the story and ask questions. Follow along.
2. **Bud and Al went on a trip. Al said, "We will stop for lunch."** (Call on a student.) What did Al say? *We will stop for lunch.*
- (Call on a student.) What time of day do you think it was? (Idea: *Around noon.*)
3. **They sat on a hill next to the pond. They did not see that the hill was an ant hill.** (Call on a student.) What kind of hill did they sit on? *An ant hill.*
- (Call on a student.) What is an ant hill? (Idea: *A small hill in the ground made by ants to live in.*)
4. **The ants got cold cuts and chips. Al got ants in his pants.** (Call on a student.) What did the ants get? *Cold cuts and chips.*
- (Call on a student.) Where did those cold cuts and chips come from? (Idea: *From Bud and Al's lunch.*)
- (Call on a student.) What did Al get? (Idea: *Ants in his pants.*)
- (Call on a student.) How do you think that felt? (Accept a reasonable response.)

Lesson 57   181

Lesson 57

EXERCISE 11
MATCHING COMPLETION

1. Everybody, touch part 7. ✓
2. First word. What word? (Signal.) *Singer.*
3. Next word. What word? (Signal.) *Ship.*
4. (Repeat step 3 for **desk, clock, this.**)
5. Later, you'll complete the matching words.

EXERCISE 12
CIRCLE GAME

1. Everybody, touch part 8. ✓
2. What word will you circle in the first line? (Signal.) *In.*
3. What word will you circle in the second line? (Signal.) *It.*
4. What word will you circle in the third line? (Signal.) *Was.*
5. Circle the words and finish the rest of your Workbook lesson.

EXERCISE 13
WORKBOOK CHECK

1. (Check each student's Workbook.)
2. (Award points for Workbook performance.)
3. (Record the student's total points in Box B.)

0–3 errors	8 points
4–5 errors	4 points
6 errors	2 points
7 or more errors	0 points

INDIVIDUAL READING CHECKOUTS

EXERCISE 14
TIMED STORY-READING CHECKOUT

- Study the story. If you read the story with no more than 3 errors and read it in 1 minute or less, you'll earn 6 points.
- If you make more than 3 errors, or if you take more than 1 minute to read the story, you won't earn any points.
- If you don't earn points the first time you read the story, you can try again. If you succeed the second time you try, you'll earn 3 points.
- (Check the students individually.)
- (Record either 6, 3, or 0 points in Box C.)

Lesson point total

(Tell students to write the point total in the last box at the top of the Workbook page. Maximum = 20 points.)

Point Summary Chart

(Tell students to write this point total in the box for Lesson 57 in the Point Summary Chart.)

END OF LESSON 57

Lesson 58

WORD-ATTACK SKILLS

EXERCISE 1
SOUND IDENTIFICATION

1. (Point to **o**:) One sound you learned for this letter is the letter name. Everybody, what's that sound? (Touch.) *ōōō.* Yes, **ōōō.**
- What's the other sound? (Touch.) *ŏŏŏ.* Yes, **ŏŏŏ.**
2. (Point to **e**:) One sound you learned for this letter is the letter name. Everybody, what's that sound? (Touch.) *ēēē.* Yes, **ēēē.**
- What's the other sound? (Touch.) *ĕĕĕ.* Yes, **ĕĕĕ.**
3. (Point to **t**:) What sound? (Touch.) *t.* Yes, **t.**
4. (Repeat step 3 for **j, s, ch, ck, sh, ŭ, p, d, ă**.)

o e t j
s ch
ck sh u
p d a

> **Individual test**
> (Call on two or three students. Touch under each sound. Each student says all the sounds, including two sounds for **o** and two sounds for **e**.)

EXERCISE 2
PRONUNCIATIONS

Task A Sat, sap, sack
1. Listen: **sat, sap, sack.** Say those words. (Signal.) *Sat, sap, sack.* (Repeat until firm.)
2. Listen: **sat, sap, sack.** One of those words means **a bag.**
- (Pause.) Which word? (Signal.) *Sack.* Yes, **sack.**
3. One of those words means **an action that somebody did.**
- (Pause.) Which word? (Signal.) *Sat.* Yes, **sat.**
4. One of those words means **the sticky stuff that comes from trees.**
- (Pause.) Which word? (Signal.) *Sap.* Yes, **sap.**
5. (Repeat steps 2–4 until firm.)

Task B
1. Listen: **even.** Say it. (Signal.) *Even.*
2. Next word: **rested.** Say it. (Signal.) *Rested.*
3. Next word: **licked.** Say it. (Signal.) *Licked.*
4. (Repeat the words until firm.)

Task C Tell, teal, toll
1. Listen: **tell, teal, toll.** Say those words. (Signal.) *Tell, teal, toll.* (Repeat until firm.)
2. One of those words has the middle sound **ōōō.** I'll say the words again: **tell, teal, toll.**
3. Which word has the middle sound **ōōō**? (Signal.) *Toll.* Yes, **toll.**
- Which word has the middle sound **ĕĕĕ**? (Signal.) *Tell.* Yes, **tell.**
- Which word has the middle sound **ēēē**? (Signal.) *Teal.* Yes, **teal.**
4. Listen: **tĕĕĕll.** What's the middle sound in the word **tell**? (Signal.) *ĕĕĕ.* Yes, **ĕĕĕ.**
- Listen: **tēēēl.** What's the middle sound in the word **teal**? (Signal.) *ēēē.* Yes, **ēēē.**
- Listen: **tōōōll.** What's the middle sound in the word **toll**? (Signal.) *ōōō.* Yes, **ōōō.**
5. (Repeat step 4 until firm.) Good job.

Lesson 58

Lesson 58

EXERCISE 3
IRREGULAR WORDS

Task A What

1. (Touch the ball of the arrow for **what:**) Sound out this word. Get ready. (Touch under **wh, a, t:**) *wwwăăăt.* (Repeat until the students say the sounds without pausing.)
2. That's how we sound out the word. But how do we say the word? (Signal.) *Wut.*
3. Sound it out. Get ready. (Touch under **wh, a, t:**) *wwwăăăt.* (Repeat until firm.)
4. Everybody, say the word. (Signal.) *Wut.* Yes, **wut.** Remember that word.

what

Task B You

1. (Touch the ball of the arrow for **you:**) Sound out this word. Get ready. (Touch under **y, o, u:**) *yēēēŏŏŏŭŭŭ.* (Repeat until the students say the sounds without pausing.)
2. That's how we sound out the word. But how do we say the word? (Signal.) *Yue.*
3. Sound it out. Get ready. (Touch under **y, o, u:**) *yēēēŏŏŏŭŭŭ.* (Repeat until firm.)
4. Everybody, say the word. (Signal.) *Yue.* Yes, **yue.** Remember that word.

you

Task C Of

1. (Touch the ball of the arrow for **of:**) Sound out this word. Get ready. (Touch under **o, f:**) *ŏŏŏfff.* (Repeat until the students say the sounds without pausing.)
2. That's how we sound out the word. But how do we say the word? (Signal.) *Uv.*
3. Sound it out. Get ready. (Touch under **o, f:**) *ŏŏŏfff.* (Repeat until firm.)
4. Everybody, say the word. (Signal.) *Uv.* Yes, **uv.** Remember that word.

of

EXERCISE 4
WORD READING THE FAST WAY

1. You're going to read these words the fast way.
2. (For each word: Touch the ball of the arrow. Pause.) What word? (Slash right.)
3. (Repeat the column until firm.)

seeds

send

grabs

born

sled

do

ship

Lesson 58

4. (For each word: Touch the ball of the arrow. Pause.) **What word?** (Slash right.)
5. (Repeat each list until firm.)

to

chip

next

was

told

last

jets

fast

left

swims

sunny

van

very

lunch

shelf

hub

Lesson 58

WORKBOOK EXERCISES

> **Note:** Pass out the Workbooks. Direct the students to open to Lesson 58.

(Award 6 points if the group worked well during the word attack. Remind the students of the points they can earn in their Workbook.)

EXERCISE 5
SOUND DICTATION

1. I'll say the sounds. You write the letters in part 1 in your Workbook.
2. First sound. (Pause.) ĕĕĕ. What sound? (Signal.) ĕĕĕ.
- Write it in the first blank.
 (Observe students and give feedback.)
3. Next sound. (Pause.) ĭĭĭ. What sound? (Signal.) ĭĭĭ.
- Write it.
 (Observe students and give feedback.)
4. (Repeat step 3 for vvv, ch, j, b, ŏŏŏ, ăăă, ōōō, shshsh, fff, d.)
5. (Repeat sounds students had trouble with.)

EXERCISE 6
SPELLING FROM DICTATION

1. Touch part 2. ✓
- You're going to write words that I dictate.
2. First word: **did**. What word? (Signal.) *Did*.
- Listen again: **d . . . ĭĭĭ . . . d**. Write it in the first blank.
 (Observe students and give feedback.)
3. Next word: **sheets**. What word? (Signal.) *Sheets*.
- Listen again: **shshsh . . . ēēē . . . t . . . sss**. Write it in the next blank. Remember to write two ē's.
 (Observe students and give feedback.)
4. (Repeat step 3 for **met, bad, then, not, his, has**.)

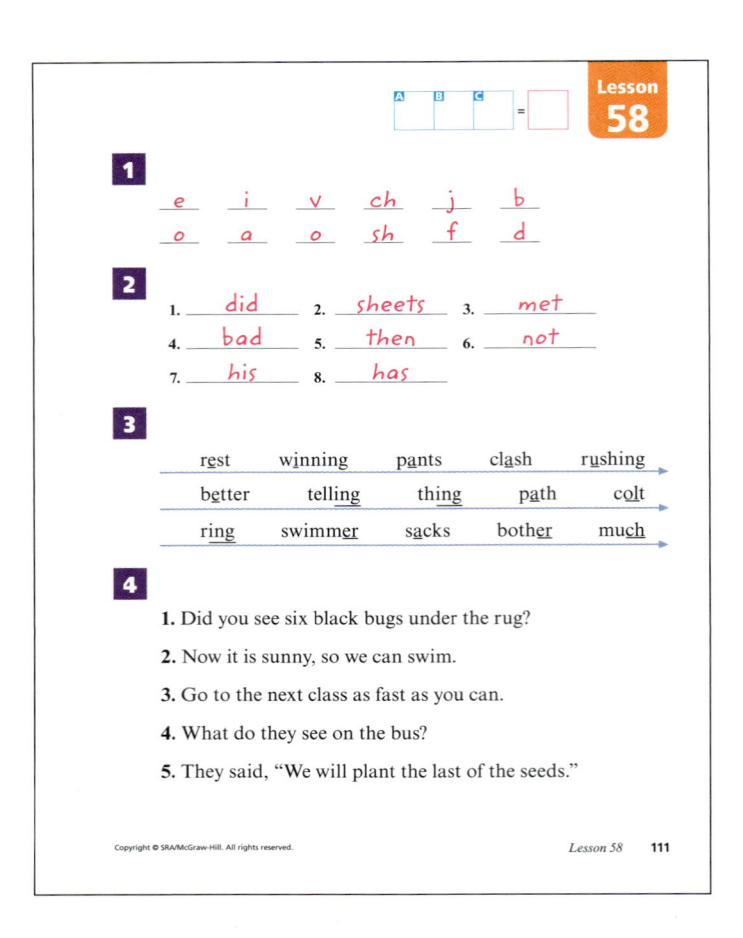

1
e i v ch j b
o a o sh f d

2
1. did 2. sheets 3. met
4. bad 5. then 6. not
7. his 8. has

3
rest   winning   pants   clash   rushing
better   telling   thing   path   colt
ring   swimmer   sacks   bother   much

4
1. Did you see six black bugs under the rug?
2. Now it is sunny, so we can swim.
3. Go to the next class as fast as you can.
4. What do they see on the bus?
5. They said, "We will plant the last of the seeds."

EXERCISE 7
WORD READING: Workbook

1. Touch the first word in part 3. ✓
2. Look at the underlined sound in the first word. (Pause.) What sound? (Signal.) ĕĕĕ.
- (Pause.) What word? (Signal.) *Rest*.
3. Next word. (Pause.) What sound? (Signal.) ĭĭĭ.
- (Pause.) What word? (Signal.) *Winning*.
4. (Repeat step 3 for remaining words.)

EXERCISE 8
SENTENCE READING

1. Everybody, touch sentence 1 in part 4. ✓
2. You're going to read the fast way. Read a word each time I clap.
3. First word. ✓
- Get ready. (Clap for each word. Pause about 2 seconds between claps.) *Did . . . you . . . see . . . six . . . black . . . bugs . . . under . . . the . . . rug?*
4. (Repeat step 3 until the students correctly identify all the words in the sentence in order.)

5. (Repeat steps 3 and 4 for each remaining sentence:
- 2. Now it is sunny, so we can swim.
- 3. Go to the next class as fast as you can.
- 4. What do they see on the bus?
- 5. They said, "We will plant the last of the seeds.")

> **Individual test**
> (Give each student a chance to read one of the sentences. Praise students who read accurately without long pauses.)

EXERCISE 9
WORD COMPLETION

1. Touch the first word in part 5. ✓
- Fix it up to say (pause) **cans.** What word? (Signal.) *Cans.*
- Fix it up.
  (Observe students and give feedback.)
2. Touch the second word. ✓
- Fix it up to say (pause) **hits.** What word? (Signal.) *Hits.*
- Fix it up.
  (Observe students and give feedback.)
3. (Repeat step 2 for **trim, slip, rocks, grab.**)

EXERCISE 10
STORY READING

Task A

1. Everybody, touch part 6. ✓
- You're going to read this story.
2. First word. ✓
- Get ready. (Clap for each word. Pause about 2 seconds between claps.) *He . . . said, . . . "We . . . must . . . get . . . a . . . gift . . . for . . . Pam."*
3. (Repeat step 2 until the students correctly identify all the words in the sentence in order.)
4. Next sentence. ✓
- Get ready. (Clap for each word:) *She . . . said, . . . "We . . . can . . . get . . . her . . . a . . . green . . . frog . . . or . . . a . . . pet . . . fish."*

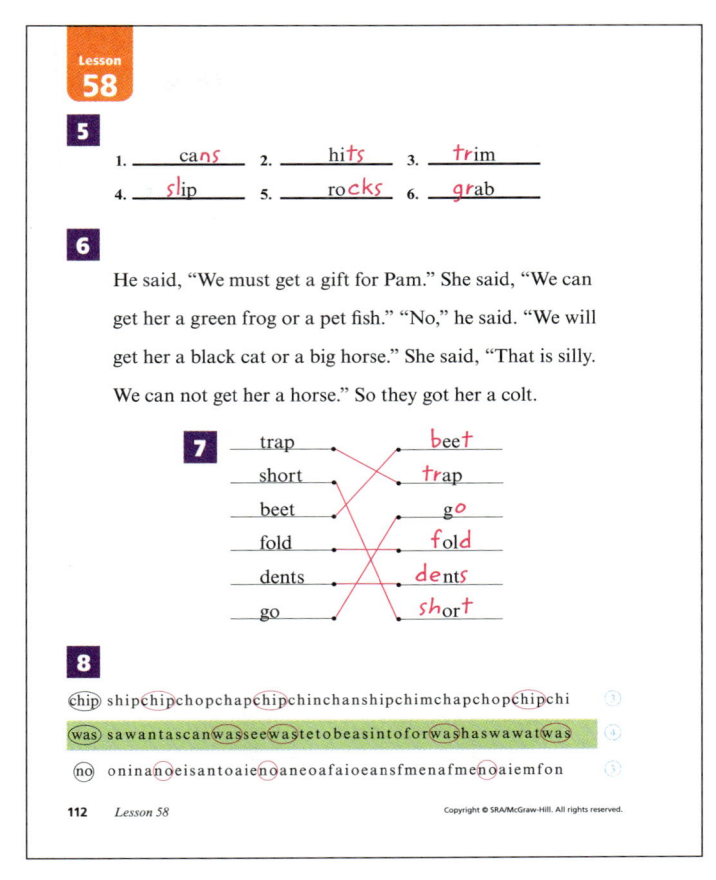

5. (Repeat step 4 until students correctly identify all the words in the sentence in order.)
6. (Repeat steps 4 and 5 for each remaining sentence: **"No," he said. "We will get her a black cat or a big horse." She said, "That is silly. We can not get her a horse." So they got her a colt.**)
7. (If the students miss more than four words, repeat the story reading from the beginning.)

Task B

1. Now I'll read the story and ask questions. Follow along.
2. **He said, "We must get a gift for Pam."** (Call on a student.) What did he say? *We must get a gift for Pam.*
3. **She said, "We can get her a green frog or a pet fish."** (Call on a student.) What did she say? *We can get her a green frog or a pet fish.*

Lesson 58

Lesson 58

4. **"No," he said. "We will get her a black cat or a big horse."** (Call on a student.) Say everything that he said. *No. We will get her a black cat or a big horse.*
5. **She said, "That is silly. We can not get her a horse."** (Call on a student.) Say everything that she said. *That is silly. We can not get her a horse.*
6. **So they got her a colt.** Everybody, what did they get her? (Signal.) *A colt.*
- (Call on a student.) **What is a colt?** (Idea: *A young horse.*)

EXERCISE 11
MATCHING COMPLETION

1. **Everybody, touch part 7.** ✓
2. **First word. What word?** (Signal.) *Trap.*
3. **Next word. What word?** (Signal.) *Short.*
4. (Repeat step 3 for **beet, fold, dents, go.**)
5. **Later, you'll complete the matching words.**

EXERCISE 12
CIRCLE GAME

1. **Everybody, touch part 8.** ✓
2. **What word will you circle in the first line?** (Signal.) *Chip.*
3. **What word will you circle in the second line?** (Signal.) *Was.*
4. **What word will you circle in the third line?** (Signal.) *No.*
5. **Circle the words and finish the rest of your Workbook lesson.**

EXERCISE 13
WORKBOOK CHECK

1. (Check each student's Workbook.)
2. (Award points for Workbook performance.)
3. (Record the student's total points in Box B.)

0–3 errors	8 points
4–5 errors	4 points
6 errors	2 points
7 or more errors	0 points

INDIVIDUAL READING CHECKOUTS

EXERCISE 14
TIMED STORY-READING CHECKOUT

- **Study the story. If you read the story with no more than 3 errors and read it in 1 minute or less, you'll earn 6 points.**
- **If you make more than 3 errors, or if you take more than 1 minute to read the story, you won't earn any points.**
- **If you don't earn points the first time you read the story, you can try again. If you succeed the second time you try, you'll earn 3 points.**
- (Check the students individually.)
- (Record either 6, 3, or 0 points in Box C.)

Lesson point total

(Tell students to write the point total in the last box at the top of the Workbook page. Maximum = 20 points.)

Point Summary Chart

(Tell students to write this point total in the box for Lesson 58 in the Point Summary Chart.)

END OF LESSON 58

Lesson 59

WORD-ATTACK SKILLS

EXERCISE 1
SOUND INTRODUCTION

1. (Point to **z:**) This letter makes the sound **zzz.** What sound? (Touch.) *zzz.*
2. (Point to **o:**) One sound you learned for this letter is the letter name. Everybody, what's that sound? (Touch.) *ōōō.* Yes, **ōōō.**
   - What's the other sound? (Touch.) *ŏŏŏ.* Yes, **ŏŏŏ.**
3. (Point to **e:**) One sound you learned for this letter is the letter name. Everybody, what's that sound? (Touch.) *ēēē.* Yes, **ēēē.**
   - What's the other sound? (Touch.) *ĕĕĕ.* Yes, **ĕĕĕ.**
4. (Point to **wh:**) What sound? (Touch.) *www.* Yes, **www.**
5. (Repeat step 4 for **er, j, v, c, b, l, d, ŭ.**)

z o e

wh er

j v c

b l d u

Individual test
(Call on two or three students. Touch under each sound. Each student says all the sounds, including two sounds for **o** and two sounds for **e.**)

EXERCISE 2
PRONUNCIATIONS

Note: Do not write the words on the board. This is an oral exercise.

Task A **Trap, track**

1. Listen: **trap** (pause) **track.** Say those words. (Signal.) *Trap, track.* (Repeat until firm.)
2. Listen: **trap** (pause) **track.** One of those words means **something to catch animals.**
   - (Pause.) Which word? (Signal.) *Trap.* Yes, **trap.**
3. One of those words means **something you run on.**
   - (Pause.) Which word? (Signal.) *Track.* Yes, **track.**
4. (Repeat steps 2 and 3 until firm.)

Task B

1. Listen: **trucks.** Say it. (Signal.) *Trucks.*
2. Next word: **trenches.** Say it. (Signal.) *Trenches.*
3. (Repeat step 2 for **handed, roses, missed.**)
4. (Repeat the words until firm.)

Task C **Trick, truck, track**

1. Listen: **trick, truck, track.** Say those words. (Signal.) *Trick, truck, track.* (Repeat until firm.)
2. One of those words has the middle sound **ĭĭĭ.** I'll say the words again: **trick, truck, track.**
3. Which word has the middle sound **ĭĭĭ**? (Signal.) *Trick.* Yes, **trick.**
   - Which word has the middle sound **ŭŭŭ**? (Signal.) *Truck.* Yes, **truck.**
   - Which word has the middle sound **ăăă**? (Signal.) *Track.* Yes, **track.**
4. Listen: **trĭĭĭck.** What's the middle sound in the word **trick**? (Signal.) *ĭĭĭ.* Yes, **ĭĭĭ.**
   - Listen: **trŭŭŭck.** What's the middle sound in the word **truck**? (Signal.) *ŭŭŭ.* Yes, **ŭŭŭ.**
   - Listen: **trăăăck.** What's the middle sound in the word **track**? (Signal.) *ăăă.* Yes, **ăăă.**
5. (Repeat step 4 until firm.) **Good job.**

Lesson 59

EXERCISE 3
WORD READING THE FAST WAY

1. You're going to read these words the fast way.
2. (For each word: Touch the ball of the arrow. Pause.) What word? (Slash right.)
3. (Repeat each list until firm.)

you
of
what
was

very
path
said
gift
club

stamp
smell
how
yes

blush
than
dusty
vest
town

4. (For each word: Touch the ball of the arrow. Pause.) **What word?** (Slash right.)
5. (Repeat the column until firm.)

blink
think
next
lost
just
felt
left

Lesson 59

WORKBOOK EXERCISES

> **Note:** Pass out the Workbooks. Direct the students to open to Lesson 59.

(Award 6 points if the group worked well during the word attack. Remind the students of the points they can earn in their Workbook.)

EXERCISE 4
SOUND DICTATION

1. **I'll say the sounds. You write the letters in part 1 in your Workbook.**
2. **First sound. Write a letter that says k in the first blank.**
   (Observe students and give feedback.)
3. **Next sound. Write another letter that says k.**
   (Observe students and give feedback.)
4. **Next sound. Write two letters that go together and say k.**
   (Observe students and give feedback.)
5. **Next sound. (Pause.) ch. What sound?** (Signal.) *ch.*
   - **Write it.**
   (Observe students and give feedback.)
6. (Repeat step 5 for **shshsh, ththth, vvv, fff, nnn, ĭĭĭ, p, ŭŭŭ.**)
7. (Repeat sounds students had trouble with.)

EXERCISE 5
SPELLING FROM DICTATION

1. **Touch part 2.** ✓
   - **You're going to write words that I dictate.**
2. **First word: on. What word?** (Signal.) *On.*
   - **Listen again: ŏŏŏ . . . nnn. Write it in the first blank.**
   (Observe students and give feedback.)
3. **Next word: has. What word?** (Signal.) *Has.*
   - **Listen again: h . . . ăăă . . . zzz. Write it in the next blank.**
   (Observe students and give feedback.)
4. (Repeat step 3 for **dads, if, than, when, meets, his.**)

Lesson 59

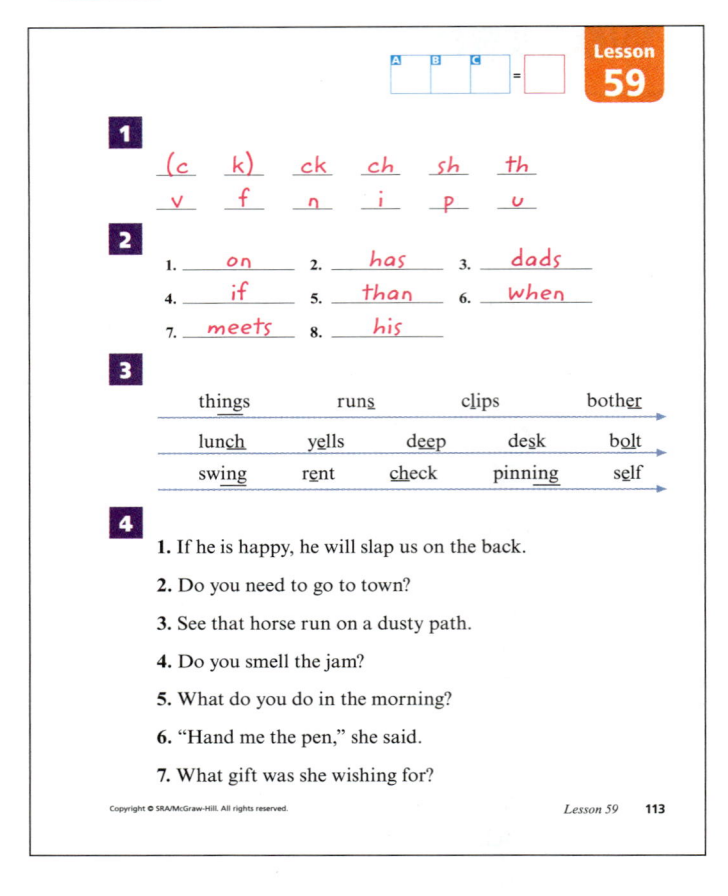

Lesson 59

Workbook Part

1

(c	k)	ck	ch	sh	th
v	f	n	i	p	u

2

1. on 2. has 3. dads
4. if 5. than 6. when
7. meets 8. his

3

things   run<u>s</u>   c<u>l</u>ips   bother
<u>l</u>unch   yells   deep   desk   b<u>o</u>lt
swi<u>ng</u>   rent   <u>ch</u>eck   pinni<u>ng</u>   self

4

1. If he is happy, he will slap us on the back.
2. Do you need to go to town?
3. See that horse run on a dusty path.
4. Do you smell the jam?
5. What do you do in the morning?
6. "Hand me the pen," she said.
7. What gift was she wishing for?

Lesson 59   113

EXERCISE 6
WORD READING: Workbook

1. Touch the first word in part 3. ✓
2. Look at the underlined sound in the first word. (Pause.) What sound? (Signal.) *ing.*
• (Pause.) What word? (Signal.) *Things.*
3. Next word. (Pause.) What sound? (Signal.) *sss.*
• (Pause.) What word? (Signal.) *Runs.*
4. (Repeat step 3 for remaining words.)

EXERCISE 7
SENTENCE READING

1. Everybody, touch sentence 1 in part 4. ✓
2. You're going to read the fast way. Read a word each time I clap.
3. First word. ✓
• Get ready. (Clap for each word. Pause about 2 seconds between claps.) If . . . he . . . is . . . happy, . . . he . . . will . . . slap . . . us . . . on . . . the . . . back.
4. (Repeat step 3 until the students correctly identify all the words in the sentence in order.)

192   Lesson 59

5. (Repeat steps 3 and 4 for each remaining sentence.)

Individual test
(Give each student a chance to read one of the sentences. Praise students who read accurately without long pauses.)

EXERCISE 8
WORD COMPLETION

1. Touch the first word in part 5. ✓
• Fix it up to say (pause) **drip.** What word? (Signal.) *Drip.*
• Fix it up.
(Observe students and give feedback.)
2. Touch the second word. ✓
• Fix it up to say (pause) **tree.** What word? (Signal.) *Tree.*
• Fix it up.
(Observe students and give feedback.)
3. (Repeat step 2 for **mast, think, left, drop, fins.**)

EXERCISE 9
STORY READING

Task A

1. Everybody, touch part 6. ✓
• You're going to read this story.
2. First word. ✓
• Get ready. (Clap for each word. Pause about 2 seconds between claps.) He . . . told . . . me . . . how . . . to . . . get . . . to . . . the . . . best . . . store . . . in . . . town.
3. (Repeat step 2 until the students correctly identify all the words in the sentence in order.)
4. Next sentence. ✓
• Get ready. (Clap for each word:) He . . . told . . . me . . . to . . . go . . . left . . . at . . . the . . . gift . . . shop . . . and . . . go . . . north.
5. (Repeat step 4 until students correctly identify all the words in the sentence in order.)

Lesson 59

Workbook page 114, Lesson 59:

5.
1. dr**ip**   2. **t**r**ee**   3. ma**st**
4. **th**ink   5. l**eft**   6. **dr**op
7. fi**ns**

6. He told me how to get to the best store in town. He told me to go left at the gift shop and go north. He said, "Then you will go six blocks to the west." He said, "Then go up the hill and down the next street." Do you think I got to the store? No. I got lost.

7.
sleep — sleep
under — under
big — big
dug — dug
sent — sent
trip — trip

8.
(when) thenthan**when**whatthey than whan **when**thethiswhat**when**tot
(to) itis**to**ofhotheonethle**to**shflaofhsthota**to**n**to**foristhefoti**o**to
(has) his ham **has** him her **has** h can tra shis his for **has** ham and his fa s to

---

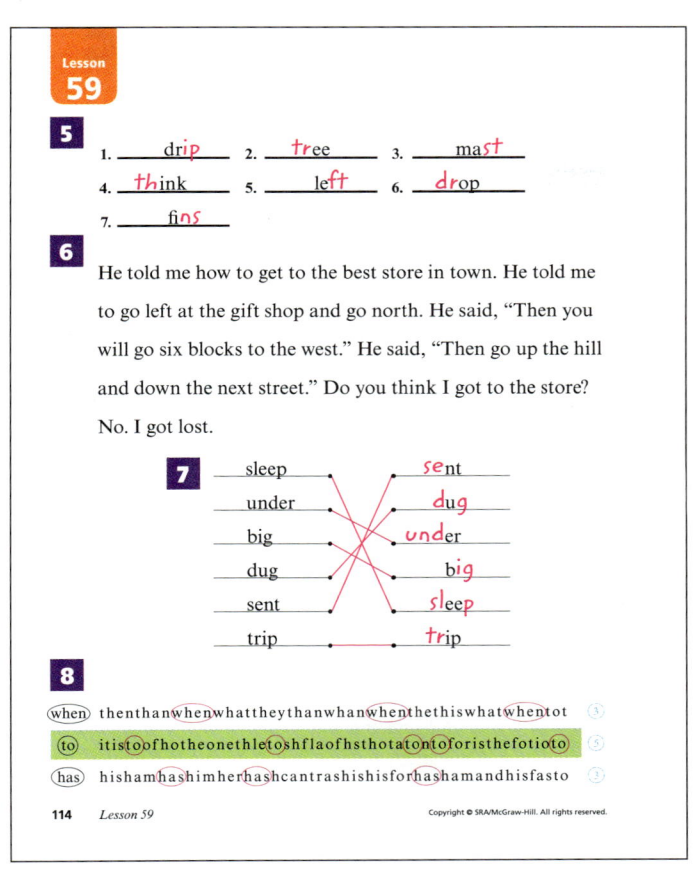

6. (Repeat steps 4 and 5 for each remaining sentence.)
7. (If the students miss more than four words, repeat the story reading from the beginning.)

Task B

1. Now I'll read the story and ask questions. Follow along.
2. **He told me how to get to the best store in town. He told me to go left at the gift shop and go north.** (Call on a student.) What did he tell me to do at the gift shop? *Go left and go north.*
3. **He said, "Then you will go six blocks to the west."** (Call on a student.) What do I do after I go north from the gift shop? *Go six blocks to the west.*
4. **He said, "Then go up the hill and down the next street."** (Call on a student.) What did he say? *Then go up the hill and down the next street.*
   - Everybody, did he tell me which way to turn at the next street? (Signal.) *No.*
5. **Do you think I got to the store? No. I got lost.** (Call on a student.) Could you follow the directions he gave?

EXERCISE 10
MATCHING COMPLETION

1. Everybody, touch part 7. ✓
2. First word. What word? (Signal.) *Sleep.*
3. Next word. What word? (Signal.) *Under.*
4. (Repeat step 3 for **big, dug, sent, trip.**)
5. Later, you'll complete the matching words.

EXERCISE 11
CIRCLE GAME

1. Everybody, touch part 8. ✓
2. What word will you circle in the first line? (Signal.) *When.*
3. What word will you circle in the second line? (Signal.) *To.*
4. What word will you circle in the third line? (Signal.) *Has.*
5. Circle the words and finish the rest of your Workbook lesson.

Lesson 59

EXERCISE 12
WORKBOOK CHECK

1. (Check each student's Workbook.)
2. (Award points for Workbook performance.)
3. (Record the student's total points in Box B.)

0–3 errors	8 points
4–5 errors	4 points
6 errors	2 points
7 or more errors	0 points

INDIVIDUAL READING CHECKOUTS

EXERCISE 13
TIMED STORY-READING CHECKOUT

- Study the story. If you read the story with no more than 3 errors and read it in 1 minute or less, you'll earn 6 points.
- If you make more than 3 errors, or if you take more than 1 minute to read the story, you won't earn any points.
- If you don't earn points the first time you read the story, you can try again. If you succeed the second time you try, you'll earn 3 points.
- (Check the students individually.)
- (Record either 6, 3, or 0 points in Box C.)

Lesson point total

(Tell students to write the point total in the last box at the top of the Workbook page. Maximum = 20 points.)

Point Summary Chart

(Tell students to write this point total in the box for Lesson 59 in the Point Summary Chart.)

END OF LESSON 59

WORD-ATTACK SKILLS

EXERCISE 1
SOUND INTRODUCTION

1. (Point to **z:**) This letter makes the sound **zzz**. What sound? (Touch.) *zzz*.
2. (Point to **e:**) One sound you learned for this letter is the letter name. Everybody, what's that sound? (Touch.) *ēēē*. Yes, **ēēē**.
   - What's the other sound? (Touch.) *ĕĕĕ*. Yes, **ĕĕĕ**.
3. (Point to **o:**) One sound you learned for this letter is the letter name. Everybody, what's that sound? (Touch.) *ōōō*. Yes, **ōōō**.
   - What's the other sound? (Touch.) *ŏŏŏ*. Yes, **ŏŏŏ**.
4. (Point to **th:**) What sound? (Touch.) *ththth*. Yes, **ththth**.
5. (Repeat step 4 for **m, n, h, v, z, x, j, ŭ, ĭ, y.**)

z e o
th m
n h v
z x j
u i y

Individual test
(Call on two or three students. Touch under each sound. Each student says all the sounds, including two sounds for **e** and two sounds for **o**.)

EXERCISE 2
PRONUNCIATIONS

Task A Slip, slick

1. Listen: **slip** (pause) **slick**. Say those words. (Signal.) *Slip, slick.* (Repeat until firm.)
2. Listen: **slip** (pause) **slick**. One of those words means **something that is very smooth**.
   - (Pause.) Which word? (Signal.) *Slick.* Yes, **slick**.
3. One of those words means **something you do on ice**.
   - (Pause.) Which word? (Signal.) *Slip.* Yes, **slip**.
4. (Repeat steps 2 and 3 until firm.)

Task B

1. Listen: **ranches**. Say it. (Signal.) *Ranches.*
2. Next word: **lasts**. Say it. (Signal.) *Lasts.*
3. (Repeat step 2 for **rested, messes, fished.**)
4. (Repeat the words until firm.)

Task C Sprung, spring, sprang

1. Listen: **sprung, spring, sprang**. Say those words. (Signal.) *Sprung, spring, sprang.* (Repeat until firm.)
2. One of those words has the middle sound **ăăă**. I'll say the words again: **sprung, spring, sprang**.
3. Which word has the middle sound **ăăă**? (Signal.) *Sprang.* Yes, **sprang**.
   - Which word has the middle sound **ĭĭĭ**? (Signal.) *Spring.* Yes, **spring**.
   - Which word has the middle sound **ŭŭŭ**? (Signal.) *Sprung.* Yes, **sprung**.
4. Listen: **sprŭŭŭng**. What's the middle sound in the word **sprung**? (Signal.) *ŭŭŭ.* Yes, **ŭŭŭ**.
   - Listen: **sprĭĭĭng**. What's the middle sound in the word **spring**? (Signal.) *ĭĭĭ.* Yes, **ĭĭĭ**.
   - Listen: **sprăăăng**. What's the middle sound in the word **sprang**? (Signal.) *ăăă.* Yes, **ăăă**.
5. (Repeat step 4 until firm.) Good job.

Lesson 60

EXERCISE 3
WORD READING THE FAST WAY

1. You're going to read these words the fast way.
2. (For each word: Touch the ball of the arrow. Pause.) What word? (Slash right.)
3. (Repeat each list until firm.)

of
was
grips
stuck
sell
jumping

you
north
to
master
said

check
smell
felt
what
do

4. (For each word: Touch the ball of the arrow. Pause.) What word? (Slash right.)
5. (Repeat the column until firm.)

- planting
- tramp
- trees
- clocks
- things
- fixer
- jam

WORKBOOK EXERCISES

Note: Pass out the Workbooks. Direct the students to open to Lesson 60.

(Award 6 points if the group worked well during the word attack. Remind the students of the points they can earn in their Workbook.)

EXERCISE 4
SOUND DICTATION

1. I'll say the sounds. You write the letters in part 1 in your Workbook.
2. First sound. (Pause.) **ch.** What sound? (Signal.) *ch.*
- Write it in the first blank.
(Observe students and give feedback.)
3. Next sound. Write a letter that says **k.**
(Observe students and give feedback.)
4. Next sound. Write another letter that says **k.**
(Observe students and give feedback.)
5. Next sound. Write two letters that go together and say **ck.**
(Observe students and give feedback.)
6. Next sound. (Pause.) **ĕĕĕ.** What sound? (Signal.) *ĕĕĕ.*
- Write it.
(Observe students and give feedback.)
7. (Repeat step 6 for **zzz, sss, shshsh, rrr, ĭĭĭ, ōōō, ŭŭŭ.**)
8. (Repeat sounds students had trouble with.)

Lesson 60 197

Lesson 60

Workbook Page (Lesson 60, p. 115)

1.
ch (c k) ck e z
s sh r i o u

2.
1. sit   2. had   3. see
4. set   5. this   6. if
7. then   8. has

3.
f<u>ee</u>ls   lett<u>er</u>s   b<u>l</u>ush   <u>c</u>rush   <u>j</u>elly
f<u>u</u>nny   <u>gr</u>eeting   lu<u>n</u>ch   m<u>o</u>ld
<u>r</u>inging n<u>e</u>xt   we<u>s</u>t   st<u>o</u>re   v<u>e</u>ry

4.
1. He said, "What can I do so that you will feel better?"
2. What was she picking on top of the hill?
3. They had lots of desks in the class.
4. She said, "Stand still or you will slip."
5. What will you get when you go to the store?

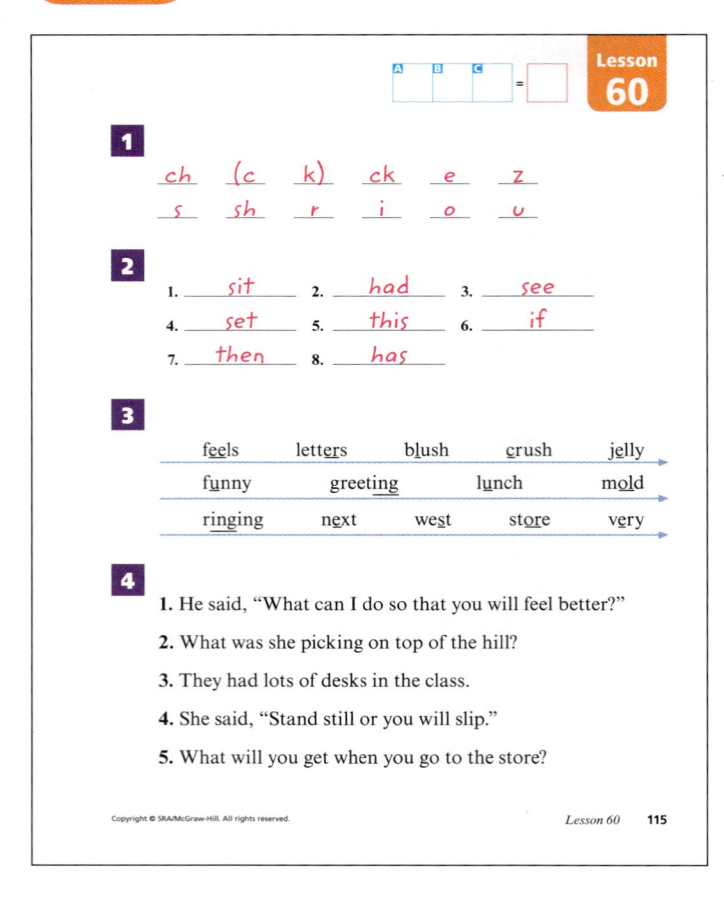

EXERCISE 5
SPELLING FROM DICTATION

1. Touch part 2. ✓
- You're going to write words that I dictate.
2. First word: **sit.** What word? (Signal.) *Sit.*
- Listen again: **sss . . . ĭĭĭ . . . t.** Write it in the first blank.
(Observe students and give feedback.)
3. Next word: **had.** What word? (Signal.) *Had.*
- Listen again: **h . . . ăăă . . . d.** Write it on the next line.
(Observe students and give feedback.)
4. (Repeat step 3 for **see, set, this, if, then, has.**)

EXERCISE 6
WORD READING: Workbook

1. Touch the first word in part 3. ✓
2. Look at the underlined sound in the first word. (Pause.) What sound? (Signal.) *ēēē.*
- (Pause.) What word? (Signal.) *Feels.*
3. Next word. (Pause.) What sound? (Signal.) *er.*
- (Pause.) What word? (Signal.) *Letters.*
4. (Repeat step 3 for remaining words.)

EXERCISE 7
SENTENCE READING

1. Everybody, touch sentence 1 in part 4. ✓
2. You're going to read the fast way. Read a word each time I clap.
3. First word. ✓
- Get ready. (Clap for each word. Pause about 2 seconds between claps.) *He . . . said, . . . "What . . . can . . . I . . . do . . . so . . . that . . . you . . . will . . . feel . . . better?"*
4. (Repeat step 3 until the students correctly identify all the words in the sentence in order.)
5. (Repeat steps 3 and 4 for each remaining sentence.)

> **Individual test**
> (Give each student a chance to read one of the sentences. Praise students who read accurately without long pauses.)

EXERCISE 8
WORD COMPLETION

1. Touch the first word in part 5. ✓
- What word? (Signal.) *Am.* Yes, **am.**
- Fix it up to say (pause) **slam.** What word? (Signal.) *Slam.*
- Fix it up.
(Observe students and give feedback.)

Lesson 60

5
1. sl_am 2. dr_ip 3. an_t
4. ho_rn 5. s_leeps 6. we_nt

6

We had a clock that did not run. We went to a clock fixer and said, "Can you fix this clock?" He said, "Yes, I can get it to run." The next morning, we went back to pick up the clock. The old man held up the clock. He said, "I stuck legs on the clock. Now it will run."

7
chop — but
then — then
jam — ship
ship — chop
fork — fork
but — jam

8
(to) forotho**to**formhas**to**beholdcoldorhas**to**beinthe**to**i**to**theof
(ship) shifthi**ship**intoshoresirshineroh the**ship**ishapely**ship**shop
(was) sawthewhat**was**hetherehasmastoben**was**away thenasmashe

---

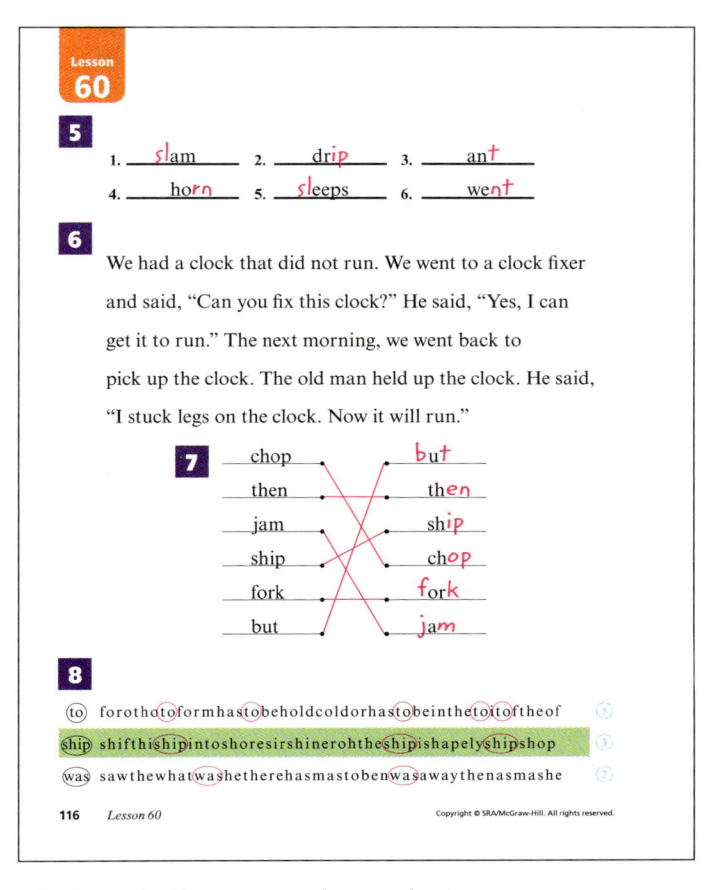

2. Touch the second word. ✓
- Fix it up to say (pause) **drip.** What word? (Signal.) *Drip.*
- Fix it up.
 (Observe students and give feedback.)
3. (Repeat step 2 for **ant, horn, sleeps, went.**)

EXERCISE 9
STORY READING

Task A

1. Everybody, touch part 6. ✓
- You're going to read this story.
2. First word. ✓
- Get ready. (Clap for each word. Pause about 2 seconds between claps.) *We . . . had . . . a . . . clock . . . that . . . did . . . not . . . run.*
3. (Repeat step 2 until the students correctly identify all the words in the sentence in order.)

4. Next sentence. ✓
- Get ready. (Clap for each word:) *We . . . went . . . to . . . a . . . clock . . . fixer . . . and . . . said, . . . "Can . . . you . . . fix . . . this . . . clock?"*
5. (Repeat step 4 until students correctly identify all words in the sentence in order.)
6. (Repeat steps 4 and 5 for each remaining sentence: **He said, "Yes, I can get it to run." The next morning, we went back to pick up the clock. The old man held up the clock. He said, "I stuck legs on the clock. Now it will run."**)
7. (If students miss more than four words, repeat the story reading from the beginning.)

Task B

1. Now I'll read the story and ask questions. Follow along.
2. **We had a clock that did not run.** (Call on a student.) **What was wrong with the clock?** (Idea: *It did not run.*)
- (Call on a student.) **What does that mean: It did not run?** (Idea: *The clock did not work.*)
3. **We went to a clock fixer and said, "Can you fix this clock?** (Call on a student.) **What did they say?** *Can you fix this clock?*
4. **He said, "Yes, I can get it to run."** (Call on a student.) **What did he say?** *Yes, I can get it to run.*
5. **The next morning, we went back to pick up the clock.** (Call on a student.) **When did they go back to the shop?** (Idea: *The next morning.*)
6. **The old man held up the clock. He said, "I stuck legs on the clock. Now it will run."** (Call on a student.) **What did the old man do to the clock?** (Idea: *Put legs on it.*)
- Everybody, did they want the clock to run that way? (Signal.) *No.*
- That old man seems to be confused!

Lesson 60   199

Lesson 60

EXERCISE 10
MATCHING COMPLETION

1. Everybody, touch part 7. ✓
2. First word. What word? (Signal.) *Chop.*
3. Next word. What word? (Signal.) *Then.*
4. (Repeat step 3 for **jam, ship, fork, but.**)
5. Later, you'll complete the matching words.

EXERCISE 11
CIRCLE GAME

1. Everybody, touch part 8. ✓
2. What word will you circle in the first line? (Signal.) *To.*
3. What word will you circle in the second line? (Signal.) *Ship.*
4. What word will you circle in the third line? (Signal.) *Was.*
5. Circle the words and finish the rest of your Workbook lesson.

EXERCISE 12
WORKBOOK CHECK

1. (Check each student's Workbook.)
2. (Award points for Workbook performance.)
3. (Record the student's total points in Box B.)

0–3 errors	8 points
4–5 errors	4 points
6 errors	2 points
7 or more errors	0 points

INDIVIDUAL READING CHECKOUTS

EXERCISE 13
TIMED STORY-READING CHECKOUT

- Study the story. If you read the story with no more than 3 errors and read it in 1 minute or less, you'll earn 6 points.
- If you make more than 3 errors, or if you take more than 1 minute to read the story, you won't earn any points.
- If you don't earn points the first time you read the story, you can try again. If you succeed the second time you try, you'll earn 3 points.
- (Check the students individually.)
- (Record either 6, 3, or 0 points in Box C.)

Lesson point total

(Tell students to write the point total in the last box at the top of the Workbook page. Maximum = 20 points.)

Point Summary Chart

(Tell students to write this point total in the box for Lesson 60 in the Point Summary Chart.)

Five-lesson point summary

(Tell students to add the point totals for Lessons 56 through 60 in the Point Summary Chart and to write the total for Block 12. Maximum for Block 12 = 100 points.)

END OF LESSON 60

MASTERY TEST 13

— AFTER LESSON 60, BEFORE LESSON 61 —

> **Note:** Use students' performance on the Lesson 60 Story reading checkout for Mastery Test 13.

Scoring the test

1. (Count each student's errors on the Story reading checkout. Write these numbers in the Test 13 boxes on the appropriate *Decoding A* Mastery Test Student Profile form. Circle **P** or **F**.)
2. (When all students have been tested, circle **P** or **F** for each student on the *Decoding A* Mastery Test Group Summary form. Determine if more than 25 percent of the students failed the Story reading checkout by dividing the number of students who failed by the total number of students in the group.)

Remedies

(If more than 25 percent of the students fail to earn 6 points for their Story reading checkout, [1] repeat the Story reading checkouts for Lessons 58 and 59, and [2] repeat all of Lesson 60. Permission is granted to reproduce the Workbook pages for Lesson 60 for classroom use.)

Lesson Objectives	LESSON 61 Exercise	LESSON 62 Exercise	LESSON 63 Exercise	LESSON 64 Exercise	LESSON 65 Exercise
Word Attack					
Phonemic Awareness					
Sound/Word Pronunciation	1, 2	1, 2	1, 2	1, 2	1, 2
Identify Sounds in Words	2	2	2	2	2
Decoding and Word Analysis					
Letter Sounds: ō, ŏ, z, er, th, v, n, j, x, y, ch, u, i	1				
Letter Sounds: qu, ē, ĕ, ō, ŏ, l, z, d, b, w, v, i, k, ch, g		1			
Letter Sounds: qu, ō, ŏ, ē, ĕ, u, ck, ing, sh, w, v, g, r, z			1		
Letter Sounds: ē, ĕ, ō, ŏ, a, i, u, ing, er, ch, sh, qu, b, p, d, h				1	
Letter Sounds: ē, ĕ, ō, ŏ, th, z, t, s, wh, j, w, h, u, er, p, d, b, g					1
Word Recognition	3	3	3	3	3
Assessment					
Ongoing: Individual Tests	1	1	1	1	
Group Reading					
Decoding and Word Analysis					
Read Decodable Text	9	9	9	9	9
Comprehension					
Access Prior Knowledge				9	
Draw Inferences	9	9	9	9	9
Note Details	9	9	9	9	9
Assessment					
Ongoing: Comprehension Check	9	9	9	9	9
Ongoing: Decoding Accuracy	9	9	9	9	9
Formal: Mastery Tests					MT 14, MT 15
Workbook Exercises					
Decoding and Word Analysis					
Word Recognition		6	6	6	6
Sentence Reading	8	7	7	7	7
Sound Combinations		6	6	6	6
Spelling: Sound/Letter Relationships	4, 6, 7	4, 8, 10	4, 8, 10	4, 8, 10	4, 8, 10
Spelling: CVC, CVCC, CCVC					5
Spelling: VC, CVC, CCVC, CVVCC				5	
Spelling: CVC, CVCC	5				
Spelling: VC, CVC, CCVC			5		
Spelling: VC, CVC, CCVC, CVCC		5			
Visual Discrimination		10, 11	10, 11	10, 11	10, 11
Assessment					
Ongoing: Individual Tests	8, 11	7, 13	7, 13	7, 13	7, 13
Ongoing: Teacher-Monitored Accuracy	11	13	13	13	13
Ongoing: Teacher-Monitored Fluency	11	13	13	13	13
Ongoing: Workcheck	10	12	12	12	12

Lessons 61–65   Objectives

Lesson 61

WORD-ATTACK SKILLS

EXERCISE 1
SOUND IDENTIFICATION

1. (Point to **o**:) One sound you learned for this letter is the letter name. Everybody, what's that sound? (Touch.) ōōō. Yes, **ōōō**.
- What's the other sound? (Touch.) ŏŏŏ. Yes, **ŏŏŏ**.
2. (Point to **z**:) What sound? (Touch.) zzz. Yes, **zzz**.
3. (Repeat step 2 for **er, th, v, n, j, x, y, ch, ŭ, ĭ**.)

o   z   er

th   v   n

j   x   y

ch   u   i

Individual test
(Call on two or three students. Touch under each sound. Each student says all the sounds, including two sounds for **o**.)

EXERCISE 2
PRONUNCIATIONS

Note: Do not write the words on the board. This is an oral exercise.

Task A

1. Listen: **chances**. Say it. (Signal.) *Chances*.
2. Next word: **casts**. Say it. (Signal.) *Casts*.
3. (Repeat step 2 for **stopped, fished**.)
4. (Repeat the words until firm.)

Task B Slum, slim, slam

1. Listen: **slum, slim, slam**. Say those words. (Signal.) *Slum, slim, slam*. (Repeat until firm.)
2. One of those words has the middle sound ĭĭĭ. I'll say the words again: **slum, slim, slam**.
3. Which word has the middle sound ĭĭĭ? (Signal.) *Slim*. Yes, **slim**.
- Which word has the middle sound ăăă? (Signal.) *Slam*. Yes, **slam**.
- Which word has the middle sound ŭŭŭ? (Signal.) *Slum*. Yes, **slum**.
4. Listen: **slŭŭŭm**. What's the middle sound in the word **slum**? (Signal.) ŭŭŭ. Yes, **ŭŭŭ**.
- Listen: **slĭĭĭm**. What's the middle sound in the word **slim**? (Signal.) ĭĭĭ. Yes, **ĭĭĭ**.
- Listen: **slăăăm**. What's the middle sound in the word **slam**? (Signal.) ăăă. Yes, **ăăă**.
5. (Repeat step 4 until firm.) **Good job.**

Lesson 61

EXERCISE 3
WORD READING THE FAST WAY

1. You're going to read these words the fast way.
2. (For each word: Touch the ball of the arrow. Pause.) What word? (Slash right.)
3. (Repeat each list until firm.)

next
under
grabs
of
check
lost
frog
held
you

smelling
just
think
town
lift
damp
belt
after
what
hold
very

4. (For each word: Touch the ball of the arrow. Pause.) What word? (Slash right.)
5. (Repeat the column until firm.)

tramp

funny

blink

lunch

sandy

Lesson 61

WORKBOOK EXERCISES

Note: Pass out the Workbooks. Direct the students to open to Lesson 61.

(Award 6 points if the group worked well during the word attack. Remind the students of the points they can earn in their Workbook.)

EXERCISE 4
SOUND DICTATION

1. I'll say the sounds. You write the letters in part 1 in your Workbook.
2. First sound. Write a letter that says **www** in the first blank.
   (Observe students and give feedback.)
3. Next sound. Write two letters that go together and say **www.**
   (Observe students and give feedback.)
4. Next sound. (Pause.) **vvv.** What sound? (Signal.) *vvv.*
   • Write it.
   (Observe students and give feedback.)
5. (Repeat step 4 for **fff, ththth, shshsh, sss, ch, j, b, ōōō, ăăă.**)
6. (Repeat sounds students had trouble with.)

EXERCISE 5
SPELLING FROM DICTATION

1. Touch part 2. ✓
   • You're going to write words that I dictate.
2. First word: **get.** What word? (Signal.) *Get.*
   • Listen again: **g . . . ĕĕĕ . . . t.** Write it in the first blank.
   (Observe students and give feedback.)
3. Next word: **cup.** What word? (Signal.) *Cup.*
   • Listen again: **c . . . ŭŭŭ . . . p.** Write it in the next blank.
   (Observe students and give feedback.)
4. (Repeat step 3 for **has, born, camp, held, fast.**)

Lesson 61 205

Lesson 61

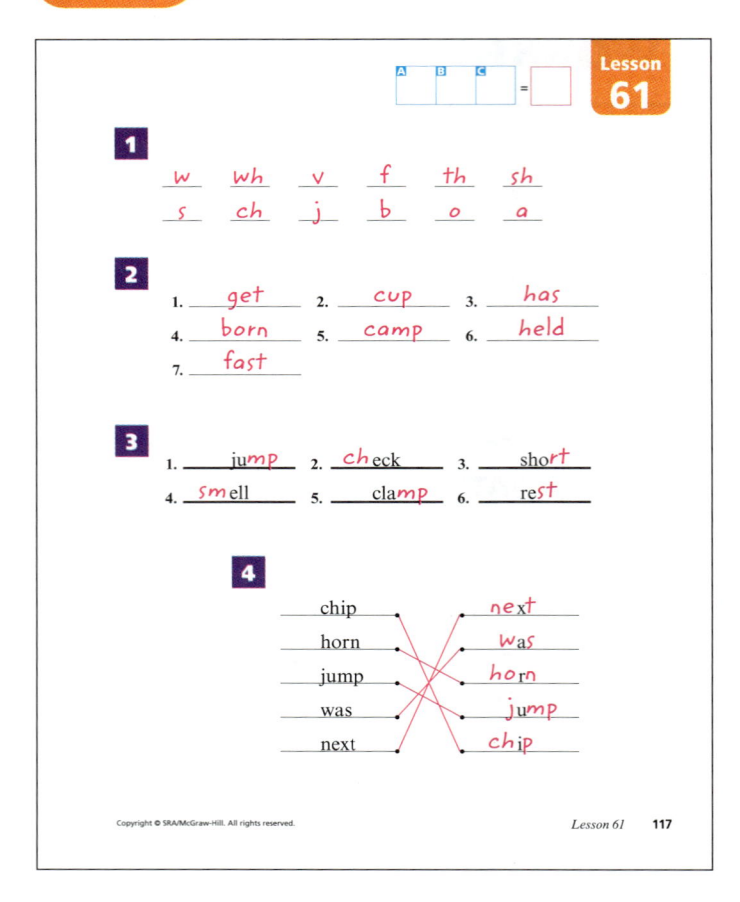

Lesson 61

1
w wh v f th sh
s ch j b o a

2
1. get 2. cup 3. has
4. born 5. camp 6. held
7. fast

3
1. ju**mp** 2. **ch**eck 3. shor**t**
4. **sm**ell 5. cla**mp** 6. re**st**

4
chip — chip
horn — horn
jump — jump
was — was
next — next

EXERCISE 6
WORD COMPLETION

1. Touch the first word in part 3. ✓
- Fix it up to say (pause) **jump.** What word? (Signal.) *Jump.* Yes, **jump.**
- Fix it up.
  (Observe students and give feedback.)
2. Touch the second word. ✓
- Fix it up to say (pause) **check.** What word? (Signal.) *Check.* Yes, **check.**
- Fix it up.
  (Observe students and give feedback.)
3. (Repeat step 2 for **short, smell, clamp, rest.**)

EXERCISE 7
MATCHING COMPLETION

1. Everybody, touch part 4. ✓
2. First word. What word? (Signal.) *Chip.*
3. Next word. What word? (Signal.) *Horn.*
4. (Repeat step 3 for **jump, was, next.**)
5. Later, you'll complete the matching words.

EXERCISE 8
SENTENCE READING

1. Everybody, touch sentence 1 in part 5. ✓
2. You're going to read the fast way.
3. First word. ✓
- Get ready. (Clap for each word. Pause about 2 seconds between claps.) *Do . . . you . . . think . . . we . . . can . . . go . . . swimming . . . if . . . it . . . gets . . . sunny?*
4. (Repeat step 3 until the students until the students read the sentence without making a mistake.)
5. (Repeat steps 3 and 4 for each remaining sentence:
- 2. Check with the man at the desk.
- 3. What did they do after dinner?
- 4. Did she keep her hands on the wheel?
- 5. You can not do math as well as I can.)

Individual test
(Give each student a chance to read one of the sentences. Praise students who read accurately without long pauses.)

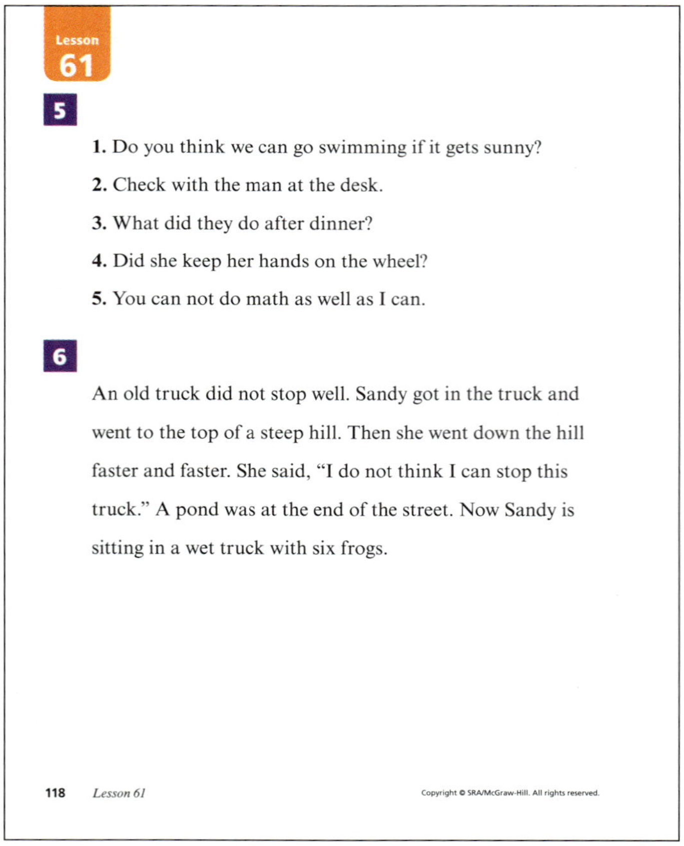

Lesson 61

5
1. Do you think we can go swimming if it gets sunny?
2. Check with the man at the desk.
3. What did they do after dinner?
4. Did she keep her hands on the wheel?
5. You can not do math as well as I can.

6
An old truck did not stop well. Sandy got in the truck and went to the top of a steep hill. Then she went down the hill faster and faster. She said, "I do not think I can stop this truck." A pond was at the end of the street. Now Sandy is sitting in a wet truck with six frogs.

Lesson 61

EXERCISE 9
STORY READING

Task A

1. Everybody, touch part 6. ✓
   - You're going to read this story.
2. First word. ✓
   - Get ready. (Clap for each word. Pause about 2 seconds between claps.) *An . . . old . . . truck . . . did . . . not . . . stop . . . well.*
3. (Repeat step 2 until the students correctly identify all the words in the sentence in order.)
4. Next sentence. ✓
   - Get ready. (Clap for each word.) *Sandy . . . got . . . in . . . the . . . truck . . . and . . . went . . . to . . . the . . . top . . . of . . . a . . . steep . . . hill.*
5. (Repeat step 4 until students correctly identify all words in the sentence in order.)
6. (Repeat steps 4 and 5 for each remaining sentence.)
7. (If students miss more than four words, repeat the story reading from the beginning.)

Task B

1. Now I'll read the story and ask questions. Follow along.
2. **An old truck did not stop well. Sandy got in the truck and went to the top of a steep hill.** (Call on a student.) Where did she go? (Idea: *To the top of a steep hill.*)
   - (Call on a student.) What is wrong with the truck? (Idea: *It didn't stop well.*)
3. **Then she went down the hill faster and faster. She said, "I do not think I can stop this truck."** (Call on a student.) What did she say? *I do not think I can stop this truck.*
4. **A pond was at the end of the street. Now Sandy is sitting in a wet truck with six frogs.** (Call on a student.) Where did the truck go? (Idea: *Into the pond.*)
   - (Call on a student.) What is Sandy doing now? (Idea: *Sitting in the truck in the pond with six frogs.*)

EXERCISE 10
WORKBOOK CHECK

1. (Check each student's Workbook.)
2. (Award points for Workbook performance.)
3. (Record the student's total points in Box B.)

0–3 errors	8 points
4–5 errors	4 points
6 errors	2 points
7 or more errors	0 points

INDIVIDUAL READING CHECKOUTS

EXERCISE 11
TIMED STORY-READING CHECKOUT

- Study the story. If you read the story with no more than 3 errors and read it in 1 minute or less, you'll earn 6 points.
- If you make more than 3 errors, or if you take more than 1 minute to read the story, you won't earn any points.
- If you don't earn points the first time you read the story, you can try again. If you succeed the second time you try, you'll earn 3 points.
- (Check the students individually.)
- (Record either 6, 3, or 0 points in Box C.)

Lesson point total

(Tell students to write the point total in the last box at the top of the Workbook page. Maximum = 20 points.)

Point Summary Chart

(Tell students to write this point total in the box for Lesson 61 in the Point Summary Chart.)

END OF LESSON 61

Lesson 62

WORD-ATTACK SKILLS

EXERCISE 1
SOUND INTRODUCTION

1. (Point to **qu:**) These letters make the sound **kwww.** What sound? (Touch.) *kwww.*
2. (Point to **e:**) One sound you learned for this letter is the letter name. Everybody, what's that sound? (Touch.) *ēēē.* Yes, **ēēē.**
   - What's the other sound? (Touch.) *ĕĕĕ.* Yes, **ĕĕĕ.**
3. (Point to **o:**) One sound you learned for this letter is the letter name. Everybody, what's that sound? (Touch.) *ōōō.* Yes, **ōōō.**
   - What's the other sound? (Touch.) *ŏŏŏ.* Yes, **ŏŏŏ.**
4. (Point to **l:**) What sound? (Touch.) *lll.* Yes, **lll.**
5. (Repeat step 4 for **z, d, b, w, v, ĭ, k, j, ch, g.**)

qu e

o l z

d b w

v i k j

ch g

Individual test
(Call on two or three students. Touch under each sound. Each student says all the sounds, including two sounds for **e** and two sounds for **o.**)

EXERCISE 2
PRONUNCIATIONS

Note: Do not write the words on the board. This is an oral exercise.

Task A Flat, flap

1. Listen: **flat** (pause) **flap.** Say those words. (Signal.) *Flat, flap.* (Repeat until firm.)
2. Listen: **flat** (pause) **flap.** One of those words means **a part that folds over.**
   - (Pause.) Which word? (Signal.) *Flap.* Yes, **flap.**
3. One of those words means **not round.**
   - (Pause.) Which word? (Signal.) *Flat.* Yes, **flat.**
4. (Repeat steps 2 and 3 until firm.)

Task B

1. Listen: **bunched.** Say it. (Signal.) *Bunched.*
2. Next word: **lasted.** Say it. (Signal.) *Lasted.*
3. (Repeat step 2 for **lived, smashes.**)
4. (Repeat the words until firm.)

Task C Swim, swum, swam

1. Listen: **swim, swum, swam.** Say those words. (Signal.) *Swim, swum, swam.* (Repeat until firm.)
2. One of those words has the middle sound **ŭŭŭ.** I'll say the words again: **swim, swum, swam.**
3. Which word has the middle sound **ŭŭŭ**? (Signal.) *Swum.* Yes, **swum.**
   - Which word has the middle sound **ăăă**? (Signal.) *Swam.* Yes, **swam.**
   - Which word has the middle sound **ĭĭĭ**? (Signal.) *Swim.* Yes, **swim.**
4. Listen: **swĭĭĭm.** What's the middle sound in the word **swim**? (Signal.) *ĭĭĭ.* Yes, **ĭĭĭ.**
   - Listen: **swŭŭŭm.** What's the middle sound in the word **swum**? (Signal.) *ŭŭŭ.* Yes, **ŭŭŭ.**
   - Listen: **swăăăm.** What's the middle sound in the word **swam**? (Signal.) *ăăă.* Yes, **ăăă.**
5. (Repeat step 4 until firm.) Good job.

EXERCISE 3
WORD READING THE FAST WAY

1. You're going to read these words the fast way.
2. (For each word: Touch the ball of the arrow. Pause.) **What word?** (Slash right.)
3. (Repeat each list until firm.)

ring

spring

junk

more

sells

greet

silly

chopping

stump

you

of

after

block

crash

clash

Lesson 62

4. (For each word: Touch the ball of the arrow. Pause.) **What word?** (Slash right.)
5. (Repeat each list until firm.)

- black
- store
- wishing
- shelf
- clapping

- down
- win
- lunch
- stuck
- cold
- mixer

WORKBOOK EXERCISES

Note: Pass out the Workbooks. Direct the students to open to Lesson 62.

(Award 6 points if the group worked well during the word attack. Remind the students of the points they can earn in their Workbook.)

EXERCISE 4
SOUND DICTATION

1. I'll say the sounds. You write the letters in part 1 in your Workbook.
2. First sound. (Pause.) **ăăă.** What sound? (Signal.) *ăăă.*
- Write it in the first blank.
  (Observe students and give feedback.)
3. Next sound. (Pause.) **b.** What sound? (Signal.) *b.*
- Write it.
  (Observe students and give feedback.)
4. (Repeat step 3 for **zzz, kss [x], vvv, ŭŭŭ, ŏŏŏ, thththt, ōōō, p, d, ĭĭĭ.**)
5. (Repeat sounds students had trouble with.)

EXERCISE 5
SPELLING FROM DICTATION

1. Touch part 2. ✓
- You're going to write words that I dictate.
2. First word: **that.** What word? (Signal.) *That.*
- Listen again: **thththt . . . ăăă . . . t.** Write it in the first blank.
  (Observe students and give feedback.)
3. Next word: **sheets.** What word? (Signal.) *Sheets.*
- Listen again: **shshsh . . . ēēē . . . t . . . sss.** Write it in the next blank. Remember to write two ē's.
  (Observe students and give feedback.)
4. (Repeat step 3 for **bad, fans, up, lip, set, his.**)

Lesson 62

1
| a | b | z | x | v | u |
| o | th | o | p | d | i |

2
1. that 2. sheets 3. bad
4. fans 5. up 6. lip
7. set 8. his

3
d<u>u</u>st	v<u>e</u>ry	b<u>i</u>g	d<u>i</u>g	b<u>u</u>st	b<u>u</u>ns
l<u>e</u>ft	s<u>u</u>ch	b<u>u</u>tter	b<u>a</u>tter	sen<u>d</u>er
f<u>o</u>lder	l<u>u</u>cky	f<u>ee</u>ling	cr<u>u</u>sh	fl<u>a</u>gs

4
1. How did so much dust get on the plants?
2. She said, "We can get more chips at the store."
3. You left lots of things on her desk.
4. What did she do when she felt bad?
5. After dinner, we will sit on the swing.

EXERCISE 6
WORD READING: Workbook

1. Touch the first word in part 3. ✓
2. Look at the underlined sound in the first word. (Pause.) What sound? (Signal.) *ŭŭŭ.*
- (Pause.) What word? (Signal.) *Dust.*
3. Next word. (Pause.) What sound? (Signal.) *ĕĕĕ.*
- (Pause.) What word? (Signal.) *Very.*
4. (Repeat step 3 for remaining words.)

EXERCISE 7
SENTENCE READING

1. Everybody, touch sentence 1 in part 4. ✓
2. You're going to read the fast way.
3. First word. ✓
- Get ready. (Clap for each word. Pause about 2 seconds between claps.) *How . . . did . . . so . . . much . . . dust . . . get . . . on . . . the . . . plants?*
4. (Repeat step 3 until the students read the sentence without a mistake.)

Lesson 62 **211**

Lesson 62

5. (Repeat steps 3 and 4 for each remaining sentence:
   - 2. She said, "We can get more chips at the store."
   - 3. You left lots of things on her desk.
   - 4. What did she do when she felt bad?
   - 5. After dinner, we will sit on the swing.)

> **Individual test**
> (Give each student a chance to read one of the sentences. Praise students who read accurately without long pauses.)

EXERCISE 8
WORD COMPLETION

1. Touch the first word in part 5. ✓
   - What word? (Signal.) *op.* Yes, **op.**
   - Fix it up to say (pause) **drop.** What word? (Signal.) *Drop.*
   - Fix it up.
     (Observe students and give feedback.)
2. Touch the second word. ✓
   - Fix it up to say (pause) **then.** What word? (Signal.) *Then.*
   - Fix it up.
     (Observe students and give feedback.)
3. (Repeat step 2 for **hand, rust, went, end.**)

EXERCISE 9
STORY READING

Task A

1. Everybody, touch part 6. ✓
   - You're going to read this story.
2. First word. ✓
   - Get ready. (Clap for each word. Pause about 2 seconds between claps.) *Ann . . . went . . . to . . . the . . . bun . . . shop . . . with . . . her . . . mixer.*
3. (Repeat step 2 until students correctly identify all the words in the sentence in order.)
4. Next sentence. ✓
   - Get ready. (Clap for each word:) *She . . . said, . . . "With . . . this . . . batter . . . mixer, . . . I . . . can . . . fix . . . the . . . best . . . batter."*
5. (Repeat step 4 until students correctly identify all words in the sentence in order.)
6. (Repeat steps 4 and 5 for each remaining sentence.)
7. (If students miss more than four words, repeat the story reading from the beginning.)

Task B

1. Now I'll read the story and ask questions. Follow along.
2. **Ann went to the bun shop with her mixer.** (Call on a student.) What do they do in a bun shop? (Idea: *Make hamburger and hot dog buns.*)
   - (Call on a student.) What is a mixer? (Idea: *A machine to mix food.*)
3. **She said, "With this batter mixer, I can fix the best batter."** (Call on a student.) What did she say? *With this batter mixer, I can fix the best batter.*
4. **"No," the men said. "We fix the best batter. It has the best butter."** (Call on a student.) Why do the men think their batter is best? (Idea: *Because it has the best butter.*)
5. **She said, "Mix the best butter with this batter mixer."** (Call on a student.) What did she want them to do with the best butter? (Idea: *Mix the butter with her batter mixer.*)
6. **So they did. They got the best buns in town.** (Call on a student.) Did they put the best butter in the batter and mix it with the batter mixer? *Yes.*
   - (Call on a student.) How did it turn out? (Idea: *They made the best buns in town.*)

Lesson 62

Workbook page (Lesson 62, p. 120)

5.
1. **dr**op
2. th**en**
3. ha**nd**
4. **ru**st
5. **we**nt
6. **en**d

6. Ann went to the bun shop with her mixer. She said, "With this batter mixer, I can fix the best batter." "No," the men said. "We fix the best batter. It has the best butter." She said, "Mix the best butter with this batter mixer." So they did. They got the best buns in town.

7.
- ship — ship
- sold — sold
- chip — chip
- tubs — tubs
- locks — locks
- creek — creek

(matching with letter endings highlighted: lo**cks**, ch**ip**, cr**eek**, sh**ip**, t**ubs**, s**old**)

8.
- (end) lendthandhenhandcan**end**sentforlendthenhasadtoends ④
- (much) suchgoodmuchcanshouldmochor**much**touchatmuchhut ③
- (on) tonforanin**on**emaosoemaosnaoe**on**asin**on**im**on**oma ④

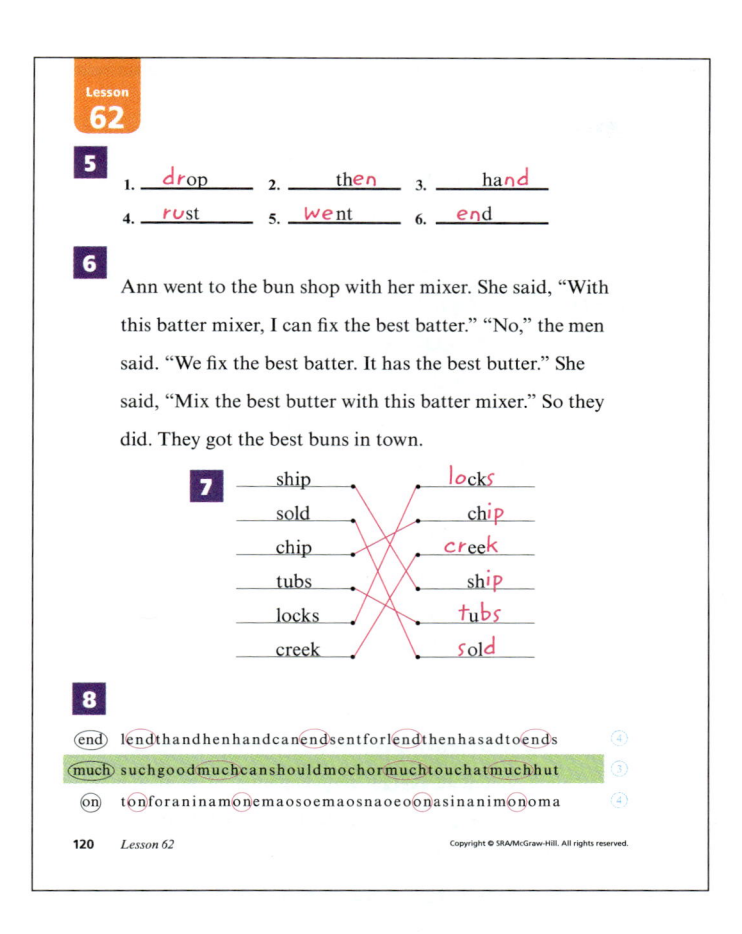

EXERCISE 10
MATCHING COMPLETION

1. Everybody, touch part 7. ✓
2. First word. What word? (Signal.) *Ship.*
3. Next word. What word? (Signal.) *Sold.*
4. (Repeat step 3 for **chip, tubs, locks, creek**.)
5. Later, you'll complete the matching words.

EXERCISE 11
CIRCLE GAME

1. Everybody, touch part 8. ✓
2. What word will you circle in the first line? (Signal.) *End.*
3. What word will you circle in the second line? (Signal.) *Much.*
4. What word will you circle in the third line? (Signal.) *On.*
5. Circle the words and finish the rest of your Workbook lesson.

EXERCISE 12
WORKBOOK CHECK

1. (Check each student's Workbook.)
2. (Award points for Workbook performance.)
3. (Record the student's total points in Box B.)

0–3 errors	8 points
4–5 errors	4 points
6 errors	2 points
7 or more errors	0 points

INDIVIDUAL READING CHECKOUTS

EXERCISE 13
TIMED STORY-READING CHECKOUT

- Study the story. If you read the story with no more than 3 errors and read it in 1 minute or less, you'll earn 6 points.
- If you make more than 3 errors, or if you take more than 1 minute to read the story, you won't earn any points.
- If you don't earn points the first time you read the story, you can try again. If you succeed the second time you try, you'll earn 3 points.
- (Check the students individually.)
- (Record either 6, 3, or 0 points in Box C.)

Lesson point total

(Tell students to write the point total in the last box at the top of the Workbook page. Maximum = 20 points.)

Point Summary Chart

(Tell students to write this point total in the box for Lesson 62 in the Point Summary Chart.)

END OF LESSON 62

Lesson 63

WORD-ATTACK SKILLS

EXERCISE 1
SOUND INTRODUCTION

1. (Point to **qu:**) These letters make the sound **kwww**. What sound? (Signal.) *kwww.*
2. (Point to **o:**) One sound you learned for this letter is the letter name. Everybody, what's that sound? (Touch.) *ōōō.* Yes, **ōōō**.
- What's the other sound? (Touch.) *ŏŏŏ.* Yes, **ŏŏŏ**.
3. (Point to **e:**) One sound you learned for this letter is the letter name. Everybody, what's that sound? (Touch.) *ēēē.* Yes, **ēēē**.
- What's the other sound? (Touch.) *ĕĕĕ.* Yes, **ĕĕĕ**.
4. (Point to **qu:**) What sound? (Touch.) *kwww.* Yes, **kwww**.
5. (Repeat step 4 for **ŭ, ck, ing, sh, w, v, g, r, z**.)

qu o
e qu u
ck ing
sh w v
g r z

Individual test
(Call on two or three students. Touch under each sound. Each student says all the sounds, including two sounds for **o** and two sounds for **e**.)

EXERCISE 2
PRONUNCIATIONS

Task A Slit, slip, slick

1. Listen: **slit, slip, slick.** Say those words. (Signal.) *Slit, slip, slick.* (Repeat until firm.)
2. Listen: **slit, slip, slick.** One of those words means **a thin cut.** (Pause.) Which word? (Signal.) *Slit.* Yes, **slit**.
3. One of those words means **something you do on ice.**
- (Pause.) Which word? (Signal.) *Slip.* Yes, **slip**.
4. One of those words means **something that is very smooth.**
- (Pause.) Which word? (Signal.) *Slick.* Yes, **slick**.
5. (Repeat steps 2–4 until firm.)

Task B

1. Listen: **splashes.** Say it. (Signal.) *Splashes.*
2. Next word: **covered.** Say it. (Signal.) *Covered.*
3. (Repeat step 2 for **equal, master**.)
4. (Repeat the words until firm.)

Task C Chimp, champ, chomp

1. Listen: **chimp, champ, chomp.** Say those words. (Signal.) *Chimp, champ, chomp.* (Repeat until firm.)
2. One of those words has the middle sound **ĭĭĭ**. I'll say the words again: **chimp, champ, chomp.**
3. Which word has the middle sound **ĭĭĭ**? (Signal.) *Chimp.* Yes, **chimp**.
- Which word has the middle sound **ŏŏŏ**? (Signal.) *Chomp.* Yes, **chomp**.
- Which word has the middle sound **ăăă**? (Signal.) *Champ.* Yes, **champ**.
4. Listen: **chĭĭĭmp.** What's the middle sound in the word **chimp**? (Signal.) *ĭĭĭ.* Yes, **ĭĭĭ**.
- Listen: **chăăămp.** What's the middle sound in the word **champ**? (Signal.) *ăăă.* Yes, **ăăă**.
- Listen: **chŏŏŏmp.** What's the middle sound in the word **chomp**? (Signal.) *ŏŏŏ.* Yes, **ŏŏŏ**.
5. (Repeat step 4 until firm.) Good job.

214 *Lesson 63*

EXERCISE 3
WORD READING THE FAST WAY

1. You're going to read these words the fast way.
2. (For each word: Touch the ball of the arrow. Pause.) What word? (Slash right.)
3. (Repeat each list until firm.)

lucky

well

you

sunny

black

slip

slippers

after

do

will

of

what

muddy

said

thorn

wish

Lesson 63

Lesson 63

4. (For each word: Touch the ball of the arrow. Pause.) What word? (Slash right.)
5. (Repeat the list until firm.)

- slick
- which
- spring
- letters
- greets
- grip

WORKBOOK EXERCISES

Note: Pass out the Workbooks. Direct the students to open to Lesson 63.

(Award 6 points if the group worked well during the word attack. Remind the students of the points they can earn in their Workbook.)

EXERCISE 4
SOUND DICTATION

1. I'll say the sounds. You write the letters in part 1 in your Workbook.
2. First sound. Write a letter that says **www** in the first blank.
   (Observe students and give feedback.)
3. Next sound. Write two letters that go together and say **www**.
   (Observe students and give feedback.)
4. Next sound. (Touch.) **lll**. What sound? (Signal.) *lll*.
- Write it.
   (Observe students and give feedback.)
5. (Repeat step 4 for **p, ŭŭŭ, shshsh, mmm, nnn, ŏŏŏ, ĭĭĭ, sss, ch.**)
6. (Repeat sounds students had trouble with.)

EXERCISE 5
SPELLING FROM DICTATION

1. Touch part 2. ✓
- You're going to write words that I dictate.
2. First word: **lips**. What word? (Signal.) *Lips.*
- Listen again: **lll . . . ĭĭĭ . . . p . . . sss.** Write it in the first blank.
   (Observe students and give feedback.)
3. Next word: **nod**. What word? (Signal.) *Nod.*
- Listen again: **nnn . . . ŏŏŏ . . . d.** Write it in the next blank.
   (Observe students and give feedback.)
4. (Repeat step 3 for **it, this, his, them, nut, if.**)

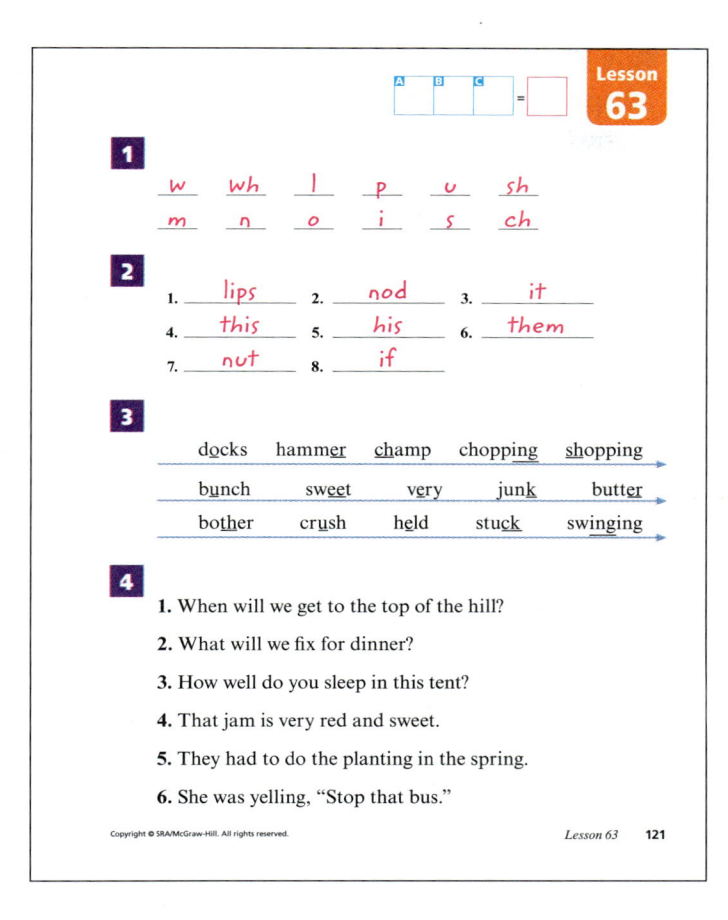

Lesson 63

Workbook Page (Lesson 63, p. 121)

1. w wh l p u sh
m n o i s ch

2.
1. lips 2. nod 3. it
4. this 5. his 6. them
7. nut 8. if

3.
d**o**cks   hamm**er**   **ch**amp   **ch**opping   **sh**opping
bun**ch**   **sw**eet   very   jun**k**   butt**er**
bo**th**er   cr**u**sh   he**l**d   stu**ck**   **sw**i**ng**ing

4.
1. When will we get to the top of the hill?
2. What will we fix for dinner?
3. How well do you sleep in this tent?
4. That jam is very red and sweet.
5. They had to do the planting in the spring.
6. She was yelling, "Stop that bus."

EXERCISE 6
WORD READING: Workbook

1. Touch the first word in part 3. ✓
2. Look at the underlined sound in the first word. (Pause.) What sound? (Signal.) ŏŏŏ.
- (Pause.) What word? (Signal.) *Docks.*
3. Next word. (Pause.) What sound? (Signal.) *er.*
- (Pause.) What word? (Signal.) *Hammer.*
4. (Repeat step 3 for remaining words.)

EXERCISE 7
SENTENCE READING

1. Everybody, touch sentence 1 in part 4. ✓
2. You're going to read the fast way.
3. First word. ✓
- Get ready. (Clap for each word. Pause about 2 seconds between claps.) *When . . . will . . . we . . . get . . . to . . . the . . . top . . . of . . . the . . . hill?*
4. (Repeat step 3 until the students until the students read the sentence without a mistake.)
5. (Repeat steps 3 and 4 for each remaining sentence.)

> **Individual test**
> (Give each student a chance to read one of the sentences. Praise students who read accurately without long pauses.)

EXERCISE 8
WORD COMPLETION

1. Touch the first word in part 5. ✓
- Fix it up to say (pause) **sleep.** What word? (Signal.) *Sleep.*
- Fix it up.
  (Observe students and give feedback.)
2. Touch the second word. ✓
- Fix it up to say (pause) **yet.** What word? (Signal.) *Yet.*
- Fix it up.
  (Observe students and give feedback.)
3. Touch the third word. ✓
- Fix it up to say (pause) **lend.** What word? (Signal.) *Lend.*
- Fix it up.
  (Observe students and give feedback.)
4. (Repeat step 3 for **hold, with, bust.**)

EXERCISE 9
STORY READING

Task A

1. Everybody, touch part 6. ✓
- You're going to read this story.
2. First word. ✓
- Get ready. (Clap for each word. Pause about 2 seconds between claps.) *Her . . . mom . . . told . . . her, . . . "The . . . street . . . is . . . slick.*
3. (Repeat step 2 until the students correctly identify all words in the sentence in order.)
4. Next sentence. ✓
- Get ready. (Clap for each word.) *So . . . do . . . not . . . go . . . on . . . it."*

Lesson 63

5. (Repeat step 4 until students correctly identify all words in the sentence in order.)
6. (Repeat steps 4 and 5 for each remaining sentence.)
7. (If students miss more than four words, repeat the story reading from the beginning.)

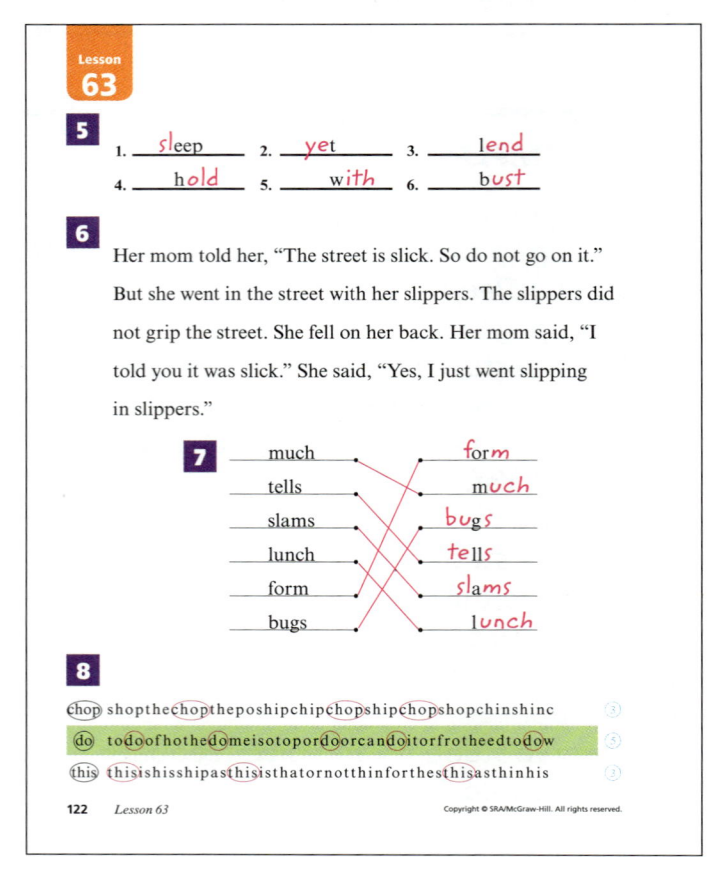

Task B

1. Now I'll read the story and ask questions. Follow along.
2. **Her mom told her, "The street is slick. So do not go on it."** (Call on a student.) What did her mom say? *The street is slick. So do not go on it.*
- (Call on a student.) **What does that mean: The street is slick?** (Idea: *It is wet or icy, and it is slippery.*)

3. **But she went into the street with her slippers. The slippers did not grip the street.** (Call on a student.) What does that mean: **The slippers did not grip the street?** (Idea: *She slid in the slick street.*)
4. **She fell on her back. Her mom said, "I told you it was slick." She said, "Yes, I just went slipping in slippers."** (Call on a student.) What did she say? *Yes, I just went slipping in my slippers.*
- (Call on a student.) **Is that what slippers are for?** *No.*

EXERCISE 10
MATCHING COMPLETION

1. Everybody, touch part 7. ✓
2. First word. What word? (Signal.) *Much.*
3. Next word. What word? (Signal.) *Tells.*
4. (Repeat step 3 for **slams, lunch, form, bugs.**)
5. Later, you'll complete the matching words.

EXERCISE 11
CIRCLE GAME

1. Everybody, touch part 8. ✓
2. What word will you circle in the first line? (Signal.) *Chop.*
3. What word will you circle in the second line? (Signal.) *Do.*
4. What word will you circle in the third line? (Signal.) *This.*
5. Circle the words and finish the rest of your Workbook lesson.

Lesson 63

EXERCISE 12
WORKBOOK CHECK

1. (Check each student's Workbook.)
2. (Award points for Workbook performance.)
3. (Record the student's total points in Box B.)

0–3 errors	8 points
4–5 errors	4 points
6 errors	2 points
7 or more errors	0 points

INDIVIDUAL READING CHECKOUTS

EXERCISE 13
TIMED STORY-READING CHECKOUT

- Study the story. If you read the story with no more than 3 errors and read it in 1 minute or less, you'll earn 6 points.
- If you make more than 3 errors, or if you take more than 1 minute to read the story, you won't earn any points.
- If you don't earn points the first time you read the story, you can try again. If you succeed the second time you try, you'll earn 3 points.
- (Check the students individually.)
- (Record either 6, 3, or 0 points in Box C.)

Lesson point total
(Tell students to write the point total in the last box at the top of the Workbook page. Maximum = 20 points.)

Point Summary Chart
(Tell students to write this point total in the box for Lesson 63 in the Point Summary Chart.)

END OF LESSON 63

Lesson 64

WORD-ATTACK SKILLS

EXERCISE 1
SOUND IDENTIFICATION

1. (Point to **e:**) **One sound you learned for this letter is the letter name. Everybody, what's that sound?** (Touch.) ēēē. **Yes, ēēē.**
   - **What's the other sound?** (Touch.) ĕĕĕ. **Yes, ĕĕĕ.**
2. (Point to **o:**) **One sound you learned for this letter is the letter name. Everybody, what's that sound?** (Touch.) ōōō. **Yes, ōōō.**
   - **What's the other sound?** (Touch.) ŏŏŏ. **Yes, ŏŏŏ.**
3. (Point to **a:**) **What sound?** (Touch.) ăăă. **Yes, ăăă.**
4. (Repeat step 3 for **ĭ, ŭ, ing, er, ch, sh, qu, b, p, d, h.**)

e o a
i u ing
er ch
sh qu b
p d h

Individual test
(Call on two or three students. Touch under each sound. Each student says all the sounds, including two sounds for **e** and two sounds for **o.**)

EXERCISE 2
PRONUNCIATIONS

Task A **Peat, peep, peak**

1. **Listen: peat, peep, peak. Say those words.** (Signal.) *Peat, peep, peak.* (Repeat until firm.)
2. **Listen: peat, peep, peak. One of those words means a sound a bird makes.**
   - (Pause.) **Which word?** (Signal.) *Peep.* **Yes, peep.**
3. **One of those words means the top of a mountain.**
   - (Pause.) **Which word?** (Signal.) *Peak.* **Yes, peak.**
4. **One of those words means something you find in a swamp.**
   - (Pause.) **Which word?** (Signal.) *Peat.* **Yes, peat.**
5. (Repeat steps 2–4 until firm.)

Task B

1. **Listen: plastered. Say it.** (Signal.) *Plastered.*
2. **Next word: painted. Say it.** (Signal.) *Painted.*
3. (Repeat step 2 for **copped, equipped, robbed, boll.**)
4. (Repeat the words until firm.)

Task C **Brunch, branch**

1. **Listen: brunch** (pause) **branch. Say those words.** (Signal.) *Brunch, branch.* (Repeat until firm.)
2. **One of those words has the middle sound ăăă. I'll say the words again: brunch** (pause) **branch.**
3. **Which word has the middle sound ăăă?** (Signal.) *Branch.* **Yes, branch.**
   - **Which word has the middle sound ŭŭŭ?** (Signal.) *Brunch.* **Yes, brunch.**
4. **Listen: brŭŭŭnch. What's the middle sound in the word brunch?** (Signal.) *ŭŭŭ.* **Yes, ŭŭŭ.**
   - **Listen: brăăănch. What's the middle sound in the word branch?** (Signal.) *ăăă.* **Yes, ăăă.**
5. (Repeat step 4 until firm.) **Good job.**

EXERCISE 3
WORD READING THE FAST WAY

1. You're going to read these words the fast way.
2. (For each word: Touch the ball of the arrow. Pause.) What word? (Slash right.)
3. (Repeat each list until firm.)

you

bother

self

jog

planting

which

what

ask

stump

think

thing

job

stick

Lesson 64   221

Lesson 64

4. (For each word: Touch the ball of the arrow. Pause.) **What word?** (Slash right.)
5. (Repeat each list until firm.)

- ink
- stink
- said
- stuck
- quick
- of
- drink
- hammer
- swinging

WORKBOOK EXERCISES

Note: Pass out the Workbooks. Direct the students to open to Lesson 64.

(Award 6 points if the group worked well during the word attack. Remind the students of the points they can earn in their Workbook.)

EXERCISE 4
SOUND DICTATION

1. I'll say the sounds. You write the letters in part 1 in your Workbook.
2. First sound. (Pause.) **kwww.** What sound? (Signal.) *kwww.*
- Write it in the first blank.
  (Observe students and give feedback.)
3. Next sound. (Pause.) **j.** What sound? (Signal.) *j.*
- Write it.
  (Observe students and give feedback.)
4. (Repeat step 3 for **g, h, nnn, rrr, t, ĭĭĭ, ĕĕĕ, ēēē, ōōō, ŏŏŏ.**)
5. (Repeat sounds students had trouble with.)

EXERCISE 5
SPELLING FROM DICTATION

1. Touch part 2. ✓
- You're going to write words that I dictate.
2. First word: **them.** What word? (Signal.) *Them.*
- Listen again: **thththh . . . ĕĕĕ . . . mmm.** Write it in the first blank.
  (Observe students and give feedback.)
3. Next word: **when.** What word? (Signal.) *When.*
- Listen again: **www . . . ĕĕĕ . . . nnn.** Write it in the next blank.
  (Observe students and give feedback.)
4. (Repeat step 3 for **did, has, us, meets, that, but.**)

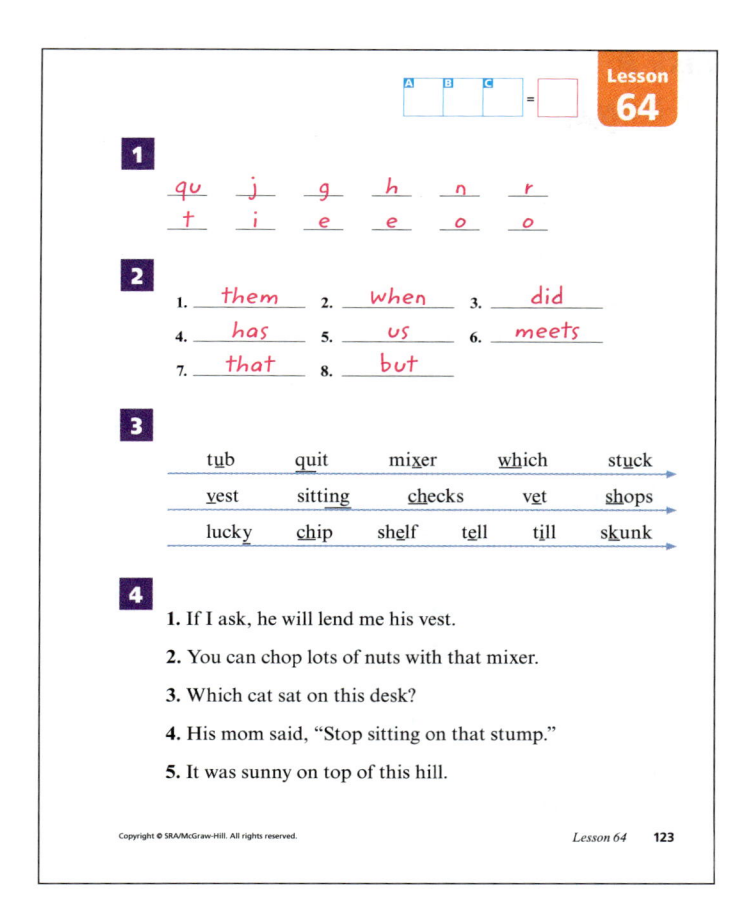

Lesson 64

Workbook page (Lesson 64)

1
qu j g h n r
t i e e o o

2
1. them   2. when   3. did
4. has   5. us   6. meets
7. that   8. but

3
tub   quit   mixer   which   stuck
vest   sitting checks   vet   shops
lucky chip   shelf   tell   till   skunk

4
1. If I ask, he will lend me his vest.
2. You can chop lots of nuts with that mixer.
3. Which cat sat on this desk?
4. His mom said, "Stop sitting on that stump."
5. It was sunny on top of this hill.

EXERCISE 6
WORD READING: Workbook

1. Touch the first word in part 3. ✓
2. Look at the underlined sound in the first word. (Pause.) What sound? (Signal.) *ŭŭŭ*.
- (Pause.) What word? (Signal.) *Tub.*
3. Next word. (Pause.) What sound? (Signal.) *kwww.*
- What word? (Signal.) *Quit.*
4. (Repeat step 3 for remaining words.)

EXERCISE 7
SENTENCE READING

1. Everybody, touch sentence 1 in part 4. ✓
2. You're going to read the fast way.
3. First word. ✓
- Get ready. (Clap for each word. Pause about 2 seconds between claps.) *If . . . I . . . ask, . . . he . . . will . . . lend . . . me . . . his . . . vest.*
4. (Repeat step 3 until the students read the sentence without a mistake.)
5. (Repeat steps 3 and 4 for each remaining sentence.)

Individual test
(Give each student a chance to read one of the sentences. Praise students who read accurately without long pauses.)

EXERCISE 8
WORD COMPLETION

1. Touch the first word in part 5. ✓
- Fix it up to say (pause) **send.** What word? (Signal.) *Send.*
- Fix it up.
  (Observe students and give feedback.)
2. Touch the second word. ✓
- Fix it up to say (pause) **mats.** What word? (Signal.) *Mats.*
- Fix it up.
  (Observe students and give feedback.)
3. (Repeat step 2 for **horn, drop, slap, trip.**)

Lesson 64

5
1. se**nd**   2. m**ats**   3. **horn**
4. **dro**p   5. **sla**p   6. **trip**

6 After lunch, Pam and her dad went to the vet with a sick frog. They sat down next to a man that had a skunk. Pam said to the man, "Can I pet that skunk?" The man said, "Do not bother this skunk. Or you will smell a big stink." Just then, the frog went hop, hop. And what do you think that skunk did?

7
tipping — better
better — just
singer — tipping
just — singer
clocks — such
such — clocks

8
(much) suchmuchtouchhutchsuchmuchmichorsickmoctouchmuch
(then) whenthenhenthanthatwhenwhatthenasthemorthanthenthe
(bad) hadtosadofbadthesadbadhadhatbatcanhadbadhatcanban

EXERCISE 9
STORY READING

Task A

1. Everybody, touch part 6. ✓
   - You're going to read this story.
2. First word. ✓
   - Get ready. (Clap for each word. Pause about 2 seconds between claps.) After . . . lunch, . . . Pam . . . and . . . her . . . dad . . . went . . . to . . . the . . . vet . . . with . . . a . . . sick . . . frog.
3. (Repeat step 2 until students correctly identify all the words in the sentence in order.)
4. Next sentence. ✓
   - Get ready. (Clap for each word:) They . . . sat . . . down . . . next . . . to . . . a . . . man . . . that . . . had . . . a . . . skunk.
5. (Repeat step 4 until students correctly identify all the words in the sentence in order.)
6. (Repeat steps 4 and 5 for each remaining sentence.)
7. (If students miss more than four words, repeat the story reading from the beginning.)

Task B

1. Now I'll read the story and ask questions. Follow along.
2. **After lunch, Pam and her dad went to the vet with a sick frog.** (Call on a student.) **When did they go to the vet?** (Idea: *After lunch.*)
   - (Call on a student.) **What did they take to the vet?** *A sick frog.*
   - (Call on a student.) **What does a vet do?** (Idea: *Helps sick animals get well.*)
3. **They sat down next to a man that had a skunk.** (Call on a student.) **Who did they sit next to?** (Idea: *A man with a skunk.*)
4. **Pam said to the man, "Can I pet that skunk?"** (Call on a student.) **What did Pam say?** *Can I pet that skunk?*
5. **The man said, "Do not bother this skunk. Or you will smell a big stink." Just then, the frog went hop, hop. And what do you think that skunk did?** (Call on a student.) **What happens if you bother a skunk?** (Idea: *It will make a stink.*)
   - **What do you think happened?** (Call on individual students to respond.)

EXERCISE 10
MATCHING COMPLETION

1. Everybody, touch part 7. ✓
2. First word. What word? (Signal.) *Tipping.*
3. Next word. What word? (Signal.) *Better.*
4. (Repeat step 3 for **singer, just, clocks, such.**)
5. Later, you'll complete the matching words.

EXERCISE 11
CIRCLE GAME

1. Everybody, touch part 8. ✓
2. What word will you circle in the first line? (Signal.) *Much.*
3. What word will you circle in the second line? (Signal.) *Then.*
4. What word will you circle in the third line? (Signal.) *Bad.*
5. Circle the words and finish the rest of your Workbook lesson.

EXERCISE 12
WORKBOOK CHECK

1. (Check each student's Workbook.)
2. (Award points for Workbook performance.)
3. (Record the student's total points in Box B.)

0–3 errors	8 points
4–5 errors	4 points
6 errors	2 points
7 or more errors	0 points

INDIVIDUAL READING CHECKOUTS

EXERCISE 13
TIMED STORY-READING CHECKOUT

- Study the story. If you read the story with no more than 3 errors and read it in 1 minute or less, you'll earn 6 points.
- If you make more than 3 errors, or if you take more than 1 minute to read the story, you won't earn any points.
- If you don't earn points the first time you read the story, you can try again. If you succeed the second time you try, you'll earn 3 points.
- (Check the students individually.)
- (Record either 6, 3, or 0 points in Box C.)

Lesson point total

(Tell students to write the point total in the last box at the top of the Workbook page. Maximum = 20 points.)

Point Summary Chart

(Tell students to write this point total in the box for Lesson 64 in the Point Summary Chart.)

END OF LESSON 64

Lesson 65

WORD-ATTACK SKILLS

EXERCISE 1
SOUND IDENTIFICATION

1. (Point to **e:**) One sound you learned for this letter is the letter name. Everybody, what's that sound? (Touch.) ēēē. Yes, **ēēē**.
- What's the other sound? (Touch.) ěěě. Yes, **ěěě**.
2. (Point to **o:**) One sound you learned for this letter is the letter name. Everybody, what's that sound? (Touch.) ōōō. Yes, **ōōō**.
- What's the other sound? (Touch.) ŏŏŏ. Yes, **ŏŏŏ**.
3. (Point to **th:**) What sound? (Touch.) ththth. Yes, **ththth**.
4. (Repeat step 3 for **z, t, s, wh, j, w, h, ŭ, er, p, d, b, g.**)

e o th
z t s
wh j w
h u er
p d b g

Individual test
(Call on two or three students. Touch under each sound. Each student says all the sounds, including two sounds for **e** and two sounds for **o**.)

EXERCISE 2
PRONUNCIATIONS

Task A **Quick, quit**
1. Listen: **quick** (pause) **quit.** Say those words. (Signal.) *Quick, quit.* (Repeat until firm.)
2. Listen: **quick** (pause) **quit.** One of those words means **stop.**
- (Pause.) Which word? (Signal.) *Quit.* Yes, **quit.**
3. One of those words means **fast.**
- (Pause.) Which word? (Signal.) *Quick.* Yes, **quick.**
4. (Repeat steps 2 and 3 until firm.)

Task B
1. Listen: **bothered.** Say it. (Signal.) *Bothered.*
2. Next word: **brunch.** Say it. (Signal.) *Brunch.*
3. (Repeat step 2 for **vested, robber.**)
4. (Repeat the words until firm.)

Task C **Send, sand, sinned**
1. Listen: **send, sand, sinned.** Say those words. (Signal.) *Send, sand, sinned.* (Repeat until firm.)
2. One of those words has the middle sound **ăăă.** I'll say the words again: **send, sand, sinned.**
3. Which word has the middle sound **ăăă**? (Signal.) *Sand.* Yes, **sand.**
- Which word has the middle sound **ĭĭĭ**? (Signal.) *Sinned.* Yes, **sinned.**
- Which word has the middle sound **ěěě**? (Signal.) *Send.* Yes, **send.**
4. Listen: **sěěěnd.** What's the middle sound in the word **send**? (Signal.) ěěě. Yes, **ěěě.**
- Listen: **săăănd.** What's the middle sound in the word **sand**? (Signal.) ăăă. Yes, **ăăă.**
- Listen: **sĭĭĭnned.** What's the middle sound in the word **sinned**? (Signal.) ĭĭĭ. Yes, **ĭĭĭ.**
5. (Repeat step 4 until firm.) Good job.

EXERCISE 3
WORD READING THE FAST WAY

1. You're going to read these words the fast way.
2. (For each word: Touch the ball of the arrow. Pause.) What word? (Slash right.)
3. (Repeat each list until firm.)

what

quit

slipping

you

gift

sink

which

said

best

crash

cash

clash

Lesson 65

WORKBOOK EXERCISES

Note: Pass out the Workbooks. Direct the students to open to Lesson 65.

(Award 6 points if the group worked well during the word attack. Remind the students of the points they can earn in their Workbook.)

EXERCISE 4
SOUND DICTATION

1. I'll say the sounds. You write the letters in part 1 in your Workbook.
2. First sound. (Pause.) ăăă. What sound? (Signal.) ăăă.
- Write it in the first blank.
   (Observe students and give feedback.)
3. Next sound. (Pause.) ŭŭŭ. What sound? (Signal.) ŭŭŭ.
- Write it.
   (Observe students and give feedback.)
4. (Repeat step 3 for ēēē, ĭĭĭ, ŏŏŏ, ōōō, ĕĕĕ, sss, shshsh, ch, ththth, b, d, p.)
5. (Repeat sounds students had trouble with.)

EXERCISE 5
SPELLING FROM DICTATION

1. Touch part 2. ✓
- You're going to write words that I dictate.
2. First word: **hits**. What word? (Signal.) *Hits*.
- Listen again: **h . . . ĭĭĭ . . . t . . . sss**. Write it in the first blank.
   (Observe students and give feedback.)
3. Next word: **red**. What word? (Signal.) *Red*.
- Listen again: **rrr . . . ĕĕĕ . . . d**. Write it in the next blank.
   (Observe students and give feedback.)
4. (Repeat step 3 for **rod, them, nets, ship, when, nut**.)

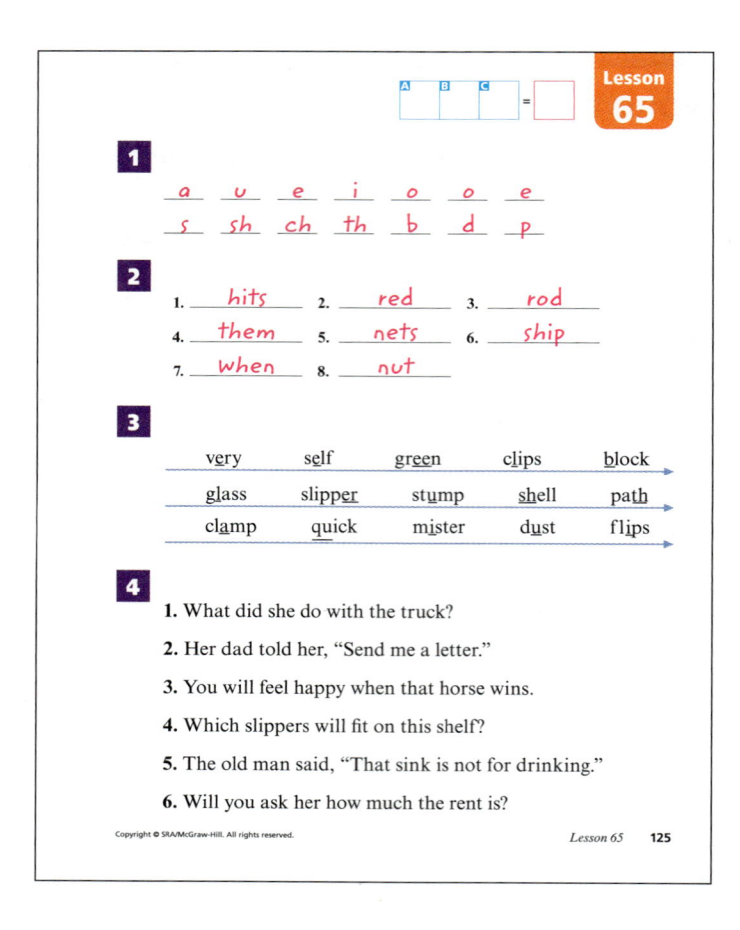

Workbook Page (Lesson 65)

Part 1:
a u e i o o e
s sh ch th b d p

Part 2:
1. hits   2. red   3. rod
4. them   5. nets   6. ship
7. when   8. nut

Part 3:
very   self   green   clips   block
glass   slipper   stump   shell   path
clamp   quick   mister   dust   flips

Part 4:
1. What did she do with the truck?
2. Her dad told her, "Send me a letter."
3. You will feel happy when that horse wins.
4. Which slippers will fit on this shelf?
5. The old man said, "That sink is not for drinking."
6. Will you ask her how much the rent is?

EXERCISE 6
WORD READING: Workbook

1. Touch the first word in part 3. ✓
2. Look at the underlined sound in the first word. (Pause.) What sound? (Signal.) ĕĕĕ.
- (Pause.) What word? (Signal.) *Very*.
3. Next word. (Pause.) What sound? (Signal.) ĕĕĕ.
- What word? (Signal.) *Self*.
4. (Repeat step 3 for remaining words.)

EXERCISE 7
SENTENCE READING

1. Everybody, touch sentence 1 in part 4. ✓
2. You're going to read the fast way.
3. First word. ✓
- Get ready. (Clap for each word. Pause about 2 seconds between claps.) *What . . . did . . . she . . . do . . . with . . . the . . . truck?*
4. (Repeat step 3 until the students read the sentence without a mistake.)

5. (Repeat steps 3 and 4 for each remaining sentence:
- 2. Her dad told her, "Send me a letter."
- 3. You will feel happy when that horse wins.
- 4. Which slippers will fit on this shelf?
- 5. The old man said, "That sink is not for drinking."
- 6. Will you ask her how much the rent is?)

> **Individual test**
> (Give each student a chance to read one of the sentences. Praise students who read accurately without long pauses.)

EXERCISE 8
WORD COMPLETION

1. **Touch the first word in part 5.** ✓
- **Fix it up to say** (pause) **tree. What word?** (Signal.) *Tree.*
- **Fix it up.**
  (Observe students and give feedback.)
2. **Touch the second word.** ✓
- **Fix it up to say** (pause) **fast. What word?** (Signal.) *Fast.*
- **Fix it up.**
  (Observe students and give feedback.)
3. (Repeat step 2 for **mend, drop, slip, sheep, cats.**)

EXERCISE 9
STORY READING

Task A

1. **Everybody, touch part 6.** ✓
- **You're going to read this story.**
2. **First word.** ✓
- **Get ready.** (Clap for each word. Pause about 2 seconds between claps.) *A . . . green . . . frog . . . was . . . in . . . a . . . bath . . . tub.*
3. (Repeat step 2 until students correctly identify all the words in the sentence in order.)
4. **Next sentence.** ✓
- **Get ready.** (Clap for each word:) *A . . . red . . . bug . . . said, . . . "Can . . . I . . . get . . . in . . . the . . . tub . . . with . . . you?"*

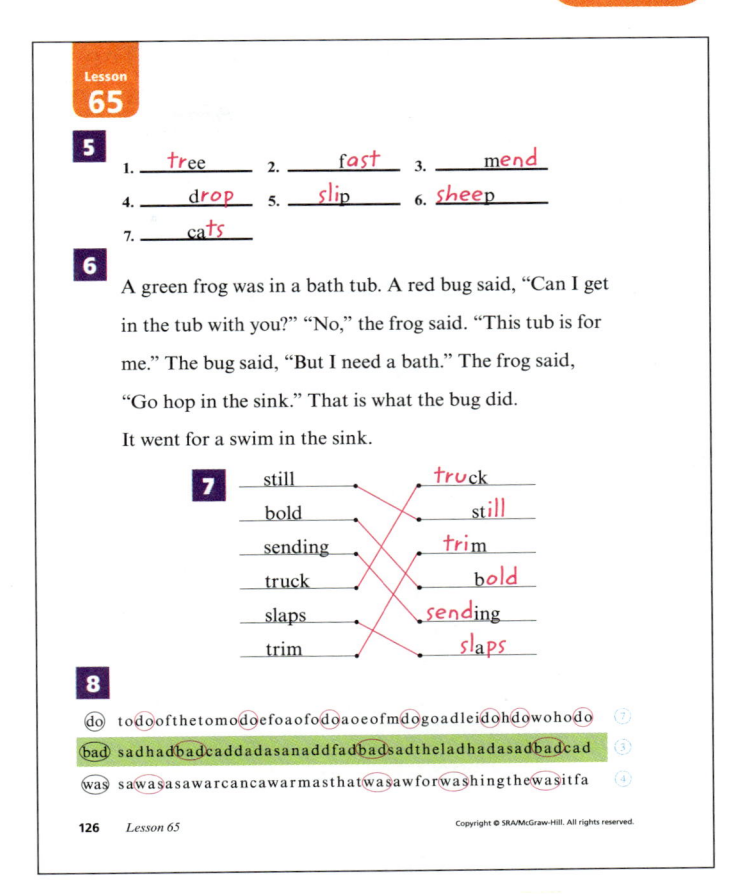

5. (Repeat step 4 until students correctly identify all the words in the sentence in order.)
6. (Repeat steps 4 and 5 for each remaining sentence.)
7. (If students miss more than four words, repeat the story reading from the beginning.)

Task B

1. **Now I'll read the story and ask questions. Follow along.**
2. **A green frog was in a bath tub. A red bug said, "Can I get in the tub with you?** (Call on a student.) **What did the red bug say?** *Can I get in the tub with you?*
- **Who was the bug talking to?** (Idea: *The green frog.*)
3. **"No," the frog said. "This tub is for me."** (Call on a student.) **Say everything the frog said.** *No. This tub is for me.*

Lesson 65   229

Lesson 65

4. **The bug said, "But I need a bath." The frog said, "Go hop in the sink."** (Call on a student.) Why does the bug want to get into the tub? (Idea: *It needs a bath.*)
- (Call on a student.) What did the frog tell the bug to do? *Go hop in the sink.*
5. **That is what the bug did. It went for a swim in the sink.** (Call on a student.) What did the bug do? *It went for a swim in the sink.*

EXERCISE 10
MATCHING COMPLETION

1. Everybody, touch part 7. ✓
2. First word. What word? (Signal.) *Still.*
3. Next word. What word? (Signal.) *Bold.*
4. (Repeat step 3 for **sending, truck, slaps, trim.**)
5. Later, you'll complete the matching words.

EXERCISE 11
CIRCLE GAME

1. Everybody, touch part 8. ✓
2. What word will you circle in the first line? (Signal.) *Do.*
3. What word will you circle in the second line? (Signal.) *Bad.*
4. What word will you circle in the third line? (Signal.) *Was.*
5. Circle the words and finish the rest of your Workbook lesson.

EXERCISE 12
WORKBOOK CHECK

1. (Check each student's Workbook.)
2. (Award points for Workbook performance.)
3. (Record the student's total points in Box B.)

0–3 errors	8 points
4–5 errors	4 points
6 errors	2 points
7 or more errors	0 points

INDIVIDUAL READING CHECKOUTS

EXERCISE 13
TIMED STORY-READING CHECKOUT

- Study the story. If you read the story with no more than 3 errors and read it in 1 minute or less, you'll earn 6 points.
- If you make more than 3 errors, or if you take more than 1 minute to read the story, you won't earn any points.
- If you don't earn points the first time you read the story, you can try again. If you succeed the second time you try, you'll earn 3 points.
- (Check the students individually.)
- (Record either 6, 3, or 0 points in Box C.)

Lesson point total

(Tell students to write the point total in the last box at the top of the Workbook page. Maximum = 20 points.)

Point Summary Chart

(Tell students to write this point total in the box for Lesson 65 in the Point Summary Chart.)

Five-lesson point summary

(Tell students to add the point totals for Lessons 61 through 65 in the Point Summary Chart and to write the total for Block 13. Maximum for Block 13 = 100 points.)

END OF LESSON 65

MASTERY TEST 14
AFTER LESSON 65

Note: Use students' performance on the Lesson 65 Story reading checkout for Mastery Test 14.

Scoring the test

1. (Count each student's errors on the Story reading checkout. Write these numbers in the Test 14 boxes on the appropriate *Decoding A* Mastery Test Student Profile form. Circle **P** or **F**.)
2. (When all students have been tested, circle **P** or **F** for each student on the *Decoding A* Mastery Test Group Summary form. Determine if more than 25 percent of the students failed the Story reading checkout by dividing the number of students who failed by the total number of students in the group.)

Remedies

(If more than 25 percent of the students fail to earn 6 points for their Story reading checkout, [1] repeat the Story reading checkouts for Lessons 61 through 64, and [2] repeat all of Lesson 65. Permission is granted to reproduce the Workbook pages for Lesson 65 for classroom use.)

Mastery Test 15

Note: Place students who successfully complete *Decoding A* at Lesson 8 of *Decoding B1*.

END-OF-PROGRAM MASTERY TEST 15
AFTER LESSON 65

- (Mastery Test 15 is located at the back of each student's Workbook.)

Note: Mastery Test 15 has both a group section (parts 1 through 5) and an individual section (parts 6 through 13). For parts 6 through 13, you will record individual errors on the student's copy as the student reads from an unmarked Workbook.

Group test

Part 1 Sound dictation

1. Turn to Mastery Test 15 on page 127 at the back of your Workbook. Write your name at the top of your Workbook page. (Wait.)
2. Ready? Everybody, touch part 1. ✓
- I'll say the sounds. You write the letters on the lines for part 1 in your Workbook.
3. First sound. (Pause.) **lll.** What sound? *lll.*
- Write it. (Observe, but do not give feedback.)
4. Next sound. (Pause.) **p.** What sound? *p.*
- Write it. (Observe.)
5. (Repeat step 4 for **g, ĭĭĭ, ŏŏŏ, d, ēēē, b, ăăă, sss, ōōō, ĕĕĕ.**)
6. Now you're going to write sound combinations.
7. Write two letters that go together and say **www.** (Pause.) What sound? *www.*
- Write it. (Observe.)
8. (Repeat step 7 for **ch, shshsh, ththth.**)

Part 2 Spelling from dictation

Note: If necessary, use the spelling word in a sentence. For example, say, "Up. The balloon went up."

1. Find part 2 in your Workbook. ✓
- You're going to write words that I dictate.
2. First word: **thē.** What word? (Signal.) *The.*
- Listen again: **thththh . . . ēēē.** Write it. (Observe.)
3. Next word: **up.** What word? (Signal.) *Up.*
- Listen again: **ŭŭŭ . . . p.** Write it on the next line. (Observe.)
4. (Repeat step 3 for **dad, men, shot, win.**)

Part 3 Word completion

1. Touch the first word in part 3. ✓
- Fix it up to say (pause) **cold.** What word? (Signal.) *Cold.*
- Fix it up. (Observe.)
2. Touch the next word. ✓
- Fix it up to say (pause) **cast.** What word? (Signal.) *Cast.*
- Fix it up. (Observe.)
3. Touch the next word. ✓
- Fix it up to say (pause) **rugs.** What word? (Signal.) *Rugs.*
- Fix it up. (Observe.)
4. Touch the next word. ✓
- Fix it up to say (pause) **sheets.** What word? (Signal.) *Sheets.*
- Fix it up. (Observe.)
5. Touch the next word. ✓
- Fix it up to say (pause) **trip.** What word? (Signal.) *Trip.*
- Fix it up. (Observe.)
6. Touch the next word. ✓
- Fix it up to say (pause) **fins.** What word? (Signal.) *Fins.*
- Fix it up. (Observe.)

Mastery Test 15

Part 4 Matching completion
1. Everybody, touch part 4. ✓
2. First word. (Pause and ✓.) What word? (Signal.) *Ship.*
3. Next word. (Pause and ✓.) What word? (Signal.) *Locks.*
4. (Repeat step 3 for **chip, creek.**)
5. Later, you'll fix up each line in the second column and match it to the word in the first column.

Part 5 Circle game
1. Everybody, touch part 5. ✓
2. What word will you circle in the first line? (Signal.) *When.*
3. What word will you circle in the second line? (Signal.) *If.*
4. Finish part 4 and part 5.

(At this time, administer the Individual section of the test to each student. Remind students to complete parts 4 and 5 of the Workbook if they have not already done so.)

Individual test
(Provide an unmarked copy for the student to read.)

Parts 6–10 Word reading
1. (Point to the words in part 6 and say:) Read all the words in part 6 as carefully as you can.
   - (Point to the first word and say:) Start here.
2. (Slash each incorrect response as the student reads.)
3. (Repeat steps 1 and 2 for parts 7–10.)

Parts 11 and 12 Story reading (timed)
1. (Point to the story in parts 11 and 12 and say:) Study this story for 2 minutes. Then you will read it aloud. Ask me about any words you don't know.
2. (After 2 minutes, or when the student is ready, say:) Read this story as carefully and as quickly as you can.
3. (Slash each incorrect response as the student reads. Record in the first box provided the time the student required to read the story. Record in the second box the total number of errors. Score 1 error for each word misidentified in the story. If there are interruptions, have the student start again. If the student has not finished the story in 1 minute, score part 11 as a fail.)

Part 13 Oral comprehension questions
1. I'll read those sentences and ask some questions. If you don't know the answer to a question, you may look back in the story, but you have to find the answer quickly. (Record the answers directly on the test. Allow the student 30 seconds to respond to each question.)
2. (Read sentences 1 and 2 from parts 11 and 12:)
   - Ann was a winner on the track.
   - And she was the best singer in town.
   - (Ask:) What are the two things that Ann could do well? (Idea: *Sing and run fast.*)
3. (Read sentences 3 and 4:)
   - She said to her self, "I need cash.
   - I can get a job running or a job singing."
   - (Ask:) Tell me what Ann said to herself. (Ideas: *I can get a job running or a job singing; I need cash; I need money.*)
4. (Read sentences 5 and 6:)
   - She got the best job.
   - She is a singer at track meets, and she is glad.
   - (Ask:) Why is that the best job for her? (Ideas: *She can both sing and run at the track; she gets to do the things she likes best.*)

(After administering the Individual section, remind the student to complete parts 4 and 5 if the student has not already done so.)

(This completes the individually administered section of *Decoding A* Mastery Test 15. Repeat parts 6 through 13 with each student.)

Mastery Test 15

SCORING THE TEST

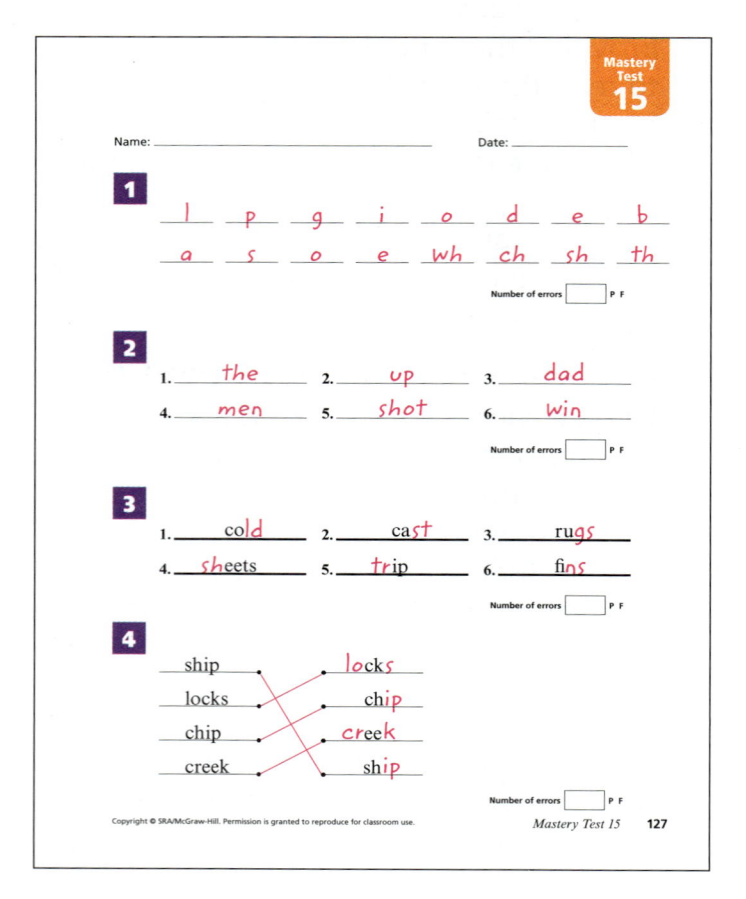

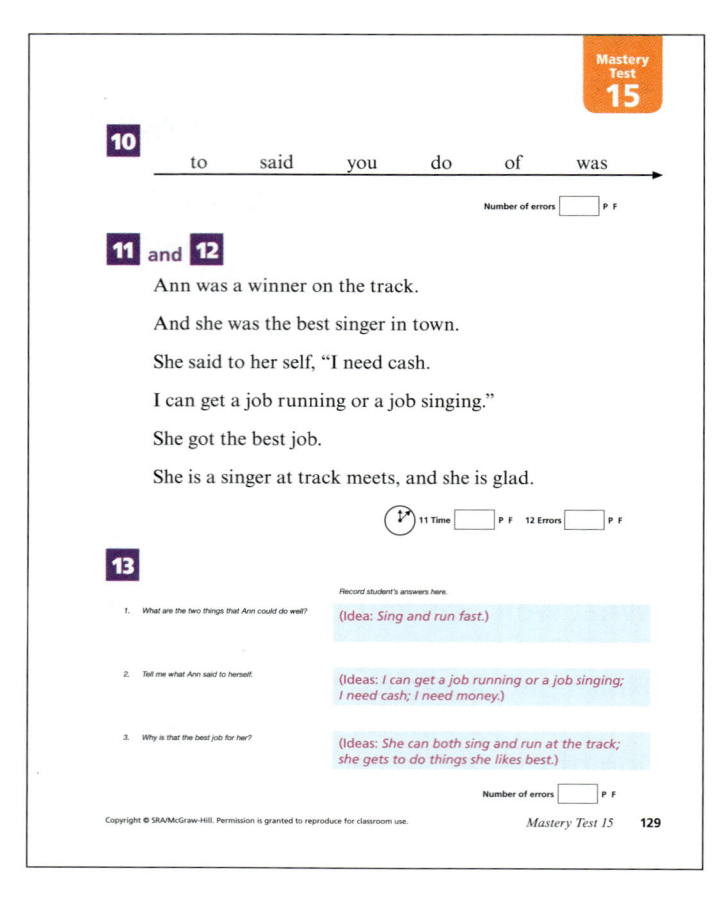

Test Page 127

1.
l p g i o d e b
a s o e wh ch sh th

2.
1. the   2. up   3. dad
4. men   5. shot   6. win

3.
1. cold   2. cast   3. rugs
4. sheets   5. trip   6. fins

4.
ship — locks (crossed to ship)
locks — chip
chip — creek
creek — ship

Test Page 128

5.
(when) thenwhenwhowhenthatthenwhentowhenwemthewhenhwenn
(if) tifthisifistibeitcafidpifinanaforiftoifitihifitisintninifiithi

6. funny letter horse happy sold torn

7.
mast went gift help rocks
hits dust seeds rags end

8.
flag crack drip crust clock
grim black street sling green

9. them mash when teeth wheel with

Test Page 129

10. to said you do of was

11 and 12
Ann was a winner on the track.
And she was the best singer in town.
She said to her self, "I need cash.
I can get a job running or a job singing."
She got the best job.
She is a singer at track meets, and she is glad.

13.
1. What are the two things that Ann could do well?
   (Idea: Sing and run fast.)
2. Tell me what Ann said to herself.
   (Ideas: I can get a job running or a job singing; I need cash; I need money.)
3. Why is that the best job for her?
   (Ideas: She can both sing and run at the track; she gets to do things she likes best.)

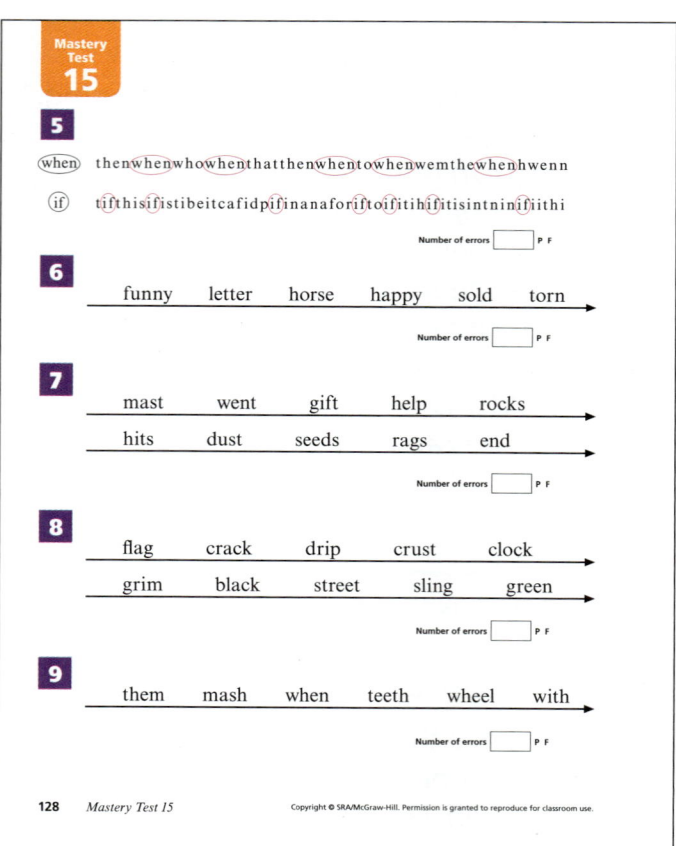

Pass criterion for Group test

Part	Pass	Fail
1	0–2 errors	3 or more errors
2	0–1 error	2 or more errors
3	0–1 error	2 or more errors
4	0 errors	1 or more errors
5	0 errors	1 or more errors

Pass criterion for Individual test

Part(s)	Pass	Fail
6–10	0–3 errors	4 or more errors
11	≤1 minute	>1 minute
11	0–2 errors	3 or more errors
12–13	0–1 error	2 or more errors

Mastery Test 15

Group test

1. (For the Group section of the test, first mark each student's Workbook page for parts 1 through 5.)
2. (Next, record the number of errors in the "Number of errors" boxes on the student's Workbook page.
   - For part 1, record the number of incorrectly written letter-sound correspondences.
   - For part 2, record the number of incorrectly spelled words.
   - For part 3, record the number of incorrectly completed words.
   - For part 4, record the number of words that have been either incorrectly matched or incorrectly spelled.
   - For part 5, count up the number of circled words in each row. **When** appears five times in the first row. **If** appears seven times in the second row. Record the number of errors.)
3. (Once each student's Workbook page has been scored, circle **P** or **F** next to each "Number of errors" box. Record the number of errors for each part in the "Number of errors" rows, and indicate whether the student passed **(P)** or failed **(F)** each part on both the **Decoding A** End-of-Program Mastery Test 15 Student Profile and the Group Summary form. Reproducible summary forms are at the back of the Teacher's Guide.)

Individual test

1. (For the individually administered section of the test, record the number of errors made in parts 6 through 10. Next, determine whether the student passed or failed the part by comparing the number of errors with the criterion for passing. Pass criterion for parts 6 through 10 is 0–3 errors for pass, 4 or more errors for fail.)
2. (For parts 11 and 12, determine whether the student passed both time [part 11] and accuracy [part 12] criteria. Count 1 error for each word. Pass criterion for time is 1 minute or less. Pass criterion for errors is 0–2 errors.)
3. (For part 13, record pass or fail based on the number of questions the student answered correctly. Pass criterion is 0–1 error.)
4. (Circle **P** or **F** next to each box. Record for each student the number of errors, time, and **P** or **F** on the Group Summary form.)

Mastery Test 15

Mastery Test 15

REMEDIES

(Students are expected to pass the major skill areas in the End-of-Program *Decoding A* Mastery Test with approximately 90 percent accuracy.)

- (If a student's overall performance is below 86 percent, it is recommended that the student be reviewed on deficit skill areas before moving on.)
- (If the entire group is weak in a skill area, all the students should be taken through the review lessons specified on the page for that skill area. After reviewing deficit skill areas with individual students or with the group, readminister those parts of Mastery Test if the students failed previously. You may want to use the student's original Workbook page for the Individual section of the test, scoring in a different color, in order to compare responses. Reproduce the Mastery Test as needed.)

(By the end of the program, students should be reading the stories at approximately 60 words per minute. The most valuable procedure for improving students' reading rate and accuracy is to repeat the reading of familiar stories.)

(Students failing only the Workbook skill areas—Matching completion and Circle game—need not be prevented from moving on, but they should receive additional seatwork activities concentrating on visual-discrimination and copying skills.)

(We strongly recommend that you consider students to have successfully completed the *Decoding A* program only after you have remediated all skill deficiencies revealed by the Mastery Tests.)

Mastery Test remedy guidelines, Test 15

Note: For these remedies, permission is granted to reproduce Workbook pages for classroom use.

Skills Tested	If No Pass, Review These Lessons
Group test	
Dictation	
1. Sound dictation	61–65
2. Spelling from dictation	54–60
Word completion	
3. Word completion	46–56
Workbook skills	
4. Matching completion	62–65
5. Circle game	54–57
Individual test	
Word identification	
6. Word reading	43–47, 50–52
7. Final blends	27, 39–42, 54–59
8. Initial blends	40–47
9. Consonant digraphs	30–32, 51, 52
10. Irregular words	49, 52, 54, 59
Story reading	
11 and 12. Time and errors	60–65
13. Oral comprehension questions	60–65